Mirages and Mad Beliefs

Mirages and Mad Beliefs

PROUST THE SKEPTIC

Christopher Prendergast

PRINCETON UNIVERSITY PRESS

PRINCETON AND OXFORD

Copyright © 2013 by Princeton University Press
Published by Princeton University Press, 41 William Street, Princeton, New Jersey 08540
In the United Kingdom: Princeton University Press, 6 Oxford Street, Woodstock, Oxford-shire OX20 1TW

press.princeton.edu

Library of Congress Cataloging-in-Publication Data
Prendergast, Christopher.
 Mirages and mad beliefs : Proust the skeptic / Christopher Prendergast.
   p. cm.
 Includes bibliographical references and index.
 ISBN 978-0-691-15520-3 (hardcover : acid-free paper)   1. Proust, Marcel, 1871–1922—Criticism and interpretation.   I. Title.
 PQ2631.R63Z8275 2013
 843'.912—dc23   2012031871

British Library Cataloging-in-Publication Data is available

This book has been composed in Sabon LT Std

Printed on acid-free paper. ∞

Printed in the United States of America

10 9 8 7 6 5 4 3 2 1

Contents

For Jane Haynes, a good friend and true Proustian

Acknowledgments

I AM GRATEFUL TO my editors at Princeton University Press, Al Bertrand and Hannah Paul, for their unfailingly engaged and generous support, as well as to my indefatigably hawkeyed copyeditor, Cathy Slovensky, who, uniquely in my experience, also helped me turn a chore into a pleasure (not least by adding to the text some wonderful lines of her own on clowns, ponies, and jugglers). My thanks are also due to a number of friends and colleagues for their encouragement and assistance: Claudia Brodsky, Tony Cascardi, Mary Ann Caws, Ian Christie, Peter de Bolla, David Ellison, Anna-Magdalena Elsner, Margaret Gray, David Hillman, Peter Jewell, Dominique Jullien, Michael Lucey, Thomas Klinkert, Nick Marston, Eric Méchoulan, Jeremy Morris, Ian Patterson, Alexander Régier, Ingrid Wassenaar, and Nicky Zeeman. I am also grateful to the institutions whose invitations to come talk about Proust helped in developing and shaping the arguments of the book: Princeton University, New York University, University of Miami, University of California, Berkeley, University of California, Santa Barbara, the Bellagio Foundation, and University of Bologna. Very special thanks go to Stanley Corngold and Michael Wood for extended and always illuminating exchanges. My good friend (and true Proustian) Jane Haynes has been a source of inspiration and support; I dedicate the book to her.

References and Abbreviations

ALL QUOTATIONS FROM and references to *À la recherche du temps perdu* are to the four-volume edition (Paris: Gallimard,1987–89). The English translation used is *In Search of Lost Time* (London: Allen Lane, 2002). I have occasionally tweaked passages quoted from the latter. Throughout I quote principally from the English translation, as some readers interested in Proust may not know French, or French to the exacting standards of Proust's original. I ruled out the compromise solution of quoting both the original and the translation on the grounds that, especially where the longer passages are concerned, this would destroy a realistically manageable rhythm of reading.

The following abbreviations are used:
ARTP *À la recherche du temps perdu*
CG *Le Côté de Guermantes*
Corr. Correspondance, ed. Philip Kolb, 21 vols. (Paris: Plon, 1970–93)
F *La Fugitive*
JF *À l'ombre des jeunes filles en fleurs*
P *La Prisonnière*
S *Du côté de chez Swann*
SG *Sodome et Gomorrhe*
T *Le Temps retrouvé*

Mirages and Mad Beliefs

CHAPTER ONE

Mad Belief

À LA RECHERCHE DU TEMPS PERDU is so constructed as to invite an argument about it to begin where it itself ends (more precisely, with that portion of the last volume occupied by the narrator's lengthy meditation on the nature of the literary vocation, the section Proust baptized as "L'Adoration perpétuelle"). This would not, however, be simply to recapitulate its own internal movement on the plausible (though contested) inference that at the end the narrator is set to embark on the writing of the novel we have just read. Nor would, or should, it be to begin at the end in the "external" sense implied by the fact that the main ideas informing the terminal meditation were there at an early stage of Proust's writing life, prior to the composition of *À la recherche* in the "essayistic" forms subsequently gathered together and published under the title *Contre Sainte-Beuve*. As Vincent Descombes explains, this would be to ignore the reasons why Proust, while proleptically hinting at them throughout, deferred the fully developed statement of these ideas until late in the novel; it was to ensure that the relation between *Contre Sainte-Beuve* and *À la recherche* would not produce a reading of the latter as just a transposition of the former.[1] On the contrary, it was to ensure that the work would be read for what it is: a novel, family member, however errant, of a genre based on a narrative through-movement and irreducible to mere derivative illustration of a schematic a priori. To begin at the end has therefore little to do with the order in which Proust wrote certain things. It is rather—banal though the remark may seem—because of a commitment built into the type of critical reading the following pages instantiate. An argued account of *À la recherche* will be, among other things, an attempt to persuade. Other kinds of less pointed account are, of course, possible, for example, commentary as pure description, or as a kind of impressionistic patchwork, or as a quasi-symbolist tone poem, forms of commentary with which the Proustian critical archive is amply stocked, the last two modes favored in particular by the Proust-cult, historically dominated by the swooning tendencies of that unhappily influential coterie bent on construing *À la recherche* as a storehouse of delicate epiphanies laced with a strong dose of class-bound aestheticism. Since Proust's own text offers the best

---

[1] Vincent Descombes, *Proust: Philosophy of the Novel* (Stanford, Calif.: Stanford University Press, 1992), 5–7.

diagnosis, part analytical, part symptomatic, of what is wrong with this construal of him as a purveyor of high-grade cultural narcotics, it is as well to have done with it once and for all.

The rationale for the approach adopted here is that there is also something *in* the work itself that seeks to persuade (marching under the banner of such terms as "truth," a term without which the whole edifice of *À la recherche* would collapse). Naturally, this does not mean that the persuasive ambitions of the account and those of the work are substantively identical, such that the former merely replicates the latter, albeit in a different idiom. What it means is that there is a match of ambitions in a purely formal sense. One might want to claim that this mischaracterizes *À la recherche*, that it is an enterprise geared not to persuasion but to another set of objectives and thus another kind of writing altogether. If that is so, then the proposed account self-defeatingly loses its point. In this scenario, the only thing coherently on offer would be to recommend reading the book, the rest being silence. However, if we can reasonably debate whether Proust's novel in general conforms to this characterization, one place where its aims are indisputably rhetorical in the sense of addressing its reader with persuasive intent is the metatextual sequence of *Le Temps retrouvé*, so often taken as housing the coda to the work as a whole. Indeed, the discourse of this sequence operates as a high-octane persuasive machine, firing on all pistons to convince us of everything that is entailed by the startling claim (in Ian Patterson's translation) from *Le Temps retrouvé*: "Real life, life finally uncovered and clarified, the only life in consequence lived to the full, is literature" (189). This is not quite what Proust wrote: "La vraie vie, la vie enfin découverte et éclaircie, la seule vie par conséquent pleinement vécue, c'est la littérature" (*À la recherche du temps perdu [ARTP]*, 4:474); while the translation makes perfect sense of the original, it is at the cost of substituting the word "real" for "true" (*la vraie vie*). While the expression "true life" falls awkwardly on English ears (as awkwardly as "true love," a concept utterly alien to Proust's world), it matters that we do not lose sight of the original French here. Combining the two versions gives us a set of propositions that bring together three very grand items from the Proustian lexicon: the "true," the "real," and the "lived."

Truth, reality, life: we shall have occasion to return to the crucial place of these terms in the novel (in the strong sense of being crux-terms, load-bearing at key junctures of the novel's articulation of its own aesthetic), along with the dense equations they sustain (to the point where "real," "true," and "lived" become virtually interchangeable). But since in its bald form the proposition is especially congenial to the swooners, let me begin irreverently, with a provocative question framed by a Proustian *plaisanterie*. There is a tongue-in-cheek joke slyly embedded in one of the many long stretches of narrative devoted to the Guermantes salon and their ilk: "I should never finish if I were to enumerate all the salons" (*Sodome et Gomorrhe* [*SG*], 144). The easy, and presumably intended, target is what is contemptuously referred to in the text as the "society novelist" (subspecies of that despised category, the "realist" writer), whose literary watchword is "I am observing" (*Du côté de chez Swann* [*S*], 329). But given that Proust himself makes a fair fist of exhaustively rendering all the minutiae of salon life, it is doubtless with not only a sigh of relief but also a raised eyebrow that we might find ourselves endorsing the self-denying ordinance, were it not for our sensing that the joke is in fact self-directed ("I am fully aware of my more manic writing habits and how they can tax the patience of even the most indulgent readers"). But what of the earnest longueurs of the coda in *Le Temps retrouvé*? No jokes of this type here. Am I alone (I doubt it) in the view that much of the prolonged meditation on the literary vocation and the redemptive conception of "literature" is simply wearing?

This is not because I am not persuaded by many of these claims (though, along with many others, I am not).[2] That, under the conditions that govern the functioning of involuntary memory, certain dead parts of ourselves can be brought back to life ("resurrected") is good news, but scarcely the Good News of promised salvation, and, as a formula for the only life worth living ("life . . . lived to the full"), it is a somewhat exiguous version of the good life. Here we might find ourselves in sympathy with William Empson's sardonic take on the great Proustian saga of remembrance and redemption: "you remember [how Empson must have savored using that talismanic Proustian verb!] how Proust, at the end of that great novel, having convinced the reader with the full sophistication of his genius that he is going to produce an apocalypse, brings out with pathetic faith, as a fact of absolute value, that sometimes when you are living in one place you are reminded of living in another place, and this, since you are now apparently living in two places, means that you are outside time, in the only state of beatitude he can imagine."[3] Empson is in no doubt that Proust is out to persuade us of something ("having convinced the reader") and there is equally no doubt on his part as to the confusion of "sophistication" with a form of sophistry. But, while it would be disingenuous to deny that my own (far less withering) parti pris will exert some pressure on the arguments I wish to make, it is not the principal cause of a degree of weariness with these pages. Nor is it because the sequence in question is relentlessly cast in a "subjectivist,"

[2] They are listed by Richard Terdiman in *Present Past: Modernity and the Memory Crisis* (Ithaca: Cornell University Press, 1993), 153.

[3] William Empson, *Seven Types of Ambiguity* (London: New Directions, 1953), 131.

theoretical idiom stamped by period tastes and tendencies unlikely to hold our attention for long today. We can, of course, approach many of the assumptions and assertions of the *Recherche* historically, in terms of that episteme of Proust's age dominated by the array of idealist idioms in circulation, some of which came Proust's way in his lycée philosophy class. But while interesting in its own terms, this sort of historical and biographical information will not take the concerns of the present book very far. In any case, as we shall see, the explicit quotation of these idioms in the novel itself suggests that, once in the mouths of his characters, they become suitably eligible candidates for inclusion in a Proustian version of Flaubert's *Dictionnaire des idées reçues*.

Dissatisfaction with the sequence in question may be said to derive from a property internal to it, namely, the fact that it is compulsively repetitive. "For nothing is ever repeated exactly," opines the narrator in *La Fugitive* ([F], 465), but the validity of the proposition is put under some strain by the disquisitions of *Le Temps retrouvé*. The same point is made over and over again: there is a world, a "reality," apart from our everyday world; it lies deep within us and is manifested as certain kinds of impressions, sensations, and memories, which it is the task of the work to express or "translate." Since the repetition of the point is not invariably or even mostly a progressive deepening of it, we must ask what it is that motivates these reprises. It is certainly not because Proust is insistently dogmatic (he is the least dogmatic of writers). Perhaps it betrays the precise opposite of self-assurance, an uncertainty as to the security of his own doctrines; Proust repeats because he is trying to convince not only his reader but also himself. But who is "himself" here? It will doubtless have been noticed that I have already started shifting between "narrator" and "Proust," thus opening a can of worms familiar to narrative theory; we will have to delve deeper into that can in due course. For now, let us simply countenance the possibility, as a working hypothesis, that the discursive machine of *Le Temps retrouvé* is itself working overtime to shore up a belief that defies rationality, a "mad belief," vital to sustaining "life," perhaps, but doing so as a pure fiction, somewhat in the spirit, if not the manner, of Nietzsche's life-protecting fictions (in the *Recherche* Saint-Loup is an enthusiastic reader of Nietzsche), a spellbinding illusion, but illusory nonetheless (in connection with art Proust will come to call it an "optical illusion").

II

Proust's novel begins, dramatically, with a hallucination, although in the context of an entirely commonplace experience. The narrator recalls a time when, drifting in and out of sleep (the so-called hypnagogic state), he has imagined himself while sleeping to have been the "subject" of the bedtime book he has been reading (probably Mignet's *Rivalité de François 1er et Charles Quint*). The experience is described, appositely, as "having taken a rather peculiar turn." First, the imagining is not a dream-induced evocation of the world of Mignet's book; rather, the narrator himself has become that world ("it seemed to me that I was myself what the book was talking about"). Second, it is not clear what it is that he has notionally "become." Commonsensically, we might posit one or more of the characters (perhaps François 1er, given the echo of the name in *François le Champi*, the bedtime novel by George Sand read by the narrator's mother). But no such restriction on the "subject" of the book applies. What the narrator actually says is that he has "become" everything (characters, settings, a building, a musical piece): "it seemed to me that I was myself what the book was talking about: a church, a quartet, the rivalry of François 1er and Charles V" (*S*, 7). This is prima facie unintelligible. It is true that in *Le Temps retrouvé* the narrator compares the self to a "book" ("the interior book of unknown signs"), but this is intended as a metaphor with a strictly semiotic import (the self as a collection of signs soliciting interpretation or "decipherment"). The opening moment is not metaphorical in this way; it is baldly literal. In what known or knowable worlds (including the more permissive worlds constructed by the dream-work) can one experience oneself as a building? There will be much more in *À la recherche* about the strange alternative domains opened up to us by sleep and dreaming, and much value is attached to them, as a counter to the dully habit-bound world of everyday conscious life.[4] But, while here seminaturalized as an effect of the dreaming self, if these projections were carried over into the waking life, they would surely qualify as examples of the deranged. And if it is felt that this is to drag a deranged red herring across Proust's "argument," let us recall that the question is raised by the narrator himself in one of several other explorations of sleep where a loss of the sense of the "reality of the common objects that surround me" induces, as it had for Descartes, an alarm over the dividing line between dream and cognition: "I was alarmed to think, however, that this dream had had the clarity of a cognition. Could cognition, by the same token, have the unreality of a dream?" (*SG*, 381).

There are lots of crazed or semicrazed beliefs in the *Recherche*. The narrator, for example, highlights our attachment to friendship and "society" (in the somewhat quaint sense of the latter term) as a mental

---

[4]In *La Prisonnière* the narrator claims that sleep provides the best stories: "I was still enjoying the last remains of sleep, that is to say, the only originality, the only novelty which exists in the telling of stories, since all waking narratives, even those embellished by literature, lack the mysterious incongruities which are the true source of beauty" (110). But if this is the standard by which we are to judge Proust's novel, it fails.

aberration (*douce folie*), which "in our heart of hearts we know is like the wanderings of a madman who believes the furniture is alive and talks to it" (*Le Temps retrouvé* [*T*], 184). This, however, is but Proustian small change, a predictable flourish in the sustained and unbending exposure of the worthlessness of our immersion in the social world. As for the invocations of madness in connection with the certifiable condition of sexual jealousy, these are simply too numerous to mention. But things may start to look unnervingly different when the view in question implicates more sensitive areas, those that the narrator ostensibly values rather than those that he despises or rejects. The man who self-deludingly believes in friendship may resemble the lunatic who converses with his furniture, but that is not so far removed from the young narrator's defamiliarized encounter with the items of furniture in his room as if they were hostile agents bent on malevolent purpose (*À l'ombre des jeunes filles en fleurs* [*JF*], 245–46). However painfully disturbing, defamiliarization for Proust is, after all, the necessary condition of escaping the deadening tyranny of Habit, and it is thus at the very least something of a complication to find the subject of this emancipating experience aligned in some important way with the image of the madman who hallucinates his furniture as animate and speech-endowed (*S*, 12).

And what of the pressure of cognitive mishap in the one area where prima facie it could exert no conceivable pressure at all, the hallowed theme of Resurrection? Diana Knight has drawn our attention to the fact that the echo toward the end of *Sodome et Gomorrhe* of the "intermittences" episode (in which the narrator's delayed grief over his grandmother's death bursts upon him as a kind of "resurrection" of the dead) takes the form of a "hallucination."[5] This is the moment in the Balbec hotel when he "sees" his grandmother in his mother "as in one of those apparitions" (520). There is, of course, a causal explanation: the mother, caught unawares, her hair in disarray, reveals the gray streaks that are normally concealed. For a split second, his mother actually appears as his grandmother, and moreover does so by way of the biological fatalism that informs Proust's treatment of the saga of the generations and the theme of "heredity," whereby we come more and more to physically resemble our parents and ancestors. But these explanatory moves, while part of the point, miss the main point: in its initial occurrence, as distinct from its post facto clarification, the experience has the force of an "optical illusion" that is truly hallucinatory. Might we then find ourselves claiming something similar of the most privileged of the privileged moments, those on which in *Le Temps retrouvé* the narrator stakes all, as

[5] "The Proustian hallucination of the grandmother's resurrection at sunrise." "The Woman without a Shadow," in *Writing the Image after Roland Barthes*, ed. Jean-Michel Rabaté (Philadelphia: University of Pennsylvania Press, 1997), 139.

precisely moments when spontaneous recollection crosses over into the illusion of something that is immediately present to vision (not Combray, Balbec, or Venice recalled, but Combray, Balbec, and Venice "there" before him, literally a resurrection, the return of the past as the deluded witnessing of a kind of "ghost")? Is there not another ghost at this feast of perceptual delights and redemptive meaning, a scene haunted by the specter of reasonable doubt? It is, of course, supposed to be the exact opposite: of the decisive epiphanies in *Le Temps retrouvé*, the narrator claims that they banish "all intellectual doubt" and bring "a joy akin to certainty" (175–76). This is what epiphany does in the ecstatic instant of its occurrence. But the moment is one thing; the totality of the narrative and the multifariousness of its voices another. Earlier I said that the naturalizing explanation of the mother/grandmother confusion, while part of the point, misses the essential point, but this requires some adjustment. That it is there at all tells us that at moments such as these Proust often has two voices speaking in counterpoint, one of them anxious to temper the intensities of the other by reference to that most prosaic of orders—the facts of the matter.

We will encounter this correcting and contextualizing voice on many occasions throughout the course of this book, most importantly, in connection with the initiatory, aesthetic education the narrator will receive from the painter Elstir. On the other hand, we should not overlook that altogether more upbeat and engaging summary of the potential of mad belief provided by the baron de Charlus. When ("slipping his arm into mine") he and the narrator stroll down the boulevard after leaving one of the Guermantes soirees, Charlus regales his young companion with a curious little story:

> "You know the story of the man who believed he had the Princess of China shut up in a bottle. It was a mad belief. He was cured of it. But as soon as he ceased to be mad, he became stupid. There are some sicknesses we must not seek to cure because they are our only protection from others that are more serious." (*Le Côté de Guermantes* [CG], 287)

This perverse recommendation of a most unusual version of therapeutic good sense may also be intended as an homage to Balzac (Charlus is Balzac's greatest fan in the *Recherche*), in particular as an echo of that moment in the concluding scene of *Illusions perdues* that so entranced both Proust and Oscar Wilde. Like Charlus slipping his arm into that of the narrator, Vautrin too seeks to charm and seduce his young protégé-to-be, Lucien de Rubempré, partly by means of an equally exotic tale, the story of a young diplomat with an unconquerable and career-destroying passion for devouring paper (including diplomatic treaties). Vautrin's narrative *curioso* is generally interpreted as a self-interested illustration of the irresistibility of "vice," and Charlus's can be read along the same lines. He certainly has plenty of mad—and dangerous—beliefs of his own with which to sustain himself, even if nothing in the end can halt his ineluctable progress to the condition of aphasic derelict.[6] But he also has another, more robustly sane bulwark against both stupidity and danger: "I have always respected those who defend grammar and logic. We realize, fifty years later, that they averted serious dangers" (*T*, 106).[7] There is, of course, an element of snobbery in this old-school defense of the virtues of clarity in thought and expression, an equivalent of which is to be found in the narrator's exasperation at the syntactic mistakes of the letter sent to him by the uneducated Aimé (dispatched on a mission to discover the truth of Albertine's suspected lesbian proclivities). Yet we should not forget that Charlus is billed as one of the most "intelligent" of the novel's characters, often—for reasons to be examined later—an ambiguous compliment in Proust, but here bestowed without a trace of equivocation. He is also billed—the Proustian accolade par excellence—as someone who could have been a "writer," the narrator lamenting the absence of the works that might have been. But if we don't have the works, we are given some idea of the putative writerly talents that would have nourished them; consistent with the attachment to the rigor of grammar and logic, they include a respect for the differentiating exactness of naming things correctly ("I am somewhat sensitive to names . . . Do you like names?" *SG*, 401) along with a corresponding view of the importance of "distinctions" (where this means less the social than the analytical kind, based on an understanding of the world as a place in which everything is either "p" or "not-p"): "he could have done us all a great service in writing, for not only could he make the finest distinctions, but when he distinguished a thing he always knew its name" (*La Prisonnière* [*P*], 190).

While contextually exotic, it should nevertheless come as no great surprise to find Charlus's pronunciamento on the value of grammar and logic making an appearance as epigraph in a work of philosophy bearing the title *Truth and Truthfulness* (by Bernard Williams). Truth and truthfulness, while close kin, are not the same. Truth, according to Williams, is a property of descriptions and representations of the world, whose prime criterion is "accuracy." Truthfulness designates the virtue of "sincerity," an intentional and humanly valued disposition to telling the truth as one

---

[6] "I came to the conclusion . . . that M de Charlus must be a trifle mad" is one of the narrator's great understatements (*CG*, 378).

[7] Even in the hugely deranged brothel scene of *Le Temps retrouvé*, Charlus evinces a respect for truth (namely, the truth of who is actually beating him, a grotesque travesty of the sadistic brute the sexual fantasy demands). *T*, 125.

sees it even if, by the "accuracy" test, it turns out to be false.[8] Both values matter hugely to Proust; both are problematic. There is, for example, one substantial impediment to Proust making a claim on truthfulness: his assertion that most of the time we lie, not only to others but also—indeed, above all—to ourselves (*SG*, 276) and yet that the practice of lying is what propels us along the road of "discovery"; lying and being lied to are the fertile spawners of curiosity, of the epistemophiliac will to know (*SG*, 198). Naturally, this is a logically opaque (as well as an ethically dubious) assertion. Is it an exception to the rule it enunciates (telling the truth about the truth-revealing possibilities of lying), or is it itself an instance of the rule? If the latter, we are left stranded (for the first time, there are others still to come) in the quicksands of the Cretan Liar Paradox. Even if we skirt the quicksands, it does not follow that lies cannot be bearers or disclosers of truth, as will be clear to anyone familiar with, say, Nietzsche's naturalistic anatomy of the moral life or Freud's psychoanalysis of the fables we tell to make sense of ourselves. What, however, is certain is that such a view of truth-telling is incompatible with "sincerity" as normally understood. But in many ways these are finicky quibbles; as Malcolm Bowie pointed out, Proust's bravura statement about lying is inconsistent with other statements in the text, such that we should perhaps not get too excited by it.[9] Generally speaking, it would be simply bizarre to construe Proust's address to his readers as one extended and intended exercise in sheer mendacity; by and large, there is no good reason to question his sincerity-credentials (susceptibility to self-deceiving rationalization is another matter).

But how do things stand relative to the principle of "accuracy"? In connection with most of the "stuff" of *À la recherche*, from the description of things to the presentation of characters, it would be fatuously irrelevant to say that these are in some sense "inaccurate." What could the term conceivably mean in these fictional contexts? But when it comes to, say, the narrator seeing a wall as a street, or land as sea (an axial example for the whole argument of this book), if here we are to reach for the principle of accuracy, we are going to have ask the question—accurate of what? An account that is an accurate reflection of a perception of the world is not necessarily an accurate reflection of the world, insofar as the experience or perception can embody an illusory or false representation. This distinction, elementary in itself, is going to take us very far in our inquiries.

[8] Bernard Williams, *Truth and Truthfulness: An Essay in Genealogy* (Princeton: Princeton University Press, 2002), 44–45.

[9] Malcolm Bowie, *Freud, Proust, and Lacan: Theory as Fiction* (Cambridge: Cambridge University Press, 1987), 48.

III

The question of "truth"—what, in the abandon with which he uses the term, Proust variously and often bewilderingly understood by it—is fundamental to the following pages, under the general umbrella of a version of philosophical "skepticism" (Charlus is also a great skeptic, especially in his withering denunciation of the patriotic nonsense induced by war fever). There are several very familiar senses in which Proust can be described as a skeptic, most obviously that centered on his doubts as to the "knowability" of other people. More generally, the notion of "literary" skepticism sketched by Graham Bradshaw in connection with Shakespeare might, suitably adapted, be applicable to Proust. Literary skepticism signifies double seeing, ambiguity, differential point of view, not just as a "position" but as a device—in Shakespeare's case, a dramatic device in the service of the generic and structural requirements of what Bradshaw calls "dramatic thinking," a perspectival mode in which a dramatic speech is relativized not simply to a point of view (that of the speaking character) but also to its place in the temporal unfolding of the play.[10] In *La Prisonnière* there is a programmatic statement, rising to a magnificent crescendo in one of Proust's most resonant and cherished metaphors, that we could, roughly, interpret as the narrative equivalent of Bradshaw's gloss, with a modernist add-on (since Proust himself proposes it) for painting and music: "The only true voyage . . . would be . . . to see the universe through the eyes of another, of a hundred others, to see the hundred universes that each of them sees, that each of them is; and this we can do with an Elstir, with a Vinteuil; with men like these we really do fly from star to star" (236–37).

This is Proust at his most genuinely appealing, and only the churlishly flat-footed would look askance at his star-spangled celebration of the plurality of universes and its artistic promise. But where this travels over to the respects in which Proust has been associated, even in its informal and diluted guises, with *philosophical* skepticism, we enter more contestable territory. Few of these associations are my concern here in any central way, and some are of no concern at all. One reason for this derives from the portrait of Swann:

> For Swann was reaching an age at which one's philosophy—encouraged by the current philosophy of the day, and also by that of the circle in which Swann had spent so much of his life, that of the social set attached to the Princesse des Laumes, where it was agreed that intelligence was in direct ratio to scepticism and nothing was real and incontestable except the individual tastes of each person—is no longer that of youth, but a positive, almost medical philosophy,

[10] Graham Bradshaw, *Shakespeare's Scepticism* (Brighton: Palgrave Macmillan, 1987).

the philosophy of men who, exteriorizing the objects of their aspirations, try to derive from the years that have already elapsed a stable residue of habits and passions they can regard as characteristic and permanent and which they will deliberately make it their primary concern that the kind of life they adopt may satisfy. (*S*, 282)

Anyone tempted to read Proust through the lens of skepticism is likely to find their wish decisively inhibited by this deft take on the surrender of the intellect, cognate with Swann's "ironic" mode of speaking as if all of his utterances were made in quotation marks, the manner that so baffles and irritates the young narrator. And there is stronger stuff still to encourage that inhibition. Apart from the flirtation of the spiritually jaded Swann with philosophical fashion, as little more than a cover for middle-aged abdication of the challenge of thought and judgment, there is the bracing view in praise of skepticism enunciated by the ineffable Cottard: "The wise man is of necessity a sceptic . . . when all's said and done, Socrates isn't so extraordinary. They're people who had nothing to do, who spent their whole day walking about logic-chopping" (*P*, 445). And in the Verdurin circle to which both Swann (briefly) and Cottard (permanently) belong, there is, according to another member of the circle (the Princesse Sherbatoff), a living incarnation of the skeptical mind, the pedant Brichot: "with the professor, the mordant irony of the complete sceptic never loses its rights" (*P*, 445), while Brichot in turn has his own model or ideal, "our gentle master of exquisite scepticism," Anatole France (*T*, 100).

Since, on the question of skepticism, or indeed anything else, the doctor, the professor, and the princess are not natural Proust company, we would perhaps do well to sidestep the pitfalls of formal definition and take our cue from Nietzsche's sprightly remark in *The Gay Science*: "I approve of any form of scepticism to which I can reply 'let's try it.' "[11] Trying it (some might say trying it on) is the experimental drift of this book. But, within this liberally pragmatic frame, let us set the stage with two preliminary clarifications, the first to do with the nature of Proustian skepticism, the second to do with its object. For the first of these clarifications, I want to draw briefly (and lightly) on the distinction in philosophy between radical skepticism and mitigated (or, as it is sometimes alternatively called, constructive) skepticism.[12] Radical skepticism is the project that turns on the notoriously self-defeating proposition "I

[11] Friedrich Nietzsche, *The Gay Science* (Cambridge: Cambridge University Press, 2001), 62.

[12] The term "mitigated" skepticism derives from Hume, who contrasts it with "excessive" skepticism. Christopher Hookway, *Scepticism* (London: Routledge, 1998); Neil Gascoigne, *Scepticism* (London: McGill Queens University Press, 2002).

know nothing," and generally ends by skirting, when not enthusiastically entering, the zones of relativism and solipsism. There are, of course, accounts of Proust that align him with both relativism and solipsism, but to my mind these versions are both unpersuasive and uninteresting if taken to mean that Proust's novel is best understood in these terms or something very like them (quite why, I shall explain in due course).[13] Mitigated or constructive skepticism is a very different matter, insofar as it avoids the traps of relativism and solipsism by holding fast to some standard of rationality from which to express and organize doubts as to certain descriptions of reality. It is this variety of skepticism that I shall bring to bear on the Proustian enterprise or, more precisely (and, I hope, more interestingly), maintain that Proust himself, in certain moods, brings to bear on his own enterprise. On the face of it, this will sound provocative or, more bluntly, just plain silly. The writer who conspicuously devalues acts of rational intellection (what his narrator calls "intelligence"), and who constantly opposes intuition to reason, will hardly seem a promising candidate for annexation to the camp of the classically skeptical rationalist. This indeed is why I draw on this source but lightly, and do so broadly for one reason only: to put in place a mode of skeptical inquiry that keeps intact the distinction between truth and error, the form of skepticism that serves the cause of truth in its campaign against error.[14]

The second clarification concerns the object of Proust's skepticism. This takes us into equally tricky and controversial areas. I do not mean here what is normally taken as the object or objects of skeptical critique in Proust: those thematic categories of *À la recherche* that go under the headings of love, friendship, society, travel, and so forth, the values and practices that link us to the world (in the worldly sense of world) and that the narrator renounces in the discovery of and self-dedication to the artistic vocation. By the object of skepticism, I mean not the former but

[13] If Proust's novel enters the solipsist's world at all, it is psychologically and morally rather than philosophically. In his study of Nabokov, Michael Wood writes that "the solipsist resembles one, and only one, other human type—the torturer." *The Magician's Doubts: Nabokov and the Risks of Fiction* (London: Chatto and Windus, 1995), 234. Proust's narrator is never closer to the solipsist than when torturing his "prisoner," Albertine, not least by virtue of the fact that, while his own mental pain is everywhere on display in *La Prisonnière*, that of the actual victim of "incarceration" is scarcely seen, one of the purposes of first-person narration being to obliterate it.

[14] It is one of the functions of what Benjamin calls "commentary" in the *Recherche* (as one of the components of a hybrid generic form that makes of it a "special case of literature"). Walter Benjamin, "The Image of Proust," in *Illuminations*, ed. Hannah Arendt, trans. Harry Zohn (London: Pimlico, 1999), 197. Benjamin also speaks of "the tested skepticism with which he approached things" (interpreted as an antidote to "the self-satisfied inwardness of Romanticism"). Benjamin cites Rivière's remark that "Proust approaches experience . . . without the slightest tendency to console" (himself adding that "[n]othing is truer than that"). Ibid., 208.

the latter, the very thing that is opposed to these categories, namely, the artistic vocation itself or a certain version of it, the version over which the Proustian coterie has swooned for so long. This is not to suggest that we should stop taking seriously Proust's view of the aesthetic solution to the problem of living, or, more pertinently, ascribe to Proust the intention of inviting us not to take it seriously. That would be perverse to a degree, and in the continuing flux of commentary, we can still encounter strong versions of the aesthetic solution, for instance, the terms on which Alexander Nehamas juxtaposes the idea of life as a work of art with Nietzsche's bracing, existential stylistics based on the twin notions of self-overcoming and the eternal recurrence.[15]

The target here is rather the weak or weak-kneed varieties of this reading of Proust. In many ways this is an easy target (what self-respecting reader would now wish to congregate with the erstwhile worshippers?), and has been hit many times before. The most telling include the critical reflections of Leo Bersani and Paul de Man.[16] Bersani encouraged us to question the redemptive or reparative aspect of Proust's view of artistic "symbolization," largely from the point of view of a neo-Lacanian psychoanalysis prioritizing "perishable experience" over "the essentializing inventions of art." In a very different intellectual register, de Man also urged us down the skeptical road, and for the purposes of my argument, de Man is, as we shall see on various occasions, a more complex reference, though on the whole I will want to maintain that in terms of the radical skepticism/mitigated skepticism distinction, de Man situates himself more on the side of the former, albeit on a very special set of terms (deconstruction). Were he still with us, I don't think he would take kindly to being described as a rationalist skeptic.

The swooners thus find themselves beleaguered. But if they have become an object of ridicule by virtue of having so often been ridiculous, they are not solely to blame for having confused daintiness with spirituality and narcissism with criticism. It is no accident that of all the great early modern writers, it is to Proust that they have gone as to a shrine (not even the more overtly religious Eliot has been revered in the same way). Proust's doctrine, if that is what it can be called, and its attempted instantiation in the *Recherche* rest on a paradox—a proclaimed renunciation of the world that remains in and of the world. The means for the accomplishment of this paradoxical task Proust variously called "art"

[15] Alexander Nehamas, *Nietzsche: Life as Literature* (Cambridge, Mass.: Harvard University Press, 1985), 167–68.

[16] Leo Bersani, *Marcel Proust: The Fictions of Life and of Art* (New York: Oxford University Press, 1969) and *The Culture of Redemption* (Cambridge, Mass.: Harvard University Press, 1990); Paul de Man, "Reading (Proust)," in *Allegories of Reading* (New Haven: Yale University Press, 1979), 57–78.

or "literature" or "beauty." An ascesis was to be achieved through the aesthetic, where the latter entails not just the specialized meaning of the Beautiful but the full spectrum of *aesthesis*, the sphere of sense-based experiences and intuitions prior to or "below" rational cognition. This was a difficult, if not impossible, project, an ascesis that isn't one, shadowed by idolatry and bad faith. It is no surprise, therefore, that Proust acquired a swooning readership, especially from an age and a social world in which wrought sensitivity and jaded appetite were often indistinguishable, in which the beauty-merchants (collectors, connoisseurs, dealers) hawked their wares around the marketplace, the whole business backed by the discreet rustle of banknotes and share certificates (one of Proust's gags has share certificates as art objects).[17] On the other hand, since Proust took both his master, Ruskin, and himself to task for confusing the aesthetic and the spiritual, we must not only listen to an alternative, more taxing, and self-critical Proustian voice but begin by actually identifying and locating it.

In the de Manian view this other voice is anonymous; it belongs to something called the "text" and is in fact less a distinctive voice, in the sense of attributable to a determinate speaker, than a textual force, a power to counter the declared ambitions of the text's author, as a reflection of how language itself works irrespective of the intentions of any particular user. I take a different view, at least of the intentions of Marcel Proust. If they may not always be precisely determinable (crucially, what Proust intentionally determined as the relation between himself and his narrator), they matter. But the plural also matters, that is, the form in which they matter is indeed double, which generates the novel as home to two warring voices, albeit unequally pitched: the celebratory and the skeptical.[18] The former is noisy and insistent, laden with persuasive energy and confident of its message; the other is low-key, intermittent, oblique, a sotto voce emanation from the margins, and often audible only in the tones of ironic indirection. Nevertheless, although quiet, that voice is there to be heard. It would, of course, make no sense whatsoever to suggest that Proust asks us to take no heed of his version of the "aesthetic solution," and that is most certainly not the claim of this book. It would, however, be most unlikely to detain anyone other than the light-headed

[17] M. de Norpois "did not hesitate to congratulate my father on the 'composition' of his portfolio, 'very stylish, very neat, very handsome.' It sounded as though he endowed the difference between the market values of shares, and even the shares themselves, with something like aesthetic merit" (*JF*, 28).

[18] Bowie was closer to the multivocal structure of the *Recherche* when, in connection with a different set of interests, he spoke of "certain neglected voices" within "the contrapuntal texture of Proustian argument." "Proust, Jealousy, Knowledge," in *Freud, Proust, and Lacan*, 59.

admirer for very long if it were offered solely from within the cocooned complacency of unquestioned belief (the stance of the pure Aesthete). If it speaks to us and moves us, it is because, while believing in it, to the point of sacrificing the entirety of a creative life to it, Proust himself is aware of the frailty of the belief, along with his gleefully comic understanding that it is in some ways completely mad.

Arguably, Proust's great achievement was to have kept those beliefs alive under the pressure of that understanding, but we do him no favors if we choose simply to ignore the pressure.[19] Proust was a secular writer, not a religious one (a question I consider at some length in chapter 4), and much of the point of his message of "redemption" through art is that, thrown into a wholly secular world, it has to acknowledge its own vulnerabilities and take its chances with those who do not think and feel in the same way. This must include the thought that, on occasion, Proust himself was among those who do not think and feel in the same way. Anyone disinclined to accept that Proust explicitly voices doubt in connection with his deepest beliefs should pause over a passage in what, along with the madeleine episode, is the most ecstatic moment in the entire novel. Indeed, as the narrator reflects on the unsuspected realms of "redemptive" imagination into which he has been swept by the Vinteuil septet, he is reminded of what happened to him on tasting the madeleine, but in terms of a worried thought the reader might not have predicted:

> I began to doubt once more, I said to myself that after all it might be that, even though Vinteuil's phrases seemed to me to be the expression of certain states of the soul—analogous to the one I had experienced on tasting the madeleine soaked in tea—nothing proved that the vagueness of these states was a sign of their profundity, rather than of our inability, so far, to analyze them: there would therefore be nothing more real in them than in others. (P, 352)

He does not dwell on the thought and its potential implications. It is mentioned and then shunted to one side; and the caveat "so far" is entered by Proust in the knowledge that at the revelatory end of his novel

<hr>

[19]Vincent Descombes summarizes on the model of a "trial" undergone by the narrator that consists "in the choice between the destiny of a 'doubter' and the destiny of a man of 'faith,'." *Proust: Philosophy of the Novel*, 128. The standard view, of course, has Swann, the failed dilettante, as the doubter and the narrator, the artist-to-be, as the "man of faith." Bersani, however, radically equivocated the doubt/faith distinction, with the argument that Proust's project—the redemptive premise of its aesthetic—is umbilically joined to the recognition of its own impossibility: "Proust's novel is constantly raising doubts about its own status as a vehicle of those essences that, according to Proust, become visible in great art . . . Proust's novel defeats its redemptive project . . . only by failing to provide us with any reason for its own existence; its greatness, in short, is inseparable from the impossibility of its ever having been written." "Death and Literary Authority," in *A New History of French Literature*, ed. Denis Hollier (Cambridge, Mass.: Harvard University Press, 1989), 866–67.

in the Guermantes library, it will have evaporated. It is not a repudiation; that is not how Proustian doubt works. But however contained and short-lived, the doubting voice has spoken, not just as early hesitation reflecting the lack of self-confidence yet to be acquired but also relatively late in the day (in *La Prisonnière*), and it cannot ever be wholly banished from our reading consciousness, even after we have passed from the anxiety-charged world of *La Prisonnière* into the revelatory one of *Le Temps retrouvé*. And between the two, in *La Fugitive*, there are these throwaway lines on the subject of novels and what it means to read them:

> And sometimes reading a rather sad novel carried me suddenly backwards, for some novels are like a period of great mourning which abolishes habit and puts us once more in touch with the reality of life, but for a few hours only, as does a nightmare, for the force of habit, the oblivion that it procures and the gaiety that it restores as the brain is unable to resist them and re-establish the truth, are infinitely stronger than even the most hypnotic suggestions of a beautiful book, which, like all suggestions, have a very fleeting effect. (526)

The case made here is self-restricting; it applies only to "some novels," which do not necessarily include Proust's, and, however both "sad" and "beautiful" the latter is, the function of whiling away the odd hour ("for a few hours") in a variety of induced hypnosis does not plausibly describe either Proust's aims or our experience of reading him. On the other hand, since "mourning" is one of his deepest themes, and liberation from Habit certainly a major aim, the passage cuts closer to the Proustian bone than one might think at first sight: if the "liberation" is but a "fleeting effect," then it is hard to see how transience converts to transcendence.

IV

Passing remarks do not an entire argument make. The challenge is to take one-off moments such as these and place them in the broader context of the diverse forms and terms in which the skeptical voice can be intermittently yet persistently heard. That is what this book is about, its own argument centered on the spectacle of Proust arguing with himself. A first step here might be a backward one, into Proust's unsteady relation with the work of Ruskin. Proust famously bit the hand that fed him (the Master as source of "nourishment" is fundamental to Proust's imagining of the role of the significant predecessor), when, politely but devastatingly, he accused Ruskin of the vice Ruskin himself had denounced. Proust quotes what Ruskin had written on the "deadly function of art in its ministry to what . . . is truly, and in the deep sense, to be called idolatry," further described as "some dear and sad fantasy which we have made for ourselves."[20] Proust took full note of this admonition in more or less single-handedly resisting the uncritical French tendency, reflected in the titles chosen by his translators (*L'Esthétique anglaise*, *La Religion de la beauté*), to posit Ruskin as the aesthete's aesthete (33). Yet by the time he came to write the "Post-Scriptum" to the preface of his own translation of the *Bible of Amiens*, Proust maintained that unconsciously and against his better self, Ruskin had fallen into the idolatrous trap: "The doctrines he professed were moral doctrines, and yet he chose them for their beauty. And since he did not wish to present them as beautiful but as true, he was forced to deceive himself about the nature of the reasons that made him adopt them" (51). This is strong language from the rebellious disciple, but its strength is also an index of how deep the problem of idolatry runs. Ruskin's alleged self-deception did not stem from a mere contingent defect of Ruskin's mind, but reflected "an infirmity essential to the human mind" (54), and as such also implicated the disciple in the same web of self-deceiving blindness or "insincerity." Proust does not criticize Ruskin from the assumption of his own moral or spiritual superiority, as if claiming exemption from the condition he diagnoses. On the contrary, while stopping short of a full mea culpa, he goes out of his way to confess his own complicity, most notably in connection with the reading of a page of Ruskin in that place of glorious error and bedazzlement, the Saint Mark's baptistery (53–54).[21]

The tensions and ambivalences wound into Proust's circling around Ruskin furnish an indispensable prolegomenon to the central questions of *À la recherche*. His narrator may come close to conflating the spiritual and the aesthetic, such that the negative lesson of Ruskin—the warning issued by Ruskin and the warning about Ruskin issued by Proust—is forgotten or even nonchalantly disregarded.[22] But Proust never forgets it.

[20] Marcel Proust, *On Reading Ruskin: Prefaces to "La Bible d'Amiens" and "Sésame et les lys,"* trans. and ed. Jean Autret, William Burford, and Phillip J. Wolfe; introd. Richard Macksey (New Haven: Yale University Press, 1987), 50. Further references in this chapter are to this edition with page numbers given parenthetically in the main body of the text.

[21] I discuss this in chapter 4.

[22] Consider, for example, the narrator's flippant mockery of Nietzsche's ascetic renunciation of the seductions of Wagner: "I could admire the master of Bayreuth without any of the scruples of those who, like Nietzsche, feel that duty requires them to flee, both in art and in life, from any beauty which appeals to them, who tear themselves away from *Tristan* as they renounce *Parsifal*, and by a spiritual ascesis, piling mortification upon mortification, follow the bloodiest path of suffering until they raise themselves to the pure knowledge and perfect adoration of *The Longjumeau Postilion*" (P, 142). *The Longjumeau Postilion* was a light opera by Adam and figures nowhere in Nietzsche. The example that Nietzsche gave as an antidote to Wagner was, of course, Bizet. The narrator's tendentious replacement of Bizet by Adam's commercial bauble is evidently not a move endorsed by Proust. The example is discussed by Antoine Compagnon, *Proust Between Two Centuries* (New York: Columbia University Press, 1992), 37.

His novel does not simply proffer the aesthetic solution to the problem of living but also enacts a struggle with the solution as a problem in its own right. There can be no question but that Proust wanted to endorse it by transforming it, to save "salvation," as it were, in terms that would rescue it from those versions steeped in idolatry. The whole of the narrator's evolution is directed to that outcome. But Proust also knew that what he most wanted, while he wanted it very badly, he perhaps could never have it in a form completely immune from contamination by the idolatrous. Proust thus invites us to read him according to the rule enunciated for his own reading of Ruskin's *Bible of Amiens*: never in a manner "allowing us to believe without enquiry and to admire on faith" (55). It also became the rule for his reading of Ruskin on the topic of reading. In the preface to his translation of *Sesame and Lilies*, Proust situates the general issue of idolatry specifically in a disagreement with Ruskin on the purposes of reading. Ruskin's error, according to Proust, was to have positioned the Book as a "motionless idol" and its ideal reading as an act of "fetishistic respect" (120). This applies a fortiori to a whole class of Proust's readers, receiving and worshipping in ignorance or disregard of Proust's claim that "[r]eading is at the threshold of spiritual life; it can introduce us to it; it does not constitute it" (116).

The following chapters are about Proust's attempt to apply his rule to his own creation, as an argument, often reluctant, uncertain, and stumbling, with and against himself, in particular, his lucid refusal to take on "faith" and hence protect from "enquiry" what in other moods and enthusiasms he most cherished, namely, his own mad belief in the resurrecting, transfiguring, and redeeming powers of art. Believing literally that you have the Princess of China physically trapped in a bottle is not the same thing as the metaphorically articulated belief that you have the secret meaning of the lived life captured aesthetically in a "vessel" or a "vase" (the latter one of the most cited of Proust's metaphors for his metaphorical art). But perhaps they are not that far apart. Consider, for example, the extraordinary saga of Albertine's breast, where the "question" of metaphor is absolutely center stage. The occasion involves less what we would formally call a "belief," more a state of mind invoking a structure of belief situated on shores that reason could never dream of reaching. As one of the maddest episodes of Proustian imagining, it is of particular note for three reasons. First, it enacts a wanton unraveling of cognitive grip, embraced with the careless insouciance that is uniquely the privilege of the lunatic; second, the correcting skeptical voice is given to a figure imagined as a "philosopher," embodiment of the principle of pragmatic right reason; third, it implicates the basic procedures of Proust's art in ways both direct and fundamental. Here, in *À l'ombre des jeunes filles en fleurs*, is what happens (there are many others that we will consider further down the line) as the narrator, flushed with desire, contemplates the body of Albertine abed:

> The sight of her naked throat and her excessively pink cheeks had so intoxicated me (that is, had so transferred reality from the world of nature into the deluge of my own sensations, which I could barely contain) as to have upset the balance between the tumultuous and indestructible immensity of the life surging through me and the paltry life of the universe. The sea, which through the window could be seen beside the valley, the swelling breasts of the closest of the Maineville cliffs, the sky where the moon had not yet reached the zenith, all of this seemed to lie as light as feathers between my eyelids, at rest upon eyeballs in which I felt the pupils had expanded and become strong enough, and ready, to hold much heavier burdens, all the mountains in the world, on their delicate surface. Even the whole sphere of the horizon did not suffice to fill their orbits. Any impingement of the natural world upon my consciousness, however mighty, would have seemed insubstantial to me; a gust of air off the sea would have seemed short-winded for the vast breaths filling my breast. I leaned over to kiss Albertine. Had death chosen that instant to strike me down, it would have been a matter of indifference to me, or rather it would have seemed impossible, for life did not reside somewhere outside me; all of life was contained within me. A pitying smile would have been my only response, had a philosopher put the view that, however remote it might be now, a day was bound to come when I would die, that the everlasting forces of nature would outlive me, those forces with their divine tread grinding me like a grain of dust, that after my own extinction there would continue to be swelling-breasted cliffs, a sea, a sky and moonlight! How could such a thing be possible? How could the world outlive me, given that I was not a mere speck lost in it—it was wholly contained within me, and it came nowhere near filling me, since, somewhere among so much unoccupied space, where other vast treasures could have been stored, I could casually toss the sky, the sea and the cliffs! (508–9)

The narrative supplies a perfectly "normal" explanatory context for this remarkable extravaganza. It is, after all, well known that sexual arousal can have a peculiar effect on our sanity. But this platitude will not suffice. The relation between sexuality and the pursuit of knowledge in the *Recherche* is an unusually intimate one, and often takes the form of positing the desiring mind as the mind at its most cognitively alert and curious.[23] But it's frankly a bit of a stretch matching this cheery epistemological view to what actually takes place in the passage. The sexually excited narrator may well be disposed to leave the "philosopher"

[23]The most eloquent spokesman for this view is Malcolm Bowie, who comments on the passage in precisely these terms in *Proust Among the Stars* (London: HarperCollins, 1998), 219.

stranded on the other shore as he gaily turns "perspective" upside down and inside out, but there is no reason why we should. Or, indeed, to think that Proust does; if anything, Proust's implied position here is that of the skeptical ironist on the side of the philosopher's rational claims, wryly contemplating his narrator orbiting in the ecstasy of a solipsist *dérive*. However, there is a further complication that concerns less the content of the narrator's desiring relation to reality than Proust's writing of it, the terms of his art, crucially, the work of metaphor and syntax. Mountains implicitly represented as breasts need not detain us for long; Proust would have inherited this sort of thing from the legacy of anthropomorphic metaphor (in Lamartine, for example, though in "Le Vallon" it is the cleft of the valley rather than the mountain peaks that is associated with the idea of a welcoming woman's breast). But when conventional trope joins with the "swelling" syntax of Proust's elaborate periods to metamorphose the entire world, dissolving it into a soliloquy made from a heady mix of sex and solipsism, we are entitled to wonder whether this is a case of language gone on holiday with no intention of returning (the emotional geography of the obvious predecessor, Baudelaire's metamorphic translations of woman's breast and tropical landscape in "Parfum exotique," are, rhetorically speaking, decorously modest by comparison). It is not just the pressure of sexual appetite that can disarrange the cognitive map of the world but also the pleasures of metaphor-making underpinned by oceanic sentence structures; the manic reordering of reality is driven more by the tumescence of the writing than that of its narrating subject.

In a moment of reckless euphoria, Proust recovered something of the megalomania of the romantics, when in the preface to *La Bible d'Amiens* he wrote of Ruskin in terms of the relation between "belief" and the sovereign rights of "genius": "Whether some of these conceptions of his supernatural aesthetics be false is a matter which, in our opinion, is of no importance at all. All those who have any understanding of the laws governing the development of genius know that its force is measured more by the force of its beliefs than by what may be satisfying to common sense in the object of those beliefs" (36). It was probably just about possible still to get away with this sort of thing ("in our opinion") in the early twentieth century, but only so far. Beyond its social function as a polite substitute for a more egocentric "my," the likely reach of the plural possessive pronoun was strictly limited. And even as a wildly affirmed personal opinion, already by the time of the "Post-Scriptum" to his preface, we find Proust rebuking himself for a gesture of such flagrant hubris (55). From there to making Proust into an apostle of rational common sense is, of course, another matter altogether, although the affection bestowed in the novel on the practical wisdom of grandmother, mother, and Françoise may give us pause for thought. There are far grander models for the role of skeptic standing as watchman at the portals of the Proustian aesthetic epiphany. The grandest by far within Proust's tradition would be the father of the modern skeptical *reductio*, Descartes, a figure about whom Proust has interesting, if largely scattered, things to say, but whose sole mention in the *Recherche* is in connection with the socially shared intuitions of common sense ("the most common thing in the world," *P*, 319).[24] But since the swelling and (verbally) swollen erotic fantasia around Albertine's body sweeps the artistic imagination across the oceans of the world, let us in conclusion turn to a humbler figure with practical knowledge of the oceans, a seafaring man whom Proust encounters in the pages of Ruskin as the perfect incarnation of the commonsensical view of things.

This is Turner's naval officer, the gentleman who objects to the painter's depiction of ships without their portholes, and to whom Turner explains his artistic purposes. Proust came across Ruskin's account of this exchange in *Eagle's Nest*, and, more important, saw fit to reproduce it in the preface to the *Bible of Amiens*. It is quoted in the context of Proust's discussion of the vantage point from which to see and—in the case of Ruskin's engraving—draw the cathedral of Amiens:

> Turner, in his early life, was sometimes good-natured, and would show people what he was about. He was one day making a drawing of Plymouth harbour, with some ships at a distance of a mile or two, seen against the light. Having shown this drawing to a naval officer, the naval officer observed with surprise, and objected with very justifiable indignation, that the ships of the line had no port-holes. "No," said Turner, "certainly not. If you will walk to Mount Edgecombe, and look at the ships against the sunset, you will find that you can't see the port-holes." "Well, but," said the naval officer, still indignant, "you know the port-holes are there." "Yes," said Turner, "I know that well enough, but my business is to draw what I see, and not what I know is there." (41–42)

Wheeling this representative of robustly empirical English common sense onto the stage alongside René Descartes will hardly seem a productive move, and one most unlikely to command the intellectual sympathy, let alone the active support, of Proust. The "good-natured" Turner is courteously helpful to his companion, but it is clear that for both Ruskin

[24]The definitive, if controversial, study of the Proust-Descartes relation remains Maurice Müller's, with the imposing title *De Descartes à Marcel Proust: Essais sur la théorie des essences, le positivisme et les méthodes dialectique et réflexive* (Neufchâtel: La Baconniere, 1947). For further sources and suggestions, see Claudia Brodsky, "Remembering Swann," in *The Imposition of Form: Studies in Narrative Representation and Knowledge* (Princeton: Princeton University Press, 1987), 273.

and Proust the officer is a bit of a fool, an agreeable philistine.[25] However respectfully his inquiries and objections are treated, he is there as a mildly comic foil to a "perspectivist" aesthetic manifesto, which Proust summarizes as the principle of "distance arranging, in the deceitful but happy manner of the artist" (42). This is the aesthetic that will be imported lock, stock, and barrel into the Elstir section of À l'ombre des jeunes filles en fleurs, precisely in terms of the distinction between depicting not what you know but what you see "from a distance." Yet even as Proust summarizes what he takes to be the thought of Turner and Ruskin, the phrasing flashes a warning light. Neither Turner nor Ruskin uses the term "deceitful" (mensongère). Pleasing or exciting the eye (after the happy manner of the artist) is one thing, casting that enterprise as a deception of the eye belongs in a very different conceptual and moral register. It is the epistemological worm in the rose and raises all kinds of important questions: What is it that Turner draws—is it a ship or that curiously impossible thing, a ship that isn't one (a ship without portholes), or, arguably, a wholly new object for which a new name would be required; and what relation of reference, if any, to the world might this new object and name sustain? These will be urgent questions for us in connection with Elstir's painterly ideas and their influence on the artistic thinking of the narrator (Charlus's way with things, distinctions, and names, under the guiding aegis of grammar and logic, finds something of its point here). We might also take note here of another sailors' tale, in both its setting and its content the perfect foil to the celebrated aesthetic of the "mirage." Proust took special note of a passage in the preface by Robert de la Sizeranne to Mathilde Crémieux's translation of The Stones of Venice. It is the passage where La Sizeranne reports and comments on the collapse of the campanile of Saint Mark's in 1902 (two years after Proust's own visit to Venice) and the consternation of the sailors, arriving from Trieste in the early morning light, who think they are hallucinating the absence of the great landmark that not only guides safely into the Venetian harbor but summarizes the very essence of "Venice." Proust remarks in particular on how the seafarers "believe themselves the plaything of a mirage," and this is clearly not intended as an instance of the perceptually exciting and mind-expanding "mirage" of Elstir's painting; it is vision as unhappy and potentially catastrophic disorientation.[26]

[25] On the other hand, recall Proust writing to Marie Nordlinger in 1905 in defense of Whistler as "the painter of the rooms with the rose-strewn curtains and, above all, the sails at night belonging to Messrs Vanderbilt and Freer," but then adds, "why does one see only the sail and not the boat?" Corr., 5:261.

[26] Corr., 21:613; see Nathalie Mauriac Dyer, "Genesis of Proust's 'Ruine de Venise,' " in Proust in Perspective: Visions and Revisions, ed. Armine Kotin Mortimer and Katherine Kolb (Chicago: University of Illinois Press, 2002), 76–77.

But this is to anticipate what lies some way off. In the meantime, perhaps we might provisionally give the naval officer a bigger part in the relevant argument, as the awkwardly disruptive agent provocateur who provides the ideal antidote to the suffocating grip of hushed reverence. Let us then elect him an honorary member of Proust's society of ghosts, returning from the dead to accompany Proust's narrator, Proust himself, and us, his readers, on a walk through *À la recherche* armed with his impatiently doubtful air and his impertinently obvious questions. For Turner's answer, while entirely satisfactory on its own terms, indeed underlying and explaining the creation of some of the greatest effects of modern painting, is also incomplete. What is the meaning and the value of painting what you see rather than what you know, or, more exactly, painting what you see in the knowledge that this isn't what you know? Although these questions can come out as ponderously idiotic ("what, no portholes?"), they can also be all too airily dismissed. Incongruous though it may seem, in his sturdily naive way, the ghost of Turner's navy man may help us in confronting a blind spot in the settled reception of the canonical masters of impressionist and modern art, a celebration that sweeps to one side a whole problematic centered on an uneasy relation between vision, knowledge, and truth. Turner's friend may have missed the point about Turner's painting; he nevertheless succeeds in making a point about its point.

V

These are also possible questions for Proust's conception of literature. In the preface to his translation of *Sesame and Lilies*, Proust calls reading "the inciter whose magical keys open to our innermost selves the doors of abodes into which we would not have known how to penetrate" (118). But he is then quick to add that the risk of idolatry resides in substituting the incitement for the necessary work of the mind itself in the search for truth, confusing the turn of the key with what lies behind the door, as if a necessary condition of access were also a sufficient condition. The key is "magical" (the term is Proust's), and the magic is potent. But magic also traffics in illusions, and magicians are notoriously tricksters. At his most severe Proust refers to "the kind of trickery that a page of Ruskin's was for each one of us" (51). But, once again, it is a case of the pot calling the kettle black, and, more important, of Proust's awareness that this is so. As a first marker of Proust's skeptical lucidity, we might as well go straight into the lions' den, that place sacred to the Proust worshippers, and *the* scene of key-turning and door-opening magic in the novel. Would it be mindlessly foolish to represent the madeleine episode as, at one level, in conflict with the other level of manifest seriousness, a sort of hoax, and to guide a rereading of it in part under the auspices of one of the finest Proust cartoons (of which there are hundreds, no high-cultural writer more amenable than Proust to pop-cultural appropriation, a phenomenon worth investigating in its own right)? The cartoon in question has the invalid Proust propped up in a hospital bed as an employee comes into his room doing his rounds with the food tray. The caption: "I'm out of madeleines, how about a prune Danish?"[27] Along with two other, equally implausible candidates (whom we shall encounter later),[28] this makes of the cartoonist one of Proust's best ever critics, grasping the essential in a single, condensed, and irreverent moment of representation. In connection with Proustian pastry worship, it humorously captures what Proust himself tells us over and over again, and most notably in the passage on the "magic" of reading: that it is a source of great "danger" to the mind when "truth no longer appears to us as an ideal we can realize only through the intimate progress of our thought and the effort of our heart, but as a material thing, deposited between the leaves of books" (118).

But there is more negative freight to the madeleine episode than just the risk of fetishizing the catalyst as the thing-in-itself. For what cannier instance of narrative trickery than that anthology piece wherein a whole "world" and a whole past are, as if by a miracle, conjured out of a cake and a cup of tea to become this most substantial expanse of recollecting narrative in the modernist repertoire. The Ur-version has the cake as toast (*pain grillé*) and the early drafts of *À la recherche* have a "biscuit," but these are minor variations on the theme of pure contingency (Danish pastry would do just as well).[29] And if it has to be a madeleine rather than toast or biscuit because of the psychologically and affectively complex associations of the common noun with a suite of proper names—the sinner saint, Mary Magdalene, Madeleine Blanchet (the adoptive mother who ends by quasi-incestuously marrying her adoptive son in George Sand's *François le Champi*), Madeleine de Villeparisis, member of the aristocratic Guermantes family and mother of Saint-Loup who marries Swann's daughter, Gilberte, thus joining biologically and socially the two ways of the childhood walks in Combray—there is also the hilariously contingent element that is generally overlooked: the nineteenth-century

---

[27] "Proust orders from the cart," in Emily Eells, "Proust à l'Américaine," in *La Réception de Proust à l'étranger*, ed. Mireille Naturel (Illiers-Combray, France: Institut Marcel Proust International, 2002). For other cartoon treatments of the madeleine, see Margaret Gray, *Postmodern Proust* (Philadelphia: University of Pennsylvania Press, 1992), 161–64.

[28] They are both characters in the novel, the Prince de Foix and Dr. Cottard.

[29] *Against Sainte-Beuve and Other Essays*, ed. John Sturrock (London: Penguin Books Ltd., 1988), 3. *Esquisse* 13 has "biscotte," but in 14 it is "Madeleine" (with a capital "M"); *ARTP*, 4:695–99.

derivation of the common noun from the name of its creator, the much-appreciated pastry cook, one Madeleine Paulmier. The coup de grâce, as it were, is the distant and preposterous echo of the madeleine in Madame Verdurin's croissants, while in the Goncourt pastiche in *Le Temps retrouvé* Proust tramples all over the aura of Madeleine as proper name when he has the Goncourts claim that Madame Verdurin is the model for Madeleine, the ethereal heroine of Fromentin's novel *Dominique* (*T*, 15).[30]

So much baked into a cake, we might be tempted to say, a thought massively reinforced when we also add the truly extraordinary narrative-generating powers of the madeleine episode. In *Contre Sainte-Beuve* its capacity—albeit in this context as mere toast—to trigger involuntary memory is compared to the operations of "magic." But it is also here that the commonsense interjections of our naval officer would prove more than reasonable, backed, perhaps, by the demystifying comments of William Empson. If we ask, "What's in a pastry?," the answer has to be: only what the artist-magician puts into it. The "world" that emerges from the tasting of cake and tea is entirely an effect of artifice and craft. No one in what we must persist in calling "real life" would be able to both recall and narrate so much on the basis of a single afternoon's refreshments, however evocative. Proust is simply playing the fictional game in accordance with conventions we willingly accept, along with admiring the remarkable effects they can produce. But it is another step altogether to mask the artifice and dress up the game as offering the miracle of "resurrection" and the royal road to salvation in the domain of the "extratemporal." That is magical thinking writ large. We shall see far more of it in succeeding chapters.

Is this why after "Combray" Proust switched immediately and anomalously to a third-person narrative for the telling of Swann's story? This has always been a source of puzzlement. No one takes seriously the pathetic efforts to naturalize the telling (as a story "someone"—possibly Swann himself—imparted to the narrator; not even Swann, let alone a third party, could have told it the way it is written). The actual teller is, of course, the author of the fiction, Marcel Proust. In what is the one genuinely persuasive explanation of this perplexing shift from first to third person, Claudia Brodsky maintains that this is Proust's oblique way of stripping the fictional game of its self-naturalizing mask and exposing the box of tricks that makes the game possible, just as in the *Recherche*, while Vinteuil's music transports, the cellist performing it at the Verdurins' is shown

---

[30] The multiple sources and associations of the name "Madeleine" are listed and discussed by Julia Kristeva in *Time and Sense: Proust and the Experience of Literature* (New York: Columbia University Press, 1996), 5–18. I discuss the significance of Madame Verdurin's croissants in chapter 2.

plying his trade as if peeling a cabbage (the analogy is Proust's).[31] Narrative is not a product of "miracles" or "revelations"; and while Art, like magic, is a wonderful thing, it is something cooked up in the all-too-human kitchen of meaning, where no one recipe has the status of divine script.

The best cooks work their recipes; they are improvisers and revisers. As a writer, Proust was one of the greatest revisers of all time, as anyone can attest who has spent even a modicum of time in the tangled world of manuscript, typescript, and proof, from which the so-called definitive editions of À la recherche du temps perdu have emerged. Revision was not just tinkering and refining but fundamental to Proust's entire conception. Since we have begun with the ending—the uncertain status of the "propositions" of Le Temps retrouvé—let us stop off there one more time, at the end of the ending, the novel's magnificent last sentence. It is a statement of what will be the core subject matter of the narrator's "book": the giantlike, monstrous, and unmeasurable dimensions of our existence "in Time." The sentence we all now read is the sentence that appears in the first posthumous edition of Le Temps retrouvé, and is a distillation from a plethora of manuscript ingredients suggestive of a writer less in possession of a recipe than in search of one. In a very remarkable analysis, Kristeva takes us back into the thicket of the manuscript Cahiers, a full page and a half of scribbles, fragments, erasures, changes, and additions, after which he appended the word Fin (underlined).[32] Although, as Kristeva notes, in neither manuscript nor published text does the word "death" appear, she rightly contextualizes the material by projecting it into the imagining of a sort of deathbed scene. On the one hand, there is the dying Proust making the final touches to his life's work; on the other hand, there is his narrator's anxiety as to whether, after so much wasted time, enough time remains to execute the literary project announced in the closing pages. The project was specified in a fragment subsequently struck out by Proust: the task for which there is hopefully enough time left is, in rough translation, "to effect all the required changes in the transcription of a universe and many others, the necessity of which, if one wishes to understand reality, will have been made plain in the course of this narrative [récit]," a formulation further elaborated in a fragment also dropped: "in the misleading transcription of a universe that needed to be reworked in its entirety." The invocation, at the very end of the novel, of the necessity of a complete retranscription of the universe deceptively transcribed in the novel we have just read ("in the course of this narrative") is mind-boggling, but we catch its tantalizing drift only if we put the right question to it.

[31] Brodsky, "Remembering Swann," 269–73.
[32] Kristeva, Time and Sense, 292–304.

Kristeva pertinently asks of the envisaged changes "which changes?"; changes to what? But she fails to ask the even more important question "whose changes?"; the narrator's or the author's? Here is the first of our several encounters with the issue of the narrator-author relation in the *Recherche*. Kristeva behaves as if the question is or would be the same for both. But on the face of it this cannot be, or rather simultaneously cannot be and has to be. The temporality of the manuscript passage is marked by an indeterminate "aujourd'hui," most probably a generalized "today," the Now of whatever time is left. But otherwise the timescales of narrator and author diverge radically. For the *narrator* the correction of the "misleading transcription" is yet to come; the time of his work is the time of a beginning ("should I begin" is also in the manuscript). For Proust the *author*, however, it is the time of ends and endings, both his and his book's. The question "whose changes?"—the author's or the narrator's—thus decisively affects how we might answer the question "which changes?" For the novice writer that is the narrator, they can be only changes to the error-saturated autobiography (*récit*) that precedes his definitive discovery of the artistic vocation, the changes that will interpret and sustain the retrospective transformation of the meaning of a life as *Bildungsroman* passes over into *Künstlerroman*. In this context, the sense and reference of the discarded fragment are clear: the "misleading transcription" is another way of designating the *vanitas vanitatum* of worldly experience, whose correction will be the task of "literature"; through the book he will write, the narrator will remake the world anew "in its entirety." But since Proust has already written *his* book, bringing it now to its moment of closure and hence to last thoughts, the potential scope of those thoughts is far more radical. For us, the actual thought processes of the fading Marcel Proust can only be an object of idle speculation, but the *Cahiers* suggest they were very much reflections "on the continuation of his novel" in the perspective of an endless revision.[33] The question is not how to conclude, but whether to conclude at all.[34] An interpretation of the manuscript gropings that is tied solely to the temporal perspective of the narrator secures, perhaps a trifle smugly, the cardinal opposition of the worldly (deceptive, fallen) and the artistic (truth-telling, redemptive). Yet when brought to bear on the temporal location of its author, this opposition is blurred. Just as the *Cahiers* are the author's, not the narrator's, private notebook, so the fictional *récit*, whose course is now being brought to an end, is his *récit*, and must therefore include its celebratory

[33] See chapter 8.

[34] A few months before he died, Proust wrote to Gaston Gallimard: "I have so many books to offer you which, if I die before then, will never appear—*A la recherché du temps perdu* has hardly begun." *Corr.*, 21:56. The letter is cited by Christine Cano, in her brilliant essay, "Death as Editor," in *Proust in Perspective*, ed. Mortimer and Kolb, 46.

finale, as well as its extended *vanitas*. If the "changes" envisaged are to be to a narrative "universe" conceived in its "entirety," this must logically implicate the terms of the proposed aesthetic reordering of that universe as themselves candidates for potentially indefinite revision.

In other words, two quite different futures are being imagined here, in two distinct, syntactic registers. The narrator's reflections in the published version are about writing and what it might ultimately accomplish, gathered in a fully coherent sentence to articulate what, viewed under a certain aspect, is an improbable claim (tendentiously pushing my luck, I have called it a mad belief). Proust's thoughts, scattered and incomplete, are thoughts directed to a future of *re*writing, going back to the beginning and starting all over again. We can never know what these other Proustian universes, these other possible worlds, might have looked like; they belong in the tantalizing yet futile domain of an empty counterfactual. The experimental shots at composing the concluding sentence are opaque, physically opaque (the jungle of Proust's handwriting), syntactically broken, semantically and referentially obscure. Above all, they are caught in a flux of scratched and scratched-out formulations, thoughts, and phrases sketched and dumped, as, before appearing to settle on what subsequent editors have decided was the final version, Proust determinedly carried on not only altering his text but also making changes to the very idea of change-making. The principal theme of the changes is change itself, what is to be their precise object, focus, and, thus, meaning. Kristeva is right to say that there is a degree of arbitrariness to the later editorial decisions (for example, in order to make the final sentence coherent, they involve restoring bits that Proust excised).[35] This is also why entering the manuscript thicket at this precise point is so potentially revealing of a Proust who has in fact made up his mind about nothing, including the proclaimed belief in art. The scratchings are the scratchings of a (semilegible) pen and the scratchings-out the index of a mind still on the move, inside the paradox of the work that Blanchot called "a finished-unfinished work" (*une œuvre achevée-inachevée*).[36] But to my mind, they also evoke a scratching of the head in the way the skeptic sometimes scratches his head as he experiences puzzlement, asks questions, and entertains doubts, once more reopening to critical inspection what he had thought was a closed book and headed safely for the enchanted realm of the stars.

[35] Cano comments on "the long struggle to assert the literary against the editorial," in "Death as Editor," 46.

[36] Maurice Blanchot, *Le Livre à venir* (Paris: Gallimard, 1959), 36.

CHAPTER TWO

Proustian Jokes

MOST OF THE MAD BELIEFS in Proust's novel are droll as well as crazy, and have their place in what is often and rightly said of *À la recherche du temps perdu*, that, among so many other things, it is also a great comic novel ("an unwearying tribute to the muse of comedy").[1] The tribute assumes many guises and operates in multiple registers, testimony to Proust's superabundant comic energy and abidingly gleeful attention to the multiplicities of the human comedy itself, although we might hesitate before laying the emaciated hand of taxonomy on its diverse generic manifestations (mimicry, pastiche, parody, burlesque, satire, etc.); that is to steer perilously close to the fine and fussy distinctions that mark the language of one of Proust's magnificent comic creations, the diplomat M. de Norpois. Yet if Proust's devotion to the muse is generously catholic in kind and scope, evoking affinities with writers as stylistically different and culturally distant as Cervantes and Dickens, there is one idiom that dominates, and that places him in the singular French tradition to which he unmistakably belongs, namely, *esprit* or wit, especially of the sharply epigrammatic type that is so distinctively a stylistic feature of the seventeenth- and eighteenth-century *moralistes*.[2] The observation "it is wrong in love to talk of a bad choice, since, as soon as there is a choice, it can be only a bad one" (*F*, 575) could have easily come from the epigrammatic repertoire of La Rochefoucauld or Chamfort; and when the Guermantes butler is described as announcing dinner ("Madame is served") "in the same tone of voice he would have used to say 'Madame is in her death throes'" (*CG*, 432), we hear not just a Proustian voice but a comic discourse inherited from the memoirs of Saint-Simon.

Moreover, it is not just that Proust can be witty; wit (*esprit*) appears as a theme in its own right, most notably with reference to the speech styles of the grand social gatherings, above all the famed (and feared) "Guermantes wit," urbane, clever, and ferociously cruel.[3] Its most gifted

---

[1] Bowie, *Proust Among the Stars*, xvi.

[2] In "On Flaubert's Style," Proust explicitly aligns "my novels" with "this school." *Against Sainte-Beuve*, 262. Many of the early interpretations of the *Recherche* placed Proust in the same way; see Nicola Luckhurst, *Science and Structure in Proust's "À la recherche du temps perdu"* (Oxford: Oxford University Press, 2001), 13–25.

[3] See David Ellison, *A Reader's Guide to Proust's "In Search of Lost Time"* (Cambridge: Cambridge University Press, 2010), 90–91.

practitioner is Oriane de Guermantes.[4] Specialist in the scintillatingly caustic quip at other people's expense, in particular, those hopeless aspirants for admission to the Saint-Germain elect, her own social raison d'être consists principally in gathering around herself a group of admirers amazed by her insouciant and inventive boldness, as if the great event of the day lies in what "Oriane" might and will say next. There is already a further stroke of wit built into this scene of regal performer and slavish audience. When the members of the latter slaver in awestruck tones over what "Oriane" might come out with, they presume in the use of her first name the very social intimacy that the Duchesse de Guermantes will always deny them; the fawning listener is as much the intended object of the *boutade* as the absent person named in it. That is to say, Oriane's coruscating remark is also Proust's satirical joke, embedded and delivered in a manner—indirect and implicit—that we will later see as fundamental to the kind of Proustian joke that really matters.

Most of them do not matter, other than as implied comment on a character or a milieu. If Proust is one of the wittiest of modern writers, he is not primarily a teller of jokes. While the line separating them is a fine one, *esprit* and *blague* belong to different speech cultures. Oriane makes witty remarks but does not typically crack jokes; the former have all the sadistic refinement that comes from the long historical and cultural training of a social class in the arts of domination; the latter are on the whole altogether too coarsely jovial, especially for an aristocratic lady (Charlus by contrast takes great pleasure in the noisy verbal equivalent of rough trade and is not averse to flights of humorous obscenity).[5] Generally speaking, jokes are reserved for lesser mortals, the conversational staple, for example, of the Verdurin circle ("the jokes Madame Verdurin would make after dinner," usually directed at excommunicated "bores," *S*, 289). It is while laughing heartily at "some damn funny tale" on the subject of one of the disgraced and banished that she succeeds in dislocating her jaw (*S*, 192). Swann plays the part of obsequious courtier, laughing only because "he saw Odette laughing, laughing with him, almost inside him"; when he too joins the excommunicated and the jokes are turned on him, he revises his view—"what fetid humour!" (*S*, 289). The circle includes

---

[4] At Madame de Sainte-Euverte's soiree, General de Froberville says to Oriane, "[Y]ou're not a Guermantes for nothing. You have your share of it all right, the wit of the Guermantes family!" Oriane's reply: "They always say the wit of the Guermantes *family*. I've never been able to understand why. Do you know any *other* Guermantes who have it?" (*S*, 342; emphasis in original).

[5] Yet, like everything else in the *Recherche*, Oriane's brilliance wanes, a symptom of her fading star in the world of the aristocratic salon; the fatal moment arrives when the proffered witticism falls flat, a sure sign of a reputation on the skids ("the joke that then appeared would be completely flat," *T*, 314). By this stage of the narrative, it is essentially a question of exposing her "total ignorance of the true realities of intellectual life" (303).

Bloch and his cringingly abhorrent way with "jokes against Jews" (*SG*, 283); Saniette, whose humble and semiaudible offerings are but the occasion for his ritual humiliation; and, above all, the egregious Cottard, who thinks of jokes as a social passport, but who almost always fails to understand those of others, winks hideously when he finally gets them, and then proceeds to mangle them as so many recycled mishits.

On the other hand, scapegoating Cottard as the tedious would-be jester of a dinner party circuit implies an unmerited assumption of effortless superiority on the part of the narrator. For while the latter, along with others (in particular, Forcheville), mocks Cottard for his "travelling-salesman jokes" (*SG*, 253), his own sallies can be just as inept: "There is nothing more limited than pleasure and vice. In that sense, changing the meaning of the phrase slightly, it can truly be said that we are always going round in the same vicious circle" (*T*, 135). This is exactly the sort of stillborn pun Cottard might brightly come up with at table.[6] If, as appears to be the case, the narrator thinks this amusingly clever ("smart," both intellectually and socially), it's not. Certainly, what I have in mind under the heading of "Proustian jokes" is none of the above. It is neither the elegantly turned *bon mot*, nor the flat-footed *blague*, less the scintillatingly witty and unforgivingly other-directed than the slyly ironical and implicitly self-directed, the joke whose effect is to give pause for thought rather than to inflict a wound.

Here are some examples. The Duchesse de Guermantes declines invitations she deems to be vulgar manifestations of *arrivisme*, on the staggeringly unusual grounds that she is about to set off on a cruise—"quite fascinating, my dear!"—of the Norwegian fjords: "Society people were thunderstruck by this, and, without any notion of following the Duchesse's example, nevertheless derived from her project the sense of relief you get when you read Kant and when, after the most rigorous demonstration of determinism, it transpires that above the world of necessity there is the world of freedom" (*CG*, 475). Albertine, lying through her teeth, states when challenged: "It's very possible I contradicted myself. The sea air takes away all my powers of reason. I'm forever saying one name instead of another" (*SG*, 202). The stupidity-wrapped communicative universe of M. de Cambremer takes a surreal turn: "By a transposition of the senses, M de Cambremer looked at you with his nose . . . Hooked, polished, shiny, spanking new, it was quite prepared to make up for the spiritual insufficiency of his gaze" (*SG*, 310). The Duchesse de Guermantes (again) observes cattily of the empress of Austria that she "never managed to get a set of false teeth that fitted her properly. They

---

[6] For example, the dreadful (and mercifully untranslatable) pun around dishes cooked with milk ("au lait") and the expression "olé" (*JF*, 73).

always came loose before she'd finished a sentence, she had to stop short in case she swallowed them" (*SG*, 509).

The examples make for an incongruously assorted collection: a hypocrite, a liar, a social dyslexic, and a geriatric with ill-fitting and syntax-threatening dentures. Yet here in grotesquely deformed mode are, astonishingly, some of the key sources and terms of Proust's own aesthetic: the idioms of philosophical Idealism, the practice of naming one thing as another, the transposition of one order of sensation to another, and the drama of the unfinished or unfinishable sentence. One cannot, of course, "prove" that these moments are intended as obliquely self-directed gags, humorous representations of what elsewhere is invested with the utmost seriousness; the distance from alleged means to putative end is so great as to place demands on even the oblique that will seem wildly unreasonable. On the other hand, there are many such moments, and cumulatively they can be seen as forming patterns sufficiently consistent to qualify as a "method," a technique of indirection. But to see the patterns in this way, as indirect commentary on the premises and processes of the work in which they appear, requires mapping them further on two interconnected relations: narrator to author and character to narrator. The junctures at which the two relations mesh in turn produce the fulcrum for a third relation—the ambivalent relation of Marcel Proust to his own creation.

The first of these relations is an old chestnut, and if—with some reluctance—I pull it from the ashes of what was once upon a time a burning issue, it is because, as a bridge to understanding what it means to call a certain kind of Proustian joke "self-directed," it also houses a structural joke of its own. It should, of course, scarcely need saying (yet again) that *À la recherche* is not autobiography or a roman à clef, and its narrator is not a thinly disguised Marcel Proust. On the other hand, the dogmatic insistence of the narratological purists on erecting a firewall between the categories of "author" and "narrator" renders them oblivious to gray areas and entirely helpless before the cannily inserted "always" in the formula from the essay on Flaubert in *Contre Sainte-Beuve*: "the narrator who says 'I,' but who is not always myself."[7] "Not always myself" (as distinct from "always not myself") is the narratologist's nightmare. If not always, then sometimes, but how often, when, and where? And why this nonchalantly opportunistic disregard for the boundaries separating fiction and reality? Some of the instances are transparently opportunistic, typically when it is a case of that age-old ruse of narrators in need of narrative knowledge necessarily unavailable to them. "She never mentioned this episode, to me or anyone else" (*S*, 384). So how come it figures in the story? The narrator reliably and clearly reports what Odette's admir-

---

[7] *Against Sainte-Beuve*, ed. John Sturrock, 273.

ers murmur to her in the Bois de Boulogne "although I could not hear their comments" (*S*, 432). He also reports in great detail, without the assistance of an anonymous "informant,"[8] the sad party thrown by La Berma, which he could not possibly have attended, since it takes place on the other side of Paris and at the same time as the Guermantes *matinée*, which the narrator does attend. This is a fix to ensure that all the characters who are still alive are assembled for the grand finale in *Le Temps retrouvé* ("And today all those different threads had come together to create the web," *T*, 281), but the fixer—the actual storyteller—is Proust; only he can "know" what is going on simultaneously in different places.[9]

The truly intriguing moments, however, concern less transgressions of elementary narrative *vraisemblance* than logical impossibilities at the level of first-personal enunciation. Who speaks in the apostrophe to the dead Swann: "And yet, dear Charles Swann . . . it is already because someone whom you must have considered a little idiot has made you the hero of one of his novels that people are beginning to talk about you again" (*P*, 182)? Or what of the even stranger moment (again from *La Prisonnière*) when Françoise stumbles upon the "manuscript" sketch of a "story" about Swann among the narrator's papers: "I once found Françoise with thick glasses on her nose, poking among my papers and putting back one on which I had noted down a story about Swann and his inability to do without Odette" (338). As we have already seen, it is at least notionally possible that the narrator is the source of the third-person "story" of Swann, but, if so, then the one thing that that story could not be is a "novel"; Swann's story can't be a fiction for the fictional narrator; it can be a *fiction* only for and by its true author, namely, Marcel Proust; the actual referent of the "young idiot" who has made Swann "the hero of one of his novels" and the "I" who "had noted down a story about Swann" is the real-life writer.

So, too, is the writing persona who, in a flush of patriotic enthusiasm, disables the author/narrator firewall in order to import the Larivière family as admirably selfless supporters of the war effort. The narrator (but this designation, while formally correct, already begs the question) informs us of the following breach of narrative protocol: "In this book in which there is not a single incident which is not fictitious, not a single character who is a real person in disguise . . . I owe it to the credit of my

---

[8] For the report of something M. Verdurin is alleged to have said at a gathering where the narrator is not present, he refers to "my informant" (*P*, 301).

[9] And what of the temporality of statements such as the following: "I did once have an opportunity (to anticipate a little, as I am still at Tansonville) to observe" (*T*, 9); "Let this parenthesis on Mme de Forcheville, while I walk down the boulevards side by side with M. de Charlus" (*T*, 97). Who is at Tansonville and who is walking down the boulevards at the time of writing?

country to say that only the millionaire cousins of Françoise who came out of retirement to help their niece when she was left without support, only they are real people who exist" (*T*, 154). We make of these sentiments what we will,[10] but they are without doubt Proust's and no one else's. Strictly speaking, it is an utterance of the first-person narrator, but viewed in this way there are at least three things wrong with it: it is factually incorrect (there are other "real people who exist" in the *Recherche*—Céleste, Professor Dieulafoy); second, it is incoherent (how can a fictional character—Françoise—be "related" to persons from real life?); third, it is only under very special conditions that a fictional narrator can not only identify the people and incidents around him in the fictional universe *as* "fictional," but also step outside the fiction into the realm of the real. The confusion here between fiction and life is both casual and radical, and is only partly dispelled when we state the obvious: the speaker here is, and has to be, Marcel Proust.

The storytelling codes adopted by *À la recherche* are such that no first-person fictional narrator is empowered to operate in this fashion; to do so is to commit an unauthorized border violation at the crossing-points of fiction and autobiography. Yet the slipping between different existential and discursive worlds is not merely a clumsy slip or an oversight, a negligent form of involuntary "stumbling" (not on the cobbles of the Guermantes courtyard, but into the aporias of first-person fiction). If the text abruptly and arbitrarily switches the firewall off so as to permit a stepping from one world into another and back again, this is not a reflection of storytelling gone wrong at a very basic level. It is not a consequence of insouciance, forgetfulness, or carelessness, the kind of lapse that merits a reprimand from the narratological police. It is rather because Proust likes to not only play the fictional game but also to play teasingly *with* the game itself, with both its rules and its readers. Take the playful disingenuousness of the moment in *Sodome et Gomorrhe*, when the reader is imagined addressing the narrator as "monsieur l'Auteur" while rapping him over the knuckles (the narrator has forgotten the name of Madame d'Arpajon) by deploring just "how regrettable it is that, young as you were (or as your hero was if he is not yourself), you should already have had so little memory" (*SG*, 56). There is a double joke here: a play on the great Proustian theme of forgetting and remembering but also on the ambiguities of narration and authorship. Consider then the return of the compliment, from author to reader in *La Prisonnière*, where we find a speaker now identified as an author who addresses the reader: "the author wishes to make clear how unhappy he would be if the reader were offended" (38). On this merry-go-round of cross-border exchange,

---

[10] I return to them in chapter 8.

we have a narrator and an author as at once indistinguishably, yet impossibly, one and the same.

The best of the tease, however, comes with the proper name "Marcel." The scholars have explored how, in both published text and manuscript, "Marcel" as a first name for the narrator was caught up in a process of attribution and deletion, the naming sometimes eliminated, sometimes allowed to stand, as if Proust were constantly trying to make up his mind as to what the relationship between author and narrator is, and how, if at all, to declare it.[11] But these are not mere hesitations; rather, they are moves in a kind of now-you-see-me, now-you-don't routine, a tongue-in-cheek *fort/da* diversion. Here is Albertine with the more tantalizing instance of the two occasions on which she gives the narrator (or, more exactly and thus absurdly, the occasions on which the narrator reports her as giving) a first name: "Now she began to speak; her first words were 'darling' or 'my darling,' followed by my Christian name, which, if we give the narrator the same name as the author of this book, would produce 'darling Marcel,' or 'my darling Marcel' " (*P*, 64). "If" and "would be" are nicely tentative touches, but also throw into even sharper relief the barefaced effrontery of a narrator apparently on terms of acquaintance with his own author.[12] Construing this as a scholarly identity puzzle is, I suppose, one way to go, but hopefully without wandering too far from a glimpse of Proust quietly laughing up his sleeve at the false trails laid across the path of the fictional who's who directory. It's a send-up, a little exercise in knowing burlesque, its self-aware quality fundamental to its point. The knowingness is important in showing us one of the forms in which the Proustian joke can be self-directed. If Proust is effectively telling us that the barrier separating author and narrator is not secure, then the way is open to considering the extent to which jokes at the narrator's expense, however indirect, are also jokes at Proust's expense, and, moreover, not as casual asides or impromptu self-parody but as modes of

[11] See Eugène Nicole, "Quel Marcel!," in *The Strange M. Proust*, ed. André Benhaïm (Oxford, UK: Legenda, 2008), 36–44; Tadié, *Proust et le roman* (Paris: Gallimard, 1971), 22. Tadié, however, interprets the textual history as evidence of the "minute care" Proust takes over erecting a barrier between author and narrator.

[12] Joshua Landy highlights the conditional in the narrator's formulation ("if . . . would") to make the point that the narrator doesn't actually claim that "Marcel" *is* his name. *Philosophy as Fiction: Self, Deception, and Knowledge in Proust* (Oxford: Oxford University Press, 2004), 171. But it is an illicit inference that this is a way of "preserving the distinction" between author and narrator (the conditional doesn't "preserve" anything), and in any case still leaves the unanswerable question: How can the narrator know what the name of his author is, even if he hedges his bets over sharing it? It is, of course, theoretically possible that there are two "Marcels" (and that, astonishingly, each happens to have done a translation of Ruskin's *Sesame and Lilies*). But what isn't possible is that the narrator "Marcel" knows the author "Marcel." The whole thing is clearly a tease.

skeptical critique. At the deepest level, the target of self-directed humor in the *Recherche* is not just an empirical self (its contingent flaws, weaknesses, and vices), but the category of Self and the risk-laden practices of self-talk.

II

"The steps of thought which we take during the lonely work of artistic creation all lead us downwards, deeper into ourselves, the only direction in which we can advance, albeit with much greater travail, towards an outcome of truth" (*JF*, 484). This is a sentence no serious admirer of Proust can afford to ignore. But it is also Proustian doctrine served neat, brandishing the notorious "philosophy" of Self that allegedly justifies a particular conception of art. On one perfectly acceptable reading, the sentence does little more than parade the shopworn clichés of romantic subjectivism and philosophical idealism. Its claims can capsize at any moment, and in Proust's text often do, especially when under the influence ("intoxication" in that sense). The droll effects of alcohol in the *Recherche* are no small matter;[13] one such is the production of an oddly philosophical take on the external world: "drunkenness brings about, for the space of a few hours, subjective idealism, pure phenomenalism; all things become mere appearances, and exist only as a function of our sublime selves" (*JF*, 396). Are we then to conclude that, even though this is more or less what the narrator will often maintain when sober, it is a case of farewell Schelling (whose work the young Proust encountered at the Sorbonne), and welcome Madame de Cambremer (a great fan of Schopenhauer): "Stopping from reading John Stuart Mill only to start reading Lachelier, the less she came to believe in the reality of the external world, the greater the zeal with which she tried to create a position in it for herself before she died" (*SG*, 321)?[14] Jokes are bouncing off the walls of the text here and headed in several directions, including that of the author himself, threatening to sink the intellectual model that joins, as if by an umbilical cord, "thought," "creation," and "self."[15]

[13] Michel Sandras, "La comédie de la soif," in *Marcel Proust: Surprises de la Recherche*, ed. Raymonde Coudert and Guillaume Perrier (Paris: UFR, 2004), 183–96; see chapter 6 for further discussion.

[14] Jules Lachelier was a philosopher in the Kantian and idealist mold. He influenced Proust's philosophy teachers.

[15] Proust, with probably Schopenhauer specifically in mind, reminds us, in a robustly commonsensical manner worthy of Dr. Johnson, that dissolving the external world into self is not incompatible with acknowledging and enjoying the material reality of a good meal: "I knew of course that idealism, even subjective idealism, did not prevent great philosophers from remaining gourmands" (*CG*, 201).

For if downward and inward are the privileged tracks for the artist (another version of the Two Ways, perhaps), where does that leave the outward-bound axis? If self is everything, what of the ethical and epistemological status of non-self, and especially the reality of other people? Proust's narrator, in his guise as part-time philosopher, provides a hodgepodge of answers. One is in effect an evasive non-answer that raises the issue only to declare a preference for kicking it into touch and moving on to topics presumably felt to be more amenable ("Some philosophers argue that the external world does not exist . . . Be that as it may . . . ," *F*, 531). "Be that as it may" is one way of keeping options open. In a more doctrinaire mood, Proust's answer is terse: the essential point about "others" is their "unreality" (*T*, 183). This is not strictly speaking the voice of the solipsist. The thought is not that others have no material existence, but rather that their existence is of no importance; others are unreal (for me) by virtue of their irrelevance to my own needs and interests. The proposition takes an even crisper turn: all "thoughts directed towards the other person rather than towards myself" are so many wasted thoughts (*JF*, 315). Conversely, to the extent that we entertain thoughts about others at all, they are in fact thoughts about ourselves anyway. The other in Proust is famously "unknowable"; what we think we know or wish to believe we know is an error-filled projection of ourselves, and to maintain otherwise is a barefaced lie: "Man is a being who cannot move beyond his own boundaries, who knows others only within himself, and if he alleges the contrary, he lies" (*F*, 418).[16]

The loneliness of the modern artistic vocation or egocentricity presented as pseudophilosophical gospel and decked out as poor man's La Rochefoucauld? The narrator as literary hero or as self-absorbed neurotic? But then, if the latter, is not the description more pertinently applicable to the emotional life of the protagonist in the tale rather than to the narrating activity of its teller? Alternatively, if in fact we do mean narrator as well as protagonist, do we not also, at least on occasion (the critical question then being on *which* occasions), have to mean the author? If "thoughts directed towards the other person rather than towards myself" are fruitless, whose thought about thoughts is this? We are, of

---

[16]In that case, Proust himself must be pronounced guilty. For there is much elsewhere in his writings to counter this radical epistemological self-centeredness. In the preface to *Sesame and Lilies*, what matters most is the sphere of "non-ego": "As for me, I feel myself living and thinking only in a room where everything is the creation and the language of lives profoundly different from mine, where I find nothing of my conscious thought, where my imagination is excited to feel itself plunged into the womb of non-ego" (*On Reading Ruskin*, 106). And in *Le Temps retrouvé*, the extended subjectivist peroration modulates, as if it needed more than self as a court of appeal, to a "universalist" incorporation of others in the work that "can express for others" and that "gives to everyone, to the universal mind" (205–6).

course, back with the referential complexities of the first person in fiction, now in conjunction with the "acutely painful ethical dilemma" that, in her relentlessly penetrating analysis of the stratagems of rationalization and self-justification in Proust, Ingrid Wassenaar specifies as the question "how it is possible to take account of otherness in a (narrative) world structured and apprehended by a singular perceiving self."[17] To my knowledge, Wassenaar's reply is the best available, not least in its recognition that delivering it requires a long, intricate, and subtle argument commensurate with the complexity of its object. Nevertheless, the guiding perspective of the argument is robustly skeptical in a sense or manner different from the ways in which I have been using the term. Simply put, it is skeptical of Proust's good faith, especially in those areas of the novel that deal with the self/other relation (above all, the narrator/Albertine story); even as Proust (and, with the usual caveats, Wassenaar means *Proust*) exposes the self-serving maneuvers of his narrator-hero, he reveals his own complicity in them. There is a "dangerous proximity" of author, narrator, and protagonist, which, among the inexhaustibly many things it is, makes of Proust's text the infuriatingly intelligent devising of a get-out-of-jail card, a false pass to occupancy of the intellectual and moral high ground.

Wassenaar's case is essential reading, especially for uncritical Proust worshippers. I want, however, to suggest another perspective (in many ways no less unwelcome to the devout), namely, that Proust knows what his own complicities look like and shows us what they are via the mirroring aspect of other characters. There are two kinds of mirror effect: one is corrective, where the character holds a (nonflattering) mirror up to the weaknesses of the narrator-hero; the other is confirmatory, the mirror as duplicating mirror image.[18] The latter type is of more interest here. The former is relatively straightforward. The young "Marcel" arrives in Balbec for the first time, a bundle of nerves before such massive challenges as "the trepidation which overwhelmed me at the prospect of sleeping in an unfamiliar room" (*JF*, 249). The role of the narrator's grandmother is to comfort and cosset, but also to reflect her young charge's neurasthenia back to him in the mirror of reason: "Do you really think there's anyone else in the whole world who's as silly and anxious?" (248).[19] The narrator appears to endorse this view of his self-absorbed younger self ("my grand-mother's nature was the exact opposite of my complete egoism,"

[17] Ingrid Wassenaar, *Proustian Passions: The Uses of Self-Justification for "À la recherche du temps perdu"* (New York: Oxford University Press, 2000), 99.

[18] See Brian Rogers, "Proust's Narrator," in *The Cambridge Companion to Proust*, ed. Richard Bales (Cambridge: Cambridge University Press, 2008), 87–92.

[19] See Eddie Hughes, "The Grandmother's War on Hypersensitivity," in *Marcel Proust: A Study in the Quality of Awareness* (Cambridge: Cambridge University Press, 1983), 77–85.

431), a judgment reinforced by the sense of perspective his budding acquaintance with Saint-Loup brings ("the worries which a moment ago I had been unable to endure a second longer seemed to me as negligible as they did to him," *CG*, 87). And, in terms of the self/other relation, Saint-Loup's example is even more instructive in "being, unlike myself, free of the impossibility of finding spiritual sustenance anywhere but in myself" (360). It would seem that "downwards, deeper into ourselves" is in fact *not* "the only direction in which we can advance . . . towards an outcome of truth"; outward to the views of others in helping shape the journey of self-discovery also counts.

However, it is one thing for the older narrator to join with some of his characters in retrospectively deriding and chastising the younger protagonist for his self-centered immaturities. There remains the issue of the extent to which both narrator and author are guilty of the same failings, and whether the prose that mocks as it analyzes is also complicit in what it analyzes.[20] When, for example, the protagonist's "trepidation" on finding himself in unfamiliar rooms is generalized to something "which is felt by many," this is the narrator interpreting his adolescent emotional life as a common condition, and looks suspiciously like an attempt to "normalize" the emotionally eccentric. And then consider the role of analogy—two quite remarkable analogies in particular—in the text's staging of the self-inflation syndrome. In the first, the prospect of being forced to enter the hotel reading room in Balbec is compared to the "tortures" of the damned in Dante's inferno (*JF*, 242–43). The second figures railway stations and train departures as akin to the agonies of the Crucifixion (the station as "dense with portents of pent-up tragedy" and "an apt backdrop to the most awesome or hideous of acts, such as the Crucifixion or a departure by train," 224). The disproportionate nature of the comparisons verges on the scandalously comical. Yet before classifying them as obviously laughing matters (jokes at the protagonist's expense), we would do well to acknowledge how they appear to illustrate three of the basic principles of the Proustian aesthetic: first, liberation from the straitjacket of habit and common sense (if we find train stations less fearsome than the Passion, this is because our sensibilities have been dulled by repetition); second, inversion of received narrative hierarchies, whereby the relative values of "small" and "big," significant and insignificant, are redistributed; and third, equivalences forged by the leveling power of analogy, working to blur or close the gap between like and unlike.

In placing the anxieties of a hypersensitive adolescent departing for his first seaside holiday on the same scale of suffering as the crucified Christ, the narrator is doing what, formally speaking, the Proustian textual

[20]Wassenaar describes it as "pleasurable replay." *Proustian Passions*, 107.

"system" does all the time—reorder moral and semantic priorities. Yet substantively, the analogy is preposterous, and if the "system" is asking us to take it seriously, it is perhaps the system that is in fact preposterous and thus the actual object of the joke, a case of Proust mocking Proust. This is the perspective encouraged by what I call the confirmatory mirror image, the character who, as objectifying reflection, makes visible what is ludicrous or questionable in all the dimensions of the novel's first-personal utterances. What and whom, for example, does the pain of waiting for a train at the Gare Saint-Lazare resemble if not the neuroses of that most fussily myopic of all Proust's characters, Aunt Léonie, awaiting the arrival of Eulalie ("too prolonged, this ecstasy of waiting for Eulalie became a torment," S, 73)? When the narrator says of her that "she attributed to the least of her sensations an extraordinary importance; she endowed them with a motility that made it difficult for her to keep them to herself, and lacking a confidant to whom she could communicate them, she announced them to herself, in a perpetual monologue that was her only form of activity" (S, 53), it is surely a case of the pot calling the kettle black.[21] The figure of the Crucifixion is in fact first applied to the "sufferings" of Aunt Léonie: "She would hold out to my lips her sad, pale, dull forehead . . . where the bones showed through like the points of a crown of thorns" (55). And if at a more elevated level we take the novel to be propounding a philosophy of creative selfhood based on overwrought introspection, Proust himself calls us up short with the example of Dr. du Boulbon dispensing heartlessly asinine advice to the mortally ill grandmother: "Feel comfortable to be called a neurotic. You belong to that splendid, pitiable family which is the salt of the earth. Everything we think of as great has come to us from neurotics. They and they alone are the ones who have founded religions and created great works of art" (CG, 301).

Aunt Léonie and Dr. du Boulbon make an improbable pair (though we can amuse ourselves with imagining just how well received the good doctor's recommendation of nervous debility would have been at the bedside of the Combray invalid). What the two have in common is their having something in common with the person who created them and the persona to whom is entrusted the telling of their story. This is not to say that they are masked self-portraits, versions of Proust "in disguise"; they function rather as pointers and reminders, the caricatural display of what is either unconscionable or deplorable in the cultivation of the self's obsessions.

---

[21] Michael Taussig speaks of "a work whose writer bears an uncanny resemblance to the invalid aunt under her flowered coverlet." *What Color Is the Sacred?* (Chicago: University of Chicago Press, 2009), 201. Wassenaar comments astutely of certain "intense moments of Proustian sensorial apprehension" that "the writing of them is simultaneously absolutely comic and absolutely straight-faced." *Proustian Passions*, 107.

We find the same technique at work in that far more harrowing and exasperating account of the self/other relation, the one that dominates the novel from the last part of *Sodome et Gomorrhe* through to *La Fugitive*, between the narrator and Albertine. Wassenaar is at her most severe here, in particular unpicking the skein of awesome egocentricity and self-deception on which is woven the "mourning" process in *La Fugitive*. All the talk of "my great pity for her at this time" and the "great shame in surviving her" is but a cover for the ceaseless drip of self-pity through the filter of notional compassion, which becomes a veritable flood as the narrator fantasizes how the dead Albertine would pity *him* if only she could spring back to life in order to witness the intensity of his grief; in Wassenaar's words, this is "a fantasy of the good self, dutifully reactivating the pain of loss as a proof of remembrance," and mourning raised "to the level of martyrdom."[22]

We thus have the suffering narrator once more exhibited as martyr, like the crucified Christ in the waiting room of the Gare Saint-Lazare. But what he "suffers" after Albertine's death (even as he prepares himself for an outcome known in advance, the indifference that comes with forgetting) is as nothing alongside the "hell" of Albertine alive, the devastation randomly inflicted by the chaotic mess of lies and disclosures that tumble from her lips, as her lover-jailer squirms inside the psychopathological paradox of simultaneously wanting to know and not wanting to know. Albertine admits that the three days she had led the narrator to believe she had spent in Balbec were in fact spent in Auteuil (according to the narrator's worst fears, in a den of lesbian iniquity). It is but one of the many revelations that rain down on him like bombs from the sky. The image is Proust's: "I felt as if I were in a razed town where not a house is left standing and the naked earth is covered only with rubble" (*P*, 309). Earlier it was the Crucifixion; now it is the psychic equivalent of being reduced to rubble in a blitzkrieg. We have the same recourse to metaphorical hyperbole, but also the same ambivalently double register in which the stretched analogy is offered to the reader, at once serious and comic, a mix of the intolerable (pain) and the insufferable (self-aggrandizement). And when the narrator goes into full panic mode on having to revise the whole Albertine script (on learning of her acquaintance with the notorious Lea), we can only surmise how much Proust—the pages of his own novel strewn on bed and floor before being tidied up by Céleste Albaret—must have chuckled over his own figurative *trouvaille*: "I watched as sudden

---

[22] Aimé's letter reporting on Albertine's proclivities triggers what the narrator calls "an unexpected suffering, the most cruel I had yet experienced" (*F*, 481). But, as Wassenaar notes, it is *always* the most cruel, each new shock trumping all previous ones (*Proustian Passions*, 198–99). And we are even less inclined to be moved when the narrator takes time out from martyrdom to comment acidly on the grammatical faults of Aimé's letter.

flames tore through a novel I had spent ten million minutes composing," an image of text-combustion and soul-consumption further elaborated as complete meltdown: "it seemed to me that the unburnt part of the novel was slowly crumbling into ashes" (*SG*, 322–24).

This has to be a self-referential jest, Proust clowning it up as the "author" of a fiction in which not only are assumptions about others revealed as flawed, but also where the dividing line between real suffering and farcically exaggerated self-pity is hazy.[23] Very many of the moments of emotional crisis in the narrator's relationship with Albertine are like this, including the most desolating of them all—the revelation of Albertine's friendship with Mlle de Vinteuil. As we shall see in chapter 3, this is the high point of trauma and terror in the whole novel, in relation to which images of a crucifixion seem altogether apposite. And yet who should appear in this ravaged scene but a disconsolately weepy version of Céleste Albaret herself, shuttling across with her sister Marie Gineste from "real life" into the novel to serve as a perfect illustration of sentiment disproportionate to occasion. Armed with his new knowledge of Albertine's apparent tastes, the narrator plans to remove her from temptation and thus allay his own distress by quitting Balbec forthwith: "Balbec was like those places in which an invalid, who can no longer breathe there, has decided, even though he may die along the way, not to spend another night." So much for our suffocating and life-threatened hero. But what of the others who have grown attached to his presence in Balbec? What, for example, of Céleste and Marie (conveniently transplanted to the world of the fiction, as companions to an unnamed foreign lady summering in Balbec):

> For the rest, I was going to have to battle against entreaties *of the same kind* [emphasis added], in the hotel first of all, where Marie Gineste and Céleste Albaret were red-eyed. (Marie moreover gave vent to the urgent sobbing of a mountain torrent; the more lethargic Celeste urged her to calm; but Marie having murmured the only lines of poetry that she knew, "*Ici-bas tous les lilas meurent*," Céleste could not contain herself and a sheet of tears spilled across her lilac-coloured face; I imagine, on the other hand, that they had forgotten me by that same evening.) (*SG*, 517)

The folding of one thing into another has virtually all the elements, as well as all the appearance, of what I have named the self-directed joke—emotional intensity marked for its inane excess ("the urgent sobbing of a mountain torrent" close to the scorched earth "covered only with

---

[23] We can also read the comedy as a means of mastering the otherwise unmasterable mental pain linked to narcissism in a manner that risks overflowing the bounds of all rational negotiation of the world. Comedy is what saves the subject from that oceanic drowning, and, at the artistic level, is what makes the *novel* possible.

rubble"); the comically despoiled fate of that highly esteemed Proustian color, lilac); the cruel bathos of "forgotten," proof incontrovertible of the forgetting as the banal outcome of, and deflating rejoinder to, the process of grieving;[24] finally, the giveaway expression "of the same kind." It is, of course, the grossest of travesties. Unlike the calm, levelheaded Céleste of real life (including her sober manner as memoirist, in *Monsieur Proust*), here she seems to have been infected by the histrionics, supposedly of her sister, but in fact of the narrator ("of the same kind" signifies intensity of the same kind as the narrator's fraughtness). How do we interpret this bizarre decanting of Céleste into a personality with which in reality she had nothing in common? Is this Proust playfully yet vindictively creating a scapegoat, choreographing a pantomime of factitiously induced emotions behind which, laughing at his prey, he himself slips through the net? Or is it perhaps a reflection of what even the sternly censorious Wassenaar concedes, a moment that nudges the reader into an understanding of what Proust himself has engineered by means of comedy, a form of knowledge one of whose most important characteristics is that it is also a self-knowledge?[25]

III

The reader is thus invited not to forget that not allowing us to forget (the dangers of the self's narcissistically colonizing interpretations of reality) is also one of Proust's aims and its implementation part of his greatness as a writer. On the other hand, claiming that Proust will not allow us to forget something or other is a hazardous assertion. It is risky not because we may still have reason to doubt Proust's good faith as regards facing up to his own implication in the moral frailties of first-person discourse, but because the experience of "forgetting" is written very deep into the fabric of the novel, at all levels of its articulation, from sentence structure to plot structure. By this I do not mean "forgetting" in the sense of an emotionally cathected object or person becoming progressively decathected, as the anesthetic of "indifference" sends it on its way into the sump of oblivion (e.g., the narrator's dead feelings for Albertine). I mean

---

[24] I mean here the "grieving" for Albertine; the narrator's grief at the death of his grandmother is a different matter altogether.

[25] "Redemption or its possibility turns out to depend on Marcel's power as a narrator. And so we cannot rid ourselves of the knowledge, however repellent, that *all* of the grandiose moral speculations, psychological explanations, and justifications in the novel come from one mind, and can be returned to it, refuted, and denounced as utterly subjective whimsy. Proust will not allow us to forget this threat, and this is why he is a great writer." Wassenaar, *Proustian Passions*, 213.

rather the rhythm of forgetting and remembering, losing and refinding, that governs the essential shape of the novel and underlies its principal "message" (that of Time transfigured by virtue of the special conditions under which time lost can be refound). Forgetting is required, is good for us, not just because our survival depends on our being hardwired with the callousness necessary for putting the painful behind us. Although the pain can periodically return in a manner we cannot control, it gradually loses its force, and by the end of the process has none at all; extinction is definitive and forgetting is, with exceptions, forever. The other process involves the kind of forgetting where you are glad subsequently to remember, and where the gladness of remembering is what gives point to the original forgetting; forgetting *in order* to remember is one way of representing the Proustian telos of "redemption."

Yet the spirit of mischief stalks even this venerated sphere. Here, for example, is the first person again—but is it narrator or author?—breaking in with an amicable, readerly greeting, this time on the misadventures of telling: "I might say to the reader as if to a friend with whom one has spent so much time that one no longer remembers whether one had found the moment to tell him about a particular thing" (*P*, 215). What he cannot remember is whether he's already told the reader of the Duchesse de Guermantes's attitude during the Dreyfus affair (concerning the dreadful influence of partisanship on the composition of her social world and the content of her guest list). It is very unlikely that the reader will recall either, or care very much. A more substantial lapse in the mnemonics of narration is our being told (in *La Prisonnière*) of Cottard's death, only to find he has been brought back from the dead, alive and well in sprightly conversation chez les Verdurin. At the level of narrative and narration, this is an excellent Proustian joke.[26] The beauty of it lies in the casualness of its undecidability: Was Cottard inadvertently killed off and then deliberately hauled back into the story or was it the other way around (willfully annihilated and then unthinkingly reborn), or—a more remote yet not impossible outcome—was it a case of both the death *and* the rebirth as planned? In a lesser writer, the inconsistency would not bother us beyond registering it as a trivial failure of narrative mechanics. But given the particular interests and commitments of *À la recherche*, the glitch may well come across as a parody or a pastiche of a death-and-resurrection scene akin to the conjuror's trick of pulling a rabbit out of the hat. Consider in addition the way pastiche serves as the location of the story of a "second life," of which this time Cottard himself is the narrator: "at a gracious signal from the mistress of the house" the Verdurin dinner party

---

[26]It chimes with Beckett's corresponding joke: "Proust had a bad memory," in *Proust* (London: Grove Press, 1931), 17.

adjourns to "the Venetian smoking-room where Cottard tells us that he has witnessed veritable instances of dual personality, citing the case of one of his patients . . . whose temples he has, apparently, only to touch to awaken him to a second life, a life during which he remembers nothing of the first" (*T*, 22). This tale of amnesia and reanimation (another resurrection scene!) is also a second (or third) life for Cottard, this time his rebirth as storyteller inside that fiction within a fiction, the deadpan pastiche of the Goncourt journal at the beginning of *Le Temps retrouvé* (the killer touch in Proust's wasting of the Goncourt manner being the expression "at a gracious signal from the mistress of the house").

When we list the multiple registers of Proustian comedy, the mode that, along with "wit," figures most prominently in Proust's own vocabulary is indeed "pastiche," his genial gift for the genre reflected in the series of fictive takes on a real-life incident, the so-called Lemoine Affair imagined as narrated or discussed by Chateaubriand, Balzac, Flaubert, Sainte-Beuve, Henri de Régnier, the Goncourt brothers, Michelet, Émile Faguet, Renan, Ruskin, Maeterlinck, and—historically the odd man out—the seventeenth-century memorialist Saint-Simon (some were unpublished in Proust's lifetime). Beyond their status as a merely playful *exercices de style*, the pastiches are generally held to express an impulse of both affection and aggression. On the one hand, their mastery of a set of stylistic signatures constitutes a gesture of solidarity with the traditions of French literary prose, a sense of belonging to a community of writers and writing. On the other hand, mastery is an index of rivalrous intent, a Bloomian sign of antagonism to the predecessor, which at its sharpest marks the point at which pastiche crosses an alleged generic boundary line, veering over into parody.[27]

One of the less-remarked yet eye-catching features of Proust's interest in pastiche is its self-implicating dimension, the way in which its focus is sometimes turned back on Proust himself, with a kind of hall-of-mirrors effect. For example, in a letter to Léon Daudet in connection with reading the Goncourt journal, Proust wrote: "You can't imagine the incredible things I found in the *Journal* on the day of Victor Hugo's funeral. I thought I was reading a pastiche by you or me."[28] Given that the imitation of the Goncourt journal is the most famous of Proust's pastiches, what are we to make of this remark in the letter to Daudet? It seems to be inviting Daudet to contemplate the impossibly yet deliciously wicked spectacle of the Goncourts pastiching Proust pastiching them. Again, in the manuscript material, we find, accompanying the pastiche of the archenemy, Sainte-Beuve, two brief notes toward the sketch of a kind of

[27] Gray, *Postmodern Proust*, 16–18.
[28] *Corr.*, 14:78.

reverse pastiche, "Sainte-Beuve, juge de Proust" (a mind-boggling counterfactual imagining). Or what of the self-canceling sketch for a pastiche of a text by Taine attacking the genre of pastiche (perhaps the kind of thing Proust had in mind when his narrator speaks of "the pedantic pastiches of today's writers," *P*, 26). In the Renan example, Proust appears inside his own pastiche: "Proust" is cited by "Renan" for his lamentably flat translation of Ruskin, while in the Ruskin pastiche (of a text by Ruskin on Giotto's frescoes representing the Lemoine story), Proust the translator is politely taken to task for his defective understanding of English.

In his learned edition of the pastiches, Jean Milly maintains that the practice of "autopastiche" is imported into the *Recherche* itself,[29] although his reverence for Proust runs too deep for him to countenance its presence as the ironic inverse of the Proustian epiphany. This, however, is to stop short, especially in connection with the origins of the epiphanic in the experience of losing and refinding. Consider, for example, Proust's way with getting lost in the fog. Fog appears in *La Prisonnière* as a metaphor for the problematical readability of Albertine; the narrator's attempts at understanding her are like trying to connect up "the various lines of a construction which at first had seemed to me almost entirely lost in a fog" (344). "Fragmentary and broken," the construction metonymically attracts analogies from music (Albertine is playing the pianola), to which we might want to add a further term: construction as syntax. Albertine as blurred or illegible syntactic form can then come to stand as an analogy for actual syntax, and thus the experience of losing one's way and refinding it at the microlevel of the sentence. Franco Moretti has argued that the entire history and culture of the novel can be understood in terms of two interacting yet competing syntactic models.[30] On the one hand, there is the syntax of "anticipation," geared to suspense and the flow of what-happens-next, its basic form the simplicity of parataxis. On the other hand, there is the syntax of "complexity" or hypotaxis, where the advancing rhythm of unimpeded through-narrative is literally subordinated to the obstructive laterality of subclausal proliferation. This syntactic order is also commanded by a principle of deferral, but one that is very different from the suspenseful delay of the first model; it operates rather a suspension of suspense in favor of organized and systematic digression, and in its later developments reflects the desire to assign high literary status to the genre of the novel; no longer confined to basic storytelling, the novel becomes a true work of art. Flaubert once

---

[29] Jean Milly, *Les Pastiches de Proust* (Paris: Colin, 1970), 43–50.
[30] Franco Moretti, "The Novel: History and Theory," *New Left Review* 52 (July/August 2008): 111–24.

more is pivotal, as the writer who proclaimed that writing a sentence mattered to him far more than telling a story.

These, of course, are also crucial Proustian commitments, the elaborately modulated sentence conceived as an art form in its own right (what the dying Bergotte means by the ambition of making the sentence "precious in itself," or the narrator's judgment: "the way a literary person, simply by reading a sentence, can judge exactly the quality of its author," S, 245). In "Un amour de Swann" there is a description—almost a verbal mimesis—of Chopin's musical phrase:

> the phrases of Chopin, with their sinuous and excessively long necks, so free, so flexible, so tactile, which begin by seeking out and exploring a place for themselves far outside and away from the direction in which they started, far beyond the point which might one have expected them to reach, and which frolic in this fantasy distance only to come back more deliberately—with a more premeditated return, with more precision, as though upon a crystal glass that resonates until you cry out—to strike you in the heart. (334)[31]

This mutatis mutandis could be taken as a description of Proust's own syntax, or at least that model of it summarized in Leo Spitzer's notion of "architectonic form," which, when applied to Proust, Spitzer defined as follows: "this ability to accumulate the sentence seems to me to spring above all from Proust's ability to see connections between the most disparate things. In these complex representations there is an enormous mastery and dominion over things, which knows all about precedence and subordination and can put important and trivial things in their appropriate places."[32]

Few are going to quarrel with the view of Proust's writing practice as reflecting an "ability to see connections between the most disparate things." Yet as an account of that practice in terms of the challenges of reading it creates, questions are begged or too rapidly dispatched. Proust's syntax is not just a hierarchical system for marking through main and subordinate clause relations the relative positions of what ordinarily passes for the "important" and the "trivial." Nor are "mastery" and

---

[31] A related musical analogy informs the narrator's admiration for Bergotte: "In some of his books, there are sentence-endings in which the long-drawn-out chords resound like those dying notes of an operatic overture which, in its reluctance to close, keeps murmuring its final harmonies" (JF, 129–30).

[32] Leo Spitzer, "Le style de Marcel Proust," in Études de Style (Paris: Gallimard, 1970), 399. Jean Milly also comments on the Chopin description as a model for Proust's own syntax in La Phrase de Proust (Paris: Larousse, 1975), 55–57. Gilles Deleuze compares Proust's syntax to the river in a painting by Elstir, which "flowing under the bridges of a city was shown from a point of view that split it, spread it into a lake, narrowed it to a trickle, or blocked it by planting a hill on it" (JF, 419). Proust and Signs (London: Allen Lane, 1973), 147.

"dominion" the words that might automatically or even generally spring to mind for what Proust's readers actually experience in negotiating his more tentacular syntactic productions. A likelier outcome is sympathy with the condition of the Struldbruggs in *Gulliver's Travels*, who "can never amuse themselves with reading, because their memory will not serve to carry them from the Beginning of a Sentence to the End."[33] *À la recherche* can make Struldbruggs of most of us; all too often, by the time we have got to the end of the sentence, we have forgotten its point of departure, and so have to trace our way back and start all over again.[34] This is above all the fate that awaits us when we negotiate Proust's hypotactic structures for the first time. There is a vast difference between retroactive and cursive reading of Proust; while the former may hold the promise of mastery, the second (reading for the first time) characteristically delivers its disruptively nonmastering opposite. Just how disruptive depends, of course, on exactly how Proust distributes the components of the main clause through the labyrinth of subordination. The commonest forms in fact take few risks, by typically keeping subject and verb in adjacent positions or at the very least in close proximity (although the remainder of the predicate may well be delayed until much further out).[35] The more adventurous constructions, however, will often have a delayed subject (the sentence beginning with a subordinate clause), the verb it governs separated from it, and then a further deferred complement, that is, a triple spacing of subject, verb, and complement as the diasporic scattering of the members of a once-united syntactic family. On a cursive reading, it is indeed common to lose track of the main-clausal signposting of the sentence, thus inducing the arduous task, and ultimate consolations, of refinding what has been lost in the process of reading (no accident that

[33] Jonathan Swift, *Gulliver's Travels* (New York: Oxford University Press, 1986), 205.

[34] The "normal" rhythm of reading is illustrated by Maman's reading of *François le Champi* to the young boy, that is, in a manner that "directed the sentence that was ending towards the one that was about to begin" (*S*, 45). This is also, necessarily, a Proustian rhythm, but one that is constantly checked by its opposite, the sentence-ending that sends us back to one that has already begun. There is often a degree of social embarrassment in confessing to this. Although Proust is more "popular" (in the sense of more widely read) than ever before, it is quite common for readers to harbor the anxious belief that all Proust's other readers read him better. Far healthier to acknowledge that we are all in the same Struldbruggian boat. Proust, however, also turns the tables—another joke?—on those inclined to reproach him for having placed excessively heavy syntactic demands on their readerly capacities when he remarks on Saniette's inversion of the long-winded and the short-winded, whereby speed and brevity of utterance paradoxically come out as an impression of the interminable (*SG*, 271).

[35] Bersani has pointed to how a syntax in which "pronouns, adjectives, or subordinate clauses, precede their antecedents" serves the interests of an "impressionist" literary aesthetic. *The Fictions of Life and Art*, 234. Landy calls this a technique of "pre-predication," in *Philosophy as Fiction*, 8.

the "retrouvé" in the title of the final volume stands in deferred relation to the inaugural, front-cover "perdu" of the book's main title).[36]

This sentence-level infusion of readerly disorientation and reorientation is doubtless held by the Proustian metaphysic to be an altogether tonic experience; the syntax of detour and delay effects a translation of theme into form, abstraction into experience, that engages the reader in the kinds of searchings and struggles that beset the hero-narrator. It is not just a contingent outcome, dependent on our variable stamina and power of concentration as readers, but a centrally intended one that we forget beginnings, as this frees the reader to leave the syntactic past momentarily behind so as to strike out laterally in new directions, down the byways of mind and memory, before tracking back to the linear structure of the main clause to recover—remember—a lost point of origin. On the other hand, it is a technique that can all too easily pass into pure manner or irritating confusion, and Proust the pasticheur or parodist carries an understanding of this *en abyme* into his own text by means of displacement onto one of his characters. Getting lost in the fogbound being of Albertine does not occur only because of the perceptually fuzzy construction that is her person. The ground of confusion is linguistic as well as perceptual; Albertine's speech occasionally leaves the narrator struggling with her sentences in a manner not dissimilar to the way the narrator often leaves the reader with his: "I wished I could remember the beginning of the sentence so as to decide myself, when she shifted her ground, what the ending would have been. But as I had been listening for the end, I could hardly remember the beginning" (*P*, 137). True, Albertine's sentences are ground shifting, not as the strenuous ("muscular"[37]) effort to make complex relations visible, but rather as a method for concealing relations (both syntactic and personal). Her speech is governed the figure of anacoluthon (cited by Proust himself in the sense of the agrammatical because unfinished sentence). Albertine moves from one incomplete sentence to another as a strategy for withholding secrets and escaping the interrogating tyranny of her jailer (the pathological version of the need to exercise "mastery" and "dominion").[38] But if the narrator's bewilderment

[36]Unsurprisingly perhaps, one of the more interesting examples concerns the account of the world conjured out of the cup of tea. The most demanding "sentence" of all in the novel—the two-page sequence in the reflection on sexual inversion at the beginning of the *Sodome et Gomorrhe* (from "Their only honour" to "does not appear to them to be a vice," 19–21)—is so constructed that it is not in fact clear that it is a sentence at all.

[37]"[H]is sentences are the entire muscular activity of the intelligible body." Benjamin, "The Image of Proust," 210.

[38]The most famous example of pathological anxiety before the incomplete sentence is the moment when Albertine hovers at the edge of declaring a slang version of her taste for anal sex: "At least be brave enough to finish your sentence, you just got as far as *casser*" (*P*, 312); the complete expression is *casser le pot*.

here is fueled by the paranoid hermeneutics of jealousy, in its loss of beginnings it is also unnervingly reminiscent of what so often happens to us as Proust's readers, and may well explain why, when honest, many confess to short-circuiting and skipping. Might one of these have been James Joyce when in one of his notebooks he cryptically noted down his impression of Proust the writer: "Proust, analytic still life. Reader ends sentence before him"?[39]

The comedy of fog proves even more entertaining when drifting up from sentence to story, and across from metaphorical to literal, in particular that marvelous moment in part 11 of *Le Côté de Guermantes* when the narrator and Saint-Loup get lost in the fog on their way to a restaurant. The sequence begins with a recollection that trembles on the verge of revelation:

> If as I came downstairs I relived those evenings at Doncières, suddenly, when we reached the street, the almost total darkness, in which the fog seemed to have extinguished the street-lamps, . . . took me back to some dim memory of arrival in Combray by night, when the town was lit only at distant intervals and you groped your way through a humid, warm, holy, crib-like darkness in which the lamps flickered here and there with no more light than from a candle. Between that year (whichever year it was) and the evenings in Rivebelle, reflected a while back above the curtains in my bedroom, what a world of difference! As I took note of this I felt a sense of inspired exhilaration, which might have resulted in something had I remained alone and so avoided the detour of the many futile years I was yet to spend before discovering the invisible vocation which is the subject of this book. Had this discovery been made that evening, the carriage I found myself in would have deserved to rank as more memorable than Dr Percepied's, in which I had composed the little descriptive piece about the Martinville steeples. (395)

The moment of stepping into the street opens onto the typical palimpsest-like layering of memories within memories, the regressive or "vertical" superimposition of Paris/Doncières/Combray, which at once takes us back to the narrator's first scene of writing in *Du côté de chez*

[39] Cited in Richard Ellmann, *James Joyce* (New York: Oxford University Press, 1965), 524. See also John Coyle, "Pulp Fiction: Or, Proust and Joyce's Rhetorical Flourishes," *Glasgow Review* 3 (Summer 1995): 65. We might note in this connection Proust's (half) tongue-in-cheek letter to Robert Dreyfus in 2005: "I thought that you who know how to say so much in half a line would be exasperated by sentences that run to a hundred. Ah, how I should like to be able to write like Madame Straus" (by which Proust meant "the unattainable perfection of Madame Straus's conciseness"). *Corr.*, 5:288. Françoise Leriche has pointed out that "the long sinuous sentences are to be found especially in the parts of the novel written before 1918, while the sentences of the parts written later tend to be shorter, more concise." "Proust, an 'Art Nouveau' Writer?," in *Proust in Perspective*, ed. Mortimer and Kolb, 122.

Swann (the little sketch of the steeples of Martinville), and gestures pro-leptically to the discovery of the artistic vocation in *Le Temps retrouvé* (where "the invisible vocation which is the subject of this book" declares itself), while between the two extremes there is regret at opportunities lost (the huge "detour" that defines the whole novel and of which this particular evening in fogbound Paris is the synecdoche). The episode re-sembles that other embedded reflection of the novel's practical aesthetic, the Vinteuil septet, with its digressions and returns, losings and findings. But here context delivers something of an irreverent shock to the closed, circular system of aesthetic revelation. First, there is the urban fog, that novel admixture of the natural and the industrially man-made, which from the symbolists onward was one of the most commonplace causes or occasions of modernist epiphany. How appropriate then that the mystic possibilities afforded by the blanket of Parisian fog should evaporate the deeper the narrator is plunged into its actual reality:

> Robert had warned me when he arrived that it was very foggy outside, but as we were talking the fog had grown steadily thicker . . . Once you moved a foot or two away from them, the street-lamps were invisible . . . I was as lost as if I were on the coast of some northern sea, risking my life a score of times before reaching the safety of the solitary inn; no longer a mirage to be sought after, the fog was becoming one of those dangers to be fought off, so that finding our way safely to our destination meant that we felt the difficulties, the anxiety and finally the delight which the sense of safety—so much taken for granted by those who are not threatened by the loss of it—gives to the perplexed and disorientated traveller. (396)

There is here both echo and negation of what precedes in the mo-ment of near-epiphany. The echo consists in the repeat reference to the experience of getting lost and refinding one's way ("the detour of the many futile years" in the first moment alongside "finding our way safely to our destination" in the second). The negation consists in the transfer of the figurative meaning of journey and detour, losing and finding, back into literal meaning—the bathos of delayed access to the banal pleasures of a fancy restaurant and the creature comforts of its customers: "all these people stimulated by the comfort of the restaurant after their long wanderings through the ocean of fog . . . their faces positively glowing with the satisfaction of people who had had difficulty getting there and been afraid of getting lost" (405, 399). And the clincher comes when in the restaurant the fatuous Prince de Foix makes polite conversation with a stranger who has also lost his way: "Losing your way is nothing; the problem is finding it again" (404). Since this is exactly what *À la recher-che* is about, could it then be that the absurd prince is the novel's best critic?

IV

The Prince de Foix as philosopher of the Way (a latter-day Dante on the perils of the *selva oscura* or Bunyan on the ordeals and obstacles of pilgrimage), Cottard the sorcerer-doctor miraculously bringing the dead back to life (when not himself returning from the dead); Albertine, the nebulous "construction," whose own speech confounds elementary syntactic expectations—these must count as unusually interesting additions to the *galère* of freakish puppets Proust installed in his textual hall of mirrors, wearing the risible mask of an aesthetic turned inside out. The queen puppet, however, has to be Madame Verdurin, not least by virtue of an association (with Aunt Léonie) where autopastiche touches the very crux of the novel, namely, the relation between the narrator's madeleine and Mme Verdurin's croissant. Madame Verdurin (according to the Goncourts in Proust's pastiche, the source for Fromentin's "Madeleine" in *Dominique*) resembles Aunt Léonie in attributing to "the least of her sensations," whether agreeable or disagreeable, "an extraordinary importance." Hypochondriacs both, they milk the part of the malade imaginaire for all that it is worth. In Madame Verdurin's case, the affliction is the migraine that inevitably ensues from the unbearably raw exposure of her delicate and aesthetically discriminating nervous sensibility to the higher musical forms; via the headache-inducing agony and ecstasy of listening to music at her social gatherings, she is unique among Proust's creations in managing an epiphany almost every other week.

There is, however, a cure for the migraines—breakfast croissants, procured for her in conditions of wartime scarcity by the well-connected Cottard. As she reads in her newspaper of the sinking of the *Lusitania* ("How awful! It's worse than the most horrific tragedy"), she dips the treasured croissant into her cup of coffee, smiling beatifically at the calming effects of their combined taste on her easily agitated central nervous system: "But the loss of all those people at sea must have been a thousand million times reduced before it struck her, because even while she uttered, through a mouthful of croissant, these distressing thoughts, the look which lingered on her face, probably induced by the taste of the croissant, so valuable in preventing migraine, was more like one of quiet satisfaction" (*T*, 81).[40] The parallel with the madeleine dipped in tea that blissfully transports the narrator back to Aunt Léonie's rooms, themselves represented as a "cupboard" full of the tastes and odors of things lost and found, looks like a case of dramatically ironic "intermittences," a hugely delayed reprise that in the moment of repetition devalues the moment recalled: "A delicious pleasure had invaded me, isolated

---

[40] In the late years, Proust's everyday diet was mostly coffee and croissants!

me, without my having any notion as to its cause. It had immediately made the vicissitudes of life unimportant to me, its disasters innocuous, its brevity illusory" (S, 47). If this is perhaps to force the pace a little with the "method" of the echo or leitmotif, there is nevertheless warrant for it from Proust himself, as the writer who persistently pushes us toward juxtapositions, however commonsensically implausible they may seem. We should also remember that *Du côté de chez Swann* and *Le Temps retrouvé* were originally written together, and in that original relation of much closer proximity, any parodic echo of the dipped madeleine in the dunked croissant was presumably much more audible. The "delicious pleasure" that renders "disasters innocuous" comes to look rather different if and when the latter category is expanded to include the *Lusitania* catastrophe.

The metaphorical "cupboard" that is Aunt Léonie's dwelling also contains a memory of the lime blossom tea specially made for her by the Combray apothecary (the pharmacist is to Léonie what Cottard is to Madame Verdurin). In the resurrectional-redemptive drama of the novel, it is the madeleine that has the *beau rôle*; alongside its extraordinary evocative power, the beverage is but an enabling adjunct about which there is little as such to be said.[41] Yet in shape, substance, and texture, the herbal concoction is in fact lovingly described as a handmade artifact resembling a highly wrought work of art:

> The drying of the stems had curved them into a whimsical trellis-work in whose interlacings the pale flowers opened, as if a painter had arranged them, had made them pose in the most ornamental way. The leaves, having lost or changed their aspect, looked like the most disparate things, a fly's transparent wing, the white of a black label, a rose petal, but these things had been heaped up, crushed or woven as in the construction of a nest. A thousand small useless details—the charming prodigality of the pharmacist—that would have been eliminated in an artificial preparation gave me like a book in which one is amazed to encounter the name of the person one knows, the pleasure of realizing that these were actually the stems of real lime-blossoms, like those I saw in the avenue de la Gare, altered precisely because they were not duplicates but themselves, and because they had aged. (S, 54)

The remembering mind fondly embraces its remembered object, contemplating it in close-up as if it were a miracle of nature and culture combined; it is a characteristic form of Proustian attention to the humble things that clutter the lumber room of the past. Yet there is something about the terms of recollection that is uncomfortably close to the kind of fetishism Proust elsewhere deplores. There is a very well-known

---

[41] But see chapter 7.

passage from *Le Temps retrouvé*—by now somewhat exhausted from overquotation—that is virtually a manifesto-piece for the whole Proustian aesthetic. The passage runs a simple distinction between the wrong (sterile) and the right (creative) kinds of memory. The right kind is, of course, the involuntary, represented by the madeleine episode and "the three recollections I had just had." The wrong kind consists of the "scenes played out by our voluntary memory" that "require no more effort on our part than leafing through a picture book." As an example, the narrator refers to the day of his first visit to the Princesse de Guermantes's house: "I had idly gazed on images of my choice, of the place de l'Eglise in Combray, or the beach at Balbec, as if I had been leafing through an album of water-colours . . . enabling me to say, with the selfish pleasure of a collector, as I catalogued the illustrations of my memory: 'I've certainly seen some beautiful things in my life' . . . The same was not true of the three recollections I had just had" (*T*, 181–82).

Conscious recall as a leisured gazing on images of choice by the gratified owner of "the beautiful things" of one's past, gems of remembrance perused in the way one might pore over entries in a private album or picture book—this captures perfectly the idea of the field of memory as a connoisseur's catalog or a banker's vault that stores a portfolio of spiritual valuables that can be taken out and considered at will.[42] It is a version of sights and emotions recollected in tranquillity, where the remembering subject is assimilated to the stylish figure of the "collector," content only with the best that money can buy (the punning analogy is, of course, possible only when reading Proust in English translation; startled Wordsworthians might balk at the coarser sense of the word "collection" emerging from the hallowed term "recollection"). This is Proust's brilliant insight into the parallel logics of remembrance, aestheticism, and capital accumulation, the sense of the past returning and time refound as a "return" on an investment; you are "saved" by what you have saved. In writing of time past, how then to avoid being merely a "collector" of its "treasures"? The lime blossom tea is, of course, meant to illustrate the opposed form of memory. It is, with the madeleine, the spontaneous source or trigger of something singularly "precious" ("filling me with a precious essence," *S*, 47), like the "precious" sentences Bergotte wishes he had composed. Yet is not the opposition compromised when the precious is edged with preciosity, a "beautiful thing" whose components are described "as if a painter had arranged them, had made them pose in the most ornamental

---

[42] Contrast with the idea of memory, developed in the "Intermittences du coeur" episode, as a bank of spiritual "assets" only intermittently available to us, but that are still described as "assets" (*biens intérieurs*): "At whatever moment we may consider it, our total soul has an almost fictitious value only, for all its great wealth of assets, for now some, now others of these are unavailable" (*SG*, 158–59).

way"? It is the stuff of tisane made into imaginary art object, stamped moreover with the aura of "authenticity" and entered in the catalog of the mind as a collector's "original," artfully posed yet "real" ("the stems of real lime blossoms"), not "duplicates" or one of those derivative "artificial preparations" from the age of the mass-manufactured. Storehouse of a precious essence of Self, of what is properly me and mine, the herb is a home (a "nest") for a form of lost property subsequently found.

There are several incarnations of the "collector's" mentality in the novel, the most interesting via the family triad of Swann, Odette, and Gilberte. Swann, as *the* collector-figure of the *Recherche* and "dilettante of immaterial sensations," adds "the voluptuous pleasure of being in love" (with Odette) to his extensive collection, on the grounds of it being an item that "was increased in value for him . . . by the price he was paying her for it."[43] The observation is cruelly sharp, and made even sharper by its further elaboration as a comparison that can be taken as casting an anticipatory ironic net over the world of Balbec and the cash basis of the numerous aesthetic pleasures it will bring for the narrator: "as we see people uncertain whether the sight of the sea and the sound of its waves are delightful, convince themselves of it and also of the exceptional quality and disinterest of their own taste, by paying a hundred francs a day for a hotel room that allows them to enjoy that sight and that sound" (S, 270). We might want to remember this when, in the next volume, from his room in the doubtless very expensive Balbec hotel, the narrator enjoys the pleasures of looking at the sea in a manner that will be decisive for his initiation into the artist's way of looking at the world. Even funnier is the example of Odette who, on becoming Madame Swann bent on forging a respectable place in society, also becomes a minor collector in search of lost time, as a habitué of the Paris antique shops: "Of course she claimed she loved 'antiques' and assumed a rapturous and discriminating air when she said she adored spending a whole day 'collecting curios,' looking for 'bric-a-brac,' things 'from the past'" (247). It is quite impossible to read this poker-faced account of the rapture afforded by foraging among the things of the past without something of a double take. It is the near-perfect Proustian joke; however hard his narrator tries, and we try with him, the "things from the past," the "bric-a-brac" of lost time—the

---

[43] One of the models for Swann was the collector Charles Ephrussi, recently brought back into view by the memoir of his descendant, Edmund de Waal, *The Hare with Amber Eyes* (London: Picador, 2011). De Waal captures beautifully the ambivalence of the wealthy and obsessive collector-connoisseur. The opportunity "to collect" is the opportunity "to turn looking into having and having into knowing" (33). De Waal's tale also takes him from Paris to Tokyo and the story of the inheritance of Charles's collection of Japanese netsuke by one of de Waal's uncles. The latter was a friend of the Japanese philosopher and historian Yanagi Soetsu, who, we learn, was an avid reader of Ruskin (preface, 3).

very stuff from which the novel is made—can never look quite the same again.[44]

And then there is Gilberte and the story of the marriage and the mortgage. At the end of *La Fugitive* the narrator makes a discovery that not only turns a childhood preconception on its head but that also reverberates throughout the entire book, actively reinforcing a circular structure of which the discovered information is itself a constitutive part. Returning to spend some time on the Tansonville family estate with Gilberte de Saint-Loup, née Swann, he learns from her that the two ways—the Méséglise and the Guermantes—are joined by a short path ("a sentence which overturned all the ideas of my childhood by revealing that the two ways were not as irreconcilable as I had thought," 654). The erroneous belief not only underpinned the view of Swann's world and the Guermantes' world as separate social spheres, but also the mysterious game of losing and finding played by the narrator's father when on the family walks he pretends to get lost before triumphantly revealing the way safely refound: "Where are we?" is the routine paternal challenge, to which there is an equally routine maternal response: "Exhausted from walking but proud of him, she would admit tenderly that she had absolutely no idea" (*S*, 116); this may be how Proust sometimes fantasized his reader, as Struldbruggian at all levels.

Thus, as the novel gears up for its ending by readying itself for a return to its beginning, it also corrects that beginning. It is importantly relevant to the point (which has, of course, been made many times) that the source of the narrator's information is Gilberte. She is a narrative crossroads, also there at the beginning, as a Swann, but now, as the wife of Robert de Saint-Loup, a member of the Guermantes family. Through the marriage and its own offspring (Gilberte's daughter), the two ways and worlds converge not just topographically but also biologically and socially. Gilberte is a nodal point of what in *Le Temps retrouvé* is called "the thread of life," Proust's summarizing metaphor for a narrative finally understood, across its elaborate weave, as a set of variations on the traditional Family Plot: "Was she not, as most human beings are, like one of those 'stars' in forests, crossroads where roads converge, which have come, as they do in our lives, from the most diverse starting-points?" (*T*, 338). In these conjunctions of place, time, and family, the transmission of property is pivotal and furnishes another twist to the theme of the lost and the regained. Recall the American wife of the Comte de Farcy ("an obscure relation of the Forchevilles") at the *bal des têtes* party, who mixes up all the lines of transmission, mistakenly assuming that Forche-

---

[44]There are also the "collectors of old snuffboxes, Japanese prints or rare flowers," as the type to which Proust compares the society of Inverts (*SG*, 22).

ville is Gilberte's biological father, that Tansonville has come to her from him, and that "Forcheville" is a grander family name than "Saint-Loup": "She heard the names and repeated them without having first understood their value, and their precise significance. Somebody explained to another person, who asked whether Tansonville came to Gilberte from her father M. de Forcheville, that it did not come from him at all, that it was an estate belonging to her husband's family, that Tansonville was close to Guermantes, and had belonged to Mme de Marsantes but, being heavily mortgaged, had been redeemed out of Gilberte's dowry" (T, 269–70). Property changes hands as social fortunes fluctuate and new cross-class alliances are forged in the crucible of marriage. As a storytelling device, it is a formula straight out of Balzac (and the European novel generally), but it is also the narrative basis for the "symbolic" as well as literal meeting of the two ways, emblem for the narrator of the circular totality of a life redeemed. This already suggests an ironic tension between plot and meaning (the "Balzacian" is no friend of the high-transcendental).

But there is also a third potential perspective, one that thoroughly demystifies the very idea of "redemption." A ruinously uneconomic holding in the Guermantes family, Tansonville is a property "lost" in the sense of mortgaged to the hilt, but "regained" in the sense of bought back with Gilberte's dowry money, a debt "redeemed." As it charts its own genealogy, Proust's novel reminds one of another, even if there is no reason to believe that Proust himself had it in mind (Nietzsche's *Genealogy of Morals*, which among other things traces modern ideas of salvation and redemption back to a more primitive set of notions centered on the discharging of economic debts and obligations, and surviving in the formal contractual language of commercial exchange).[45]

Epiphany, redemption, debt, property: these are the axes along which run the less obvious "convergences" within the more familiar system of juxtapositions, parallelisms, and interconnections that is the text of *À la recherche*. The question is whether they are incidental and accidental, unforeseen and inconsequential spin-offs from the central thrust of the Proustian enterprise or fully intended by Proust as an implied skeptical commentary on some of the central emphases of his own project. There can be no definitive answer to that question. It is nevertheless worth taking note of two last jokelike reflections on time, forgetting, losing, wasting, and owning. One is sheer cheekiness; the other unself-consciously deep. The funniest manifestation of the will to remember—in this novel that begins with its narrator waking up because he has "forgotten" that he has fallen asleep—is Léonie's reminding herself not to forget that she

---

[45] The downfall of the Guermantes salon is also represented as the loss of an ability to engineer a "social redemption" (T, 328).

has not slept (her insomnia indispensable to sustaining the part of the helplessly exhausted invalid): "'I must be sure to remember that I did not sleep'; for never sleeping was her great claim." But if she remembers (the fiction of) not having slept, she does forget to take her medicine. "'What, three o'clock!' My aunt cried out suddenly, turning pale, 'Why, my goodness, Vespers has begun and I've forgotten my pepsin . . . Three o'clock! It's unbelievable how the time passes!'" (S, 103). Even when relativized to the morbid obsessions of Aunt Léonie, it takes some nerve to write this at the beginning of this book about time and its passing, including the time it is going to take to read the book. But then consider—the second reflection—Françoise's reply in an earlier exchange:

> "Françoise, now who were they ringing the passing bell for? Oh, dear God, it must have been for Mme Rousseau. I'm blessed if I hadn't forgotten that she passed away the other night. Oh, it's time for God to call me home, I don't know what I've done with my time since my poor Octave died. But I'm wasting your time, my girl."
>
> "Not at all, Madame Octave, my time is not so precious; He who made it did not sell it to us." (58)

Françoise often grumblingly rebukes her young master, but from within the permitted codes of servant–young master relations. This is a rebuke of a deeper kind. It is not, of course, directed to the narrator, and for all sorts of reasons never could be. But her words to Aunt Léonie are of Proust's devising and reverberate way beyond their immediate context. Time as not so precious in this tale of the precious essences and the precious sentences that rescue lost time from oblivion—here perhaps is Proust the ironist proposing an alternative, heterodox coda to À la recherche du temps perdu. Françoise's wisdom is peasant wisdom, anchored in religion (time is God's gift), but it is also class-based knowledge (as a domestic servant, Françoise does not "own" the time given her, just as she owns precious little else). The narrator by contrast, with the Rolls, yachts, Fortuny dresses, expensive jewelry, fancy hotels and restaurants, and so on, financed from a private income based on investments managed by his stockbroker, and who can absorb a hit when the stock market falls, is a man who can fully afford to "waste" time, but who is also in a position to "redeem" it.[46] He can redeem it in the quasi-commercial sense of paying off a debt to the self by converting time into the currency of an

---

[46] Proust himself was an active if muddled investor. The practice of borrowing on his existing holdings to speculate on the futures market went very badly wrong during the wartime crash. Proust claimed, tongue-in-cheek, of course, but not altogether in the best of taste, to have met his reverses of fortune with stoical fortitude. Corr., 14:298. See Jean-Yves Tadié, Marcel Proust: A Life (New York: Penguin, 2000), 630–31.

extratemporal "essence."[47] The fluctuating and variable value of our life in time, with its inflations and deflations, its bad investments and disappointing returns, can be transmuted into the equivalent of an imperishable "asset." It is called the Work, as the site on which grows the "grass of eternal life," the grass for future generations after the death of its creator: "Personally, I say that the cruel law of art is that human beings die and that we ourselves die after exhausting all the forms of suffering, so that not the grass of oblivion may grow, but the grass of eternal life, the vigorous grass of fruitful works of art, on which future generations will come, heedless of those asleep beneath it, to have their *déjeuner sur l'herbe*" (T, 348).

Echoing the narrator of Beckett's *First Love* as he wanders around a cemetery (in one of his best-known analogies, Proust compares his book to a graveyard),[48] one might have a bone to pick with this. One can take the view that Proustian metaphor is sacrosanct, beyond the reach of the skeptical gaze. But if not, then this has to be one of the least convincing metaphorical sequences of the whole book, especially the embarrassingly cute allusion to Manet's picture. Here among the dead we have a dead metaphor (a weak echo perhaps of the biblical "all flesh is grass"), and the incongruous image of literary immortality and salvation as a picnic (with croissants and madeleines in the picnic box?). It is peroration without inspiration. Happily, Proust has a simple and robust counterproposition, one we can unreservedly trust as the antithesis of the self-deceiving: "No doubt my book too, like my mortal being, would eventually die, one day . . . Eternal duration is no more promised to books than it is to men" (T, 353). Françoise would doubtless agree, even as, in a final incarnation, old and half-blind she works to "patch" it up.[49]

[47] Descombes comments on how in Proust "economic power is transformed into aesthetic grace." *Proust: Philosophy of the Novel*, 187.

[48] "[A] book is a great cemetery where the names have been effaced from most of the tomb and are no longer legible" (T, 212).

[49] See chapter 8.

CHAPTER THREE

Magic

IMAGINE (IF YOU CAN) A mobile geometric shape that consists of a horizontal baseline punctuated by periodic detours, each wandering from and then looping back to its point of departure, contributing cumulatively to a concentric, spiraling ensemble that is finally encompassed by a grand outer circle. If this is difficult to visualize, it is not just because of my clunky attempt to describe it. Yet such is the complex and dynamic shape of Proust's novel. For the purposes of analytical discrimination, this looping and spiraling construction can be schematically represented as unfolding on three planes: the linear, the digressive, and the circular. At one level, À la recherche is a straight-line narrative that runs from childhood to middle age and narrates the "education" of its hero in a manner broadly consistent with the traditions of the European bildungsroman. At another level, however, the linear trajectory is regularly interrupted by a series of digressive, temporal swerves, both analeptic and proleptic, at times in a form so radical and persistent that the novel threatens to become all digression, such that the term itself (presupposing a line from which to deviate) progressively loses its meaning; it is the systematic conversion into a whole narrative method of what Proust's great contemporary, Fernando Pessoa called, in The Book of Disquiet, "the asides of life."[1] The detours are not just random; in joining past, present, and future, they enact—the third plane—a set of circular movements illustrative of a more general circular design. The novel may, in some deep sense, be one vast detour (through the "wasted" years), but it ends by returning to its beginning (in "Combray"). The two ways, assumed in early life to lead in entirely different directions, are revealed as connecting paths that run back into the "center" of both village and self, the former as the basic substratum of the "mental soil" of the latter (S, 184). Ending and beginning also become one and the same as the narrator brings his story to a

---

[1] Fernando Pessoa, The Book of Disquiet (London: Penguin Classics, 2001), 5. Richard Goodwin has argued that "digression" is constitutive of À la recherche, and is linked to the creation of a narrative based on the principle of indefinite "postponement" of resolution and closure (in the transcendental epiphany). Around Proust (Princeton: Princeton University Press, 1991).

conclusion by announcing his intention to write a book that, on certain assumptions, is the book that we have just read.

Or is it? Many have questioned the assumed identity of book-just-read and book-yet-to-be-written (and hence already-written), if on very different grounds, from technical considerations based on internal chronological anomalies to extremely sophisticated theoretical accounts of a mismatch between the narrator's idealist conception of the literary vocation and the nature of narrative fiction. But even if we hold to the assumption, there remains the curious fact that in *Le Temps retrouvé* the narrator never once refers to his project as a "novel." Some novelists are mentioned, by and large in passing—Flaubert and Laclos (cited as allies in Proust's rejection of "popular" and "patriotic" fiction), Dostoyevsky (in misleading alignment with the painter, Elstir), and, of course, George Sand (whose *François le Champi* returns from the first volume, making an impressive if implausible reappearance in the Guermantes library of the last volume). One might perhaps infer from the attack on realism ("some even wanted the novel to be a sort of cinematographic stream of things," 191) that the narrator is indeed thinking in terms of the novel form, "wanting" it to be of a different kind. But these are desultory asides, and disappear from view when juxtaposed with this disparaging observation: "A man born sensitive but with no imagination might nonetheless write admirable novels" (209). Here we have an ambiguous backhander, but directed at what—the man without imagination or the genre of the novel? In any case, when it comes to describing his own project, the narrator's preferred terms are "book," "work," and "literature," this last, of course, one of the grandest terms in the Proustian lexicon, supplying the formula for the only life worth living but radically lacking in generic precision.

There is a genuine puzzle here. What explains the narrator's tight-lipped, slightly embarrassed diffidence vis-à-vis the genre of the novel? For even if we do not subscribe to the argument that what he will write is what we have read, it neither makes sense nor has a point to think of the narrator as committed to a literary undertaking utterly distinct from the novel *À la recherche* so manifestly is. For one thing, the narrator states explicitly that the characters of Proust's novel are to figure in his own work, and, while this opens the dizzying perspective wherein what are fictional beings for Proust are "real" people for the fictional narrator, the decision implicitly reflects a commitment to narrative. And yet the sparse and scattered mentions of the novel in *Le Temps retrouvé*, on a spectrum from the casual through the noncommittal to the barbed, suggest a hesitancy on the narrator's part before the question of "form," which moreover Proust seems to have shared. In the 1908 *carnet* Proust noted: "Sloth or doubt or impotence hiding behind uncertainty as to form. Should I make it a novel, a philosophical study, am I a novelist?"[2] These were early days for Proust himself, still deep in the essayistic forms of what was to become *Contre Sainte-Beuve* (presumably the reference of "philosophical study"), and similar uncertainties accompany the narrator's long, doubt-laden movement toward the deferred embrace of his vocation as writer. There is a further similarity in that intellectual doubt is tied to temperamental defects (laziness and procrastination), which makes it unclear whether the former ("uncertainty as to form") is but rationalization ("hiding behind") of the latter or their actual cause. On the other hand, Proust ends by supplying his own stunning answer to the question "am I a novelist?"; the answer is *À la recherche*. The narrator by contrast, even at the celebratory moment of the final volume, says little of note on the generic status of his projected "work."

There is another reason why this relative silence is surprising. On the train journey back from Venice with his mother in *La Fugitive*, the narrator opens two letters received shortly prior to departure. One announces the marriage of Cambremer *fils* and Jupien's niece (now Mlle d'Oléron, accorded the title courtesy of Charlus), the other announcing the marriage of Gilberte Swann and Robert de Saint-Loup. Both furnish a crux for the plot of *À la recherche*, nodal points of what in *Le Temps retrouvé* is called "the thread of life." More immediately, the news prompts a conversation between mother and son that takes the latter's thoughts toward the topic of the novel. The two announced marriages suggest two ways of telling a story, two narrative models. For the mother, the unpredictable marital conjoinings that confound the class divide separating humble and lofty evoke the fairy tale and its Cinderella-style happy ending or the idyllic aspects of Sand's *romans champêtres*. The narrator, however, takes a very different view, more realistic and even cynical, attuned to the calculations of interest that underlie cross-class alliances, and for which the appropriate narrative model is Balzac: "'It is virtue rewarded. It's a marriage from the end of a novel by George Sand,' said my mother. 'It's the wages of sin, it's a marriage from the end of a novel by Balzac,' I thought" (*F*, 622).

---

[2] *Le Carnet de 1908*, ed. Philip Kolb (Paris: Gallimard, 1976), 61. To what literary genre *À la recherche* belongs is the opening sentence of Tadié's *Proust et le roman* (Paris: Presses Universitaires de France, 1971), 17. Roland Barthes wrote of "Proust's hesitation" (between "essay" and "novel"). "Longtemps, je me suis couché de bonne heure," in *Le bruissement de la langue* (Paris: Seuil, 1984), 314. For a more detailed account, see William C. Carter, "'Am I a Novelist?': Proust's Search for a Genre," in *Proust in Perspective*, ed. Mortimer and Kolb, 32–44.

Balzac or George Sand? Given the importance of *François le Champi* for the mother-son relation in "Combray," we might be tempted to interpret the view taken at the end of "Un Séjour à Venise" in *La Fugitive* as a sign of the more adult narrator, now weaned from emotional dependence on the mother, though there is much in the Venice section itself to confute this. There is also much in *Le Temps retrouvé* to confute the downgrade given to *François le Champi*. While in the Guermantes library, hot on the heels of the triple revelation of paving stones, spoon, and napkin, the narrator randomly takes down a number of volumes and "absent-mindedly" happens to open just one of them (191). For those readers who do not know already, no prizes for the correct guess. What a coincidence that it turns out to be *François le Champi*! Think of the odds! This has to be the most opportunistically rigged scene of significant reading in the whole of Western literature. Among other things, it encourages the thought that the triple revelation—what, in the spirit of the irreverently skeptical, I am now tempted to call the triple whammy—is itself a piece of craftily engineered narrative machinery; the remarkable *speed* with which one experience succeeds the other is surely one of the keys to the climactically revelatory import attributed to them, but is secured at the price of placing immense strain on elementary considerations of verisimilitude: "It seemed . . . as if the signs, which were, on this day, to bring me out of my despondency and renew my faith in literature, were intent on multiplying themselves" (*T*, 176). Signs intent on multiplying themselves? What kind of anthropomorphic intentionality and agency are these? Tadié quotes this sentence as if it were proof beyond question of Proust's high seriousness.[3] It is in fact arguably the feeblest sentence in the whole of the *Recherche*, a transparently manipulative exercise in narrative "motivation." This is Faith ("faith in literature") as pure magical thinking.[4] Brutally put, it is a form of spiritualized melodrama, epiphany in the fast lane. As for the "accidental" reencounter with *François le Champi*, this not only recalls the time "when Mama was reading me George Sand's book" and what that "had meant in Combray"; the recollection is also connected with an earlier construal of it—or more precisely of its title, the "magic" of its Name—as having "contained the essence of the novel" (192). However, in *La Fugitive* Sand is precisely the example not to follow, and in *Le Temps retrouvé*, while the title—the "name"—might still possess a "power of resurrection" (196), the novel itself is now judged as being

[3] Tadié, *Proust et le roman*, 424.

[4] We should also note that what "brings" this blessed condition is less the miraculous power of signs to multiply of their own accord than an operation of syntax: in the earlier parts of the novel when the privileged moment is but half-glimpsed, an object of fringe vision, it is typically relegated to a subordinate clause, whereas when it becomes the object of focal vision, it leaps onto the main clausal stage of the sentence.

"not a particularly outstanding book" (192).[5] Its prestige seems to have been displaced by the magisterial authority of George Sand's contemporary, the epic, incomparable example of Balzac.

The exchange between mother and son is a turning point and a leave-taking. The narrator leaves Venice, the place that has haunted him throughout, never to come back (other than in the realm of memory, on the cobbles of the Guermantes courtyard). The only new place that awaits him in what remains of his story is the anonymous sanatorium, about which we learn nothing; narratively speaking, it is a parenthesis or a blank. Above all, it is a leave-taking from "Maman." We hear of her again, also parenthetically, just one more time: the narrator's excuse for escaping to the Guermantes *matinée* is that Maman faces the tedious social chore of afternoon tea with Madame Sazerat. The last we really see of her is on the train back from Venice in *La Fugitive*. From that point on she disappears, still alive, but basically "dead" to and for the narrative, cleared out as part of a clearing of the decks.[6] But a clearing for what? Perhaps for the artistic revelations about to come, a late assertion of independence in the discovered and assumed identity of the Artist. On the other hand, this seems odd given that Maman is so central to that project (the narrator clears her out at the very moment he will be "returning" to her in Combray via memory and art). It may well be then that his narrative dispatch of her has something to do with the conversation in the train about the respective value of Sand and Balzac, and the rejection of his mother's preference for Sand in favor of Balzac. It is as if a decision has been made that reflects a stage of maturation, related less to creating the space for transcendental epiphanies than to acknowledging the reality principle in the paradigmatic narrative form of *illusions perdues*.[7]

The respects in which the lesson of Balzac for Proust was a variant of the archetypal lesson of the Master are well established. It seems also to have been a lesson for the narrator, at least in the closing moments of *La Fugitive*, where Balzac the truth-teller, inveterate enemy of fairy-tale versions of reality, decisively trumps Sand. Yet in *Le Temps retrouvé* nothing comes of this; indeed, apart from a brief allusion (Balzac's characters are such that one always regrets not having met them in real life), noth-

[5] In his correspondence Proust is even more caustic (see *Corr.*, 9:225).

[6] There is, of course, one more mention in the closing pages, impersonal, serving purely as "analogy" but unmistakably an allusion to the actual death of Proust's own mother, probably the closest Proust could get in his novel to what for him remained the unutterable: "I felt like a son whose dying mother still feels the need to take care of him all the time, in between her injections and cuppings" (*T*, 351).

[7] There is, after all, an echo of the conversation about the Sand and the Balzac models of ending in the actual ending of Proust's novel: it is crucially a feature of the latter that Madame Verdurin marries the widower Prince de Guermantes—a Balzacian ending if ever there was one.

ing further is made of Balzac at all, whereas George Sand returns, in the Guermantes library, for one last bow, albeit as a heavily stage-managed affair. And if at the end we go back once again to the beginning, to the narrator's first perplexed wrestling with his own desire to be a writer in "Combray," what we find, or refind, there is a mental jumble (thoughts of "poems, novels, a poetic future") in which it is the first and third terms that predominate. On the same page, the hope of becoming a "writer" (écrivain) has as its immediate, virtually synonymous cognate not the term "novelist" but "poet": "my hope . . . of succeeding in becoming a writer and a poet some day" (S, 179). He fantasizes an intimacy with Mme de Guermantes in which "she would make me tell her the subjects of the poems I intended to compose" (S, 173). And his first literary effort—the only piece of writing by the narrator actually quoted in the whole of the Recherche—comes shortly after: the excited sketch of the Martinville steeples as seen from a moving carriage, subsequently described as "a little prose poem" (JF, 29).

Thus, a set of terms is launched that, as if on a magic carpet from The Thousand and One Nights, will migrate throughout the text with all the appearance of framing and defining an aesthetic program (most notably in the hymn to "poetic seeing," which the narrator will address to the paintings of Elstir and the forms of "impressionistic" perception they are held to instantiate). On the other hand, the text in which these migratory adventures take place is itself a novel, not an extended prose poem. The easy way with this contradiction or discrepancy would be to describe À la recherche as a stylistic hybrid based on a generic division of labor: the "poetic" performs certain tasks, the novelistic (or the prosaic) performs others.[8] But this would be too easy, and there is certainly nothing in the narrator's final meditations that proposes or conforms to a recipe for happily collaborative coexistence on the principle of to each its own; the narrator nowhere casts himself as a manager overseeing the efficient functioning of a literary division of labor of this type. Perhaps, therefore, it makes more sense to cast the issue in terms of competing rather than just coexisting claims on the category "literature," as a tension reflecting an instability at the heart of the Proustian aesthetic. The "uncertainty as to form," we recall, is stated as a choice between writing a "philosophical study" or a "novel," the former alternative also carried over into "Combray" at those moments when the young narrator gropes for an understanding of what "literature" is to be for him. "Philosophical study" means largely the sort of thing Proust was thinking about at the

[8]This is Tadié's view (Proust et le roman, 429). Benjamin claimed, on the back of the general principle that "all great works of literature found a genre or dissolve one," that Proust created a "structure which is fiction, autobiography and commentary in one," but as "unconstruable synthesis." "The Image of Proust," 197.

time of writing *Contre Sainte-Beuve*. This has little to do with the abstract reasoning of the philosopher and everything to do with what in one of the "projected prefaces" is repeatedly referred to as "poetry."[9] The real choice is not between the literary and the extraliterary ("philosophy"), but a choice within the general field of the literary: poetry or narrative.

It is moreover a choice or a dilemma that has a historical context: Proust's ambivalent relation to the literary options made available to the budding writer by the legacy of the nineteenth century. If in *Le Temps retrouvé* the narrator does not explicitly identify himself as a would-be novelist, this is doubtless due in large part to the historically fraught relation between the novel and "literature," in particular, the implication of the former in the subliterary print culture of what D. H. Lawrence was to term the period of the "Emotional-Democratic" (Proust's distaste reflected in his contemptuous dismissal of "popular art").[10] More profoundly still, the novel was child of and servant to the values of the disenchanted world, the form best adapted to what Hegel called the age of prose, a form that presupposes and is suited to "a reality prosaically ordered" (*eine bereits zur Prosa geordnete Wirklichkeit*).[11] In terms of the difficulties this posed for Proust's self-conception as an artist, the important predecessor was not so much Balzac as Flaubert, the novelist who, even as he charts the prosaically disenthralled character of the modern world, also seeks to extricate the novel from its entanglement in the subliterary and raise it to the status of the "aesthetic" by the sheer force of style (the dream of a "book about nothing" that would be held together by the "internal force of its style").[12] For Proust this endeavor manifested itself above all in Flaubert's use of the "various parts of speech" (crucially the imperfect tense) in the unraveling and transformation of narrative fabric into impressionistic patchwork ("what up until Flaubert had been action has become impression").[13] The (rough) equivalent in the *Recherche* is what primarily interests the narrator in Bergotte's writings. The latter are notionally "novels," but we are given no sense of what Bergotte is like as a storyteller; the focus of attention is on selected "portions" (*morceaux*), choice passages, sentences, metaphors, an effort of style that pulls away from narrative toward the prose poem. Even the recollected scene of childhood reading conforms to this set of interests. In the preface to his translation of *Sesame and Lilies*, Proust recalls the pleasure he

[9] *Against Sainte-Beuve*, ed. Sturrock, 5.

[10] D. H. Lawrence, preface to Giovanni Verga, *Mastro-don Gesualdo*, in *Phoenix: The Posthumous Papers of D. H. Lawrence*, ed. Edward D. Macdonald (London: Penguin, 1961), 226.

[11] G.W.F. Hegel, *Aesthetics: Lectures on Fine Art*, trans. T. M. Knox (Oxford: Oxford University Press, 1974), 2:1092.

[12] Gustave Flaubert, *Correspondance* (Paris: Pléiade, 1980), 2:31.

[13] "On Flaubert's Style," in *Against Sainte-Beuve*, ed. Sturrock, 263.

took in one of his favorite books, Gautier's novel, *Le Capitaine Fracasse*. A swashbuckling tale of adventure set in the seventeenth century, it is the "boy's" novel par excellence. But the twists and turns of the exciting yarn are not what fire the imagination of the boy Marcel; it is rather the "enchanted" condition wrought by the sporadically encountered, beautiful sentence: "In it I liked above all two or three sentences which seemed to me the most original and beautiful in the book."[14]

To speak of narrative prose in this way—its ability to "enchant"— was to speak of it in terms that in the nineteenth century were normally reserved for poetry, based in particular on the view of the origin and function of lyric, which the Romantics associated with the "shamanistic" figure of Orpheus and the Orphic myths that linked poetry, music, and magic. In this context, the predecessor who would have mattered most to Proust was Baudelaire. In the "noble tradition," which the narrator acknowledges as precursor of the aesthetic of "transposed sensation," "reminiscence," and "analogy," Baudelaire is accorded pride of place (*T*, 229).[15] The lines of the declared filiation run on several fronts. One such would be the parallel between, on the one hand, Baudelaire's use of the prosaic and the everyday (especially the artifacts and persons of the modern urban world) to transform the language of lyric and, on the other, Proust's inversion of the inherited hierarchies of narrative "significance," whereby what convention holds to be insignificant, so much dross and waste, becomes the occasion of revelation and epiphany. Baudelaire's model for this was alchemy, the poetic transmutation of detritus or the conversion of muck into gold.[16] Relatedly, the affinity has to do with the role of synesthesia and *correspondances* in Baudelaire's poetic practice, as attempted retreat from modernity and imagined recovery of a prelapsarian Eden. Catching an exotic landscape of ports and islands in the scent of a woman's hair or breast, poetry operates the magical recapture of "the perfumed paradise . . . the green paradise of childhood loves" (Proust's formulation was "the 'imperishable Perfume' of the Past").[17] This is what Baudelaire meant when he defined poetry as "evocative sorcery" and "suggestive magic."[18]

[14]Proust, *On Reading Ruskin*, 135, 113.

[15]For a fuller account of the importance of Baudelaire for Proust, see Compagnon, *Proust: Between Two Centuries*, 164–202.

[16]Charles Baudelaire, epilogue to *Les Fleurs du Mal*, in *Œuvres complètes*, ed. Claude Pichois (Paris: Pléiade, 1975–76), 1:191.

[17]The motif of the "paradis parfumé . . . le vert paradis des amours enfantines" is in "Moesta et Errabunda," in *Les Fleurs du Mal*, 63–64. Proust used the expression "le Parfum impérissable du Passé" in his review of Robert de Montesquiou's *Pays des aromates*, in *Contre Sainte-Beuve*, ed. Pierre Clarac and Yves Sandre (Paris: Gallimard, 1971), 445.

[18]Baudelaire, "Théophile Gautier," in *Œuvres complètes*, 2:118; "L'Art philosophique," ibid., 2:598.

II

Proust is by reputation all about lost paradises, although, in the aphoristic statement of the theme ("the only true paradise is a paradise that we have lost," *T*, 179), quite what is entailed by the term "lost" is not that clear.[19] The formulation is lawlike, made with all the assurance of a typical Proustian maxim; the loss is absolute and open to no exceptions. However, it leaves in its wake unanswered questions: If paradise is what we have lost, does this mean that we once had it; and if we once had it before losing it, is it recoverable, and, if so, under what conditions? *À la recherche* gives no unambiguously settled answer to these questions. Consider the other less well-known maxim on the topic of Paradise Lost from *Sodome et Gomorrhe*: "We dream a great deal of paradise, or rather of successive paradises, but they are all, long before we die, paradises lost, *in which we would feel lost*" (259, emphasis added). Here we have a version of paradise lost as radically lost, as loss all the way down, applicable equally to object (paradise) and subject (we). It's not just that we lose our paradises, but also that they lose us. Paradises inhabited or regained would not feel like paradise, either because they aren't really paradises at all or because we are so constituted as to be unable to recognize or appreciate them; for us, paradise is a paradoxical place, not the site of a homecoming but of a perpetual exile, the place where we would always be lost.[20]

This would seem to close the matter once and for all. Whatever it is that "lost" precisely means, lostness seems to be envisaged as both constitutive and definitive. On the other hand, when we get to the later, and better-known, formulation in *Le Temps retrouvé*, we find something altogether more ambiguous, or at least we do if we take note of the rarely quoted surrounding text in which the always-quoted apothegm is embedded: "memory . . . makes us breathe a new air, new precisely because it is an air that we have breathed before, this purer air which poets have tried in vain to make reign in paradise and which could not provide this profound feeling of renewal if it had not already been breathed, for the only true paradise is a paradise we have lost" (179). As an account of lostness, instability of meaning seems to ripple through this: what's new is new by

---

[19] Michael Wood has addressed some of the interpretive difficulties from the point of view of how to translate Proust's formulation (*les vrais paradis sont les paradis qu'on a perdus*) in "The Thing," *London Review of Books* 27, 1 (January 6, 2005): 18.

[20] In one of the "Zürau" aphorisms, Kafka expressed the same thought, if more gnomically: "The Expulsion from Paradise is eternal in its principal aspect; this makes it irrevocable, and our living in this world inevitable, but the eternal nature of the process has the effect that not only could we remain forever in Paradise, but that we are currently there, whether we know it or not." *The Zürau Aphorisms*, ed. Roberto Calasso (London: Harvill Secker, 2006), 65.

virtue of being something not new, but repeated ("new precisely because it is an air that we have breathed before"); the new air is what the poets have unsuccessfully ("in vain") tried to restore to us ("to make reign in paradise"), but, notwithstanding their failure, memory can take us there by way of "a profound feeling of renewal." Paradise, it seems, lies within our reach after all, though less as the recovery of a lost origin than in the form of a repetition, paradise gained for the first time only on the basis of an experience that occurs the second time around.[21]

However we interpret Proust on "paradise," and wherever its exact imaginative and temporal location may be,[22] the idea of literature as magic-making is part of it. Proust often uses the term "magic," along with its cognates "enchantment" and "charm." Sometimes the usage is weak, the terms little more than complimentary tokens for what, socially or aesthetically, is deemed especially delightful, and on occasion betrays contamination by the irritatingly dilettantish idiom of the Faubourg Saint-Germain (as when someone's person or possessions are deemed to be "charming"). But there is also the stronger meaning of the operations of magical thought on those moments identified, explicitly or implicitly, as embodiments of the "poetic" in experience, art, and language. Thus, certain of our sensations and impressions are the magical stardust of existence ("almost the only interest in existence lies in those days when a pinch of magic sand is mixed with the dust of reality," *JF*, 444); there is "that particular enchantment one gets from works [of art]" that capture a "charm" that is "present in the material reality of the natural world" (*JF*, 426); and then there is "the magic world of names" that confer "a new and purely poetic sense" on what they designate (*CG*, 542). All three dimensions—impression, art, name—conspire to sustain what in *Contre Sainte-Beuve* Proust terms the "magical pact" of memory and imagination as the crucible from which comes the miracle of a "poetic resurrection."[23] In many ways, this kind of literary thinking is virtually indistinguishable from the aims and beliefs underlying romantic conceptions of the objectives of lyric poetry.

---

[21]The explicit representation of this idea in *Le Temps retrouvé* is that something occurs for the second time, but, while knowing it to be the second time, we experience it as if for the first time: "the impression was so strong that the moment I was reliving seemed actually to be the present" (172).

[22]There is a third possibility: paradise as the might-have-been, in the space of the counterfactual. The Vinteuil septet is proposed as a model of what a "musicalized" human world might have been if mankind had not taken the road of language and increasing abstraction (*P*, 237). Paradise is thus not where we once were, from which we have been expelled into the long detour of exile, and to which we may one day return, but where we might have been had things been otherwise and of which we can have but intimations through the musical work.

[23]*Against Sainte-Beuve*, ed. Sturrock, 4–5.

Proustian magic comes in all shapes and sizes (the whole point is its power to transfigure even the most obdurately prosaic of things and experiences), but the preferred locales for conjuring the enchanted realm are dark or semidark, the domain of nightworld and shadowland: "True books," reflects the narrator in *Le Temps retrouvé*, "must be the product not of daylight and chitchat but of darkness and silence . . . an atmosphere of poetry will always hover around the truths that one has reached in oneself, a gentle sense of mystery which is merely the remains of the semi-darkness we have had to pass through, the indication, as precisely marked as on an altimeter, of the depth of a work" (206). There are many such locales in the *Recherche*, but the alchemist's place of darkness and silence par excellence is the "restful obscurity" of the bedroom, the world of sleep and dream, especially the liminal or threshold states of falling asleep and waking up, the midzone of the waking dream. This is where the novel begins, to be followed by several important sleeping scenes. In one of these—the "essay" or disquisition on sleep in *Sodome et Gomorrhe*—there is a striking first-personal image: "I, the strange human being who, while waiting for death to deliver him, lives behind closed shutters, knows nothing of the world, stays unmoving as an owl and, like an owl, can see with any clarity only in the dark" (377).

The ornithological is a richly varied source for the Proust analogy-machine—the sea swallow and bird nesting metaphors for the sleeping child; the "hesitant sparrows" for Gilberte's playmates; the squawking lovebirds for the ritual antics of Mlle Vinteuil and her friend; the swan for both Mme de Guermantes and Albertine; the "strongly modeled nose" of the shopgirl that "resembles the beak of a baby vulture"; the emblematic pheasants of Venice (symbolizing death and resurrection) reproduced on the Fortuny dresses; the winged angels in Giotto's frescoes figured as literally birds.[24] But the owl is surely a special case. The "I" that is likened to it, though notionally the narrator, has also—the interruptive switch of tense and context is too flagrantly peculiar for it to be otherwise—to be the person who in reality "lives behind closed shutters," the writer Marcel Proust. And although but a passing analogy, lightly drawn and unelaborated, there are reasons for pausing over it and the associations Proust might have had in mind in offering this self-description. We can presumably assume familiarity with the owl of Minerva, companion to the goddess of darkness, who was also the goddess of wisdom, science, and the arts; seen from the point of view of that classical source, Proust's owl would be primarily a figure of knowledge, the kind that comes from unblinking watchfulness, its ability to see in the dark an analogue of the pitiless lucidity of the novelist as radiographer endowed with X-ray vi-

---

[24] *S*, 11; *S*, 402; *S*, 162; *CG*, 27; *F*, 493; *P*, 124; *P*, 341; *F*, 612.

sion. But, while there is no evidence for it, one might like to think that Proust also knew of another lineage, the ancient association of the owl with magic-making, and in particular with the shamanistic practice of communicating with the dead ("resurrection").

In one of the earlier meditations on darkness and sleep, the narrator speaks of "the dense sleep which reveals to us mysteries such as youth regained, the rediscovery of years past and emotions once felt, disincarnation, the transmigration of souls, the summoning up of the dead" (*JF*, 400). This is quite a list of benefits. In the narrator's case, the dead are ourselves, our dead selves ("the darkened zones of my past life"), processionally recalled to the present as if in a magic lantern show: "each reality no sooner glimpsed than vanishing in the face of the next one, as the slides projected by a magic lantern succeed one another." The magic lantern show of sleep in *À l'ombre des jeunes filles en fleurs* is a pivotal moment for one of the great leitmotifs of *À la recherche*, matrix of a vast web of recollections and anticipations with large thematic reach: it looks forward, for example, to the effect of seeing Elstir's paintings on the walls of the Guermantes home ("like the luminous images of a magic lantern," *CG*, 417), as well as to the blackout of wartime Paris ("a mysterious semi-darkness, as of a room in a magic lantern show," *T*, 42), but the more important movement is retrospective and recapitulative, carrying us back to the magic lantern toy in the child's Combray bedroom and the fairy-tale world of "its supernatural, multicoloured apparitions" (*S*, 13). Discussions of the magic lantern in Proust usually emphasize the term "lantern," as, along with the kinetoscope, the first of the many optical instruments the *Recherche* both catalogs and metaphorically deploys.[25] But there needs to be equal stress on the term "magic," and thus on the image of Proust the magician, as well as Proust the optician.

The passage in *À l'ombre des jeunes filles en fleurs* is also of interest in alluding to a further narrative source connected with the magical; the phantasmagoria of sleep is held to unfold "after the manner of Oriental tales."[26] The tales are, of course, those of *The Arabian Nights*, which, along with the fairy-tale world of the magic lantern show, also belong in "Combray," albeit in the semicomical mode of the illustrations on Aunt Léonie's kitchenware: "These were the only plates with pictures on them, and my aunt amused herself at each meal by reading the inscription on the one she was served that day. She would put on her glasses and spell

[25] I am grateful to Peter Jewell for allowing me to see a copy of his unpublished catalogue raisonné of all the types of optical instruments and their various visual effects in Proust's novel (*The Last Belated Horsemen: Proust and Pre-cinema*).

[26] In the sleep-world of the opening pages of "Combray," the equivalent of the magic carpet from *The Arabian Nights* is the "magic armchair" that "will send him travelling at top speed through time and space" (*S*, 9).

out: Ali Baba and the Forty Thieves, Aladdin or the Magic Lamp, and smile, saying: 'Very good, very good' " (S, 59–60). Aunt Léonie's side-plates will reappear as objects of memory at the cliff-top picnic with the band of young girls outside Balbec, their "multicoloured vignettes" glowing like "the illuminations from the magic lantern in the twilight of my bedroom" (JF, 481). And if, with the narrator, we laugh affectionately at Aunt Léonie's small-world domestic rituals, nevertheless, both Aladdin's genie and Ali Baba's magic spell will be assigned major roles, analogically speaking, in the revelatory moment at the Guermantes matinée. As the narrator wipes his mouth with the napkin handed him by the butler, "like the character in the Arabian Nights who, without knowing it, performs precisely the ritual which makes appear, visible to himself alone, a docile genie ready to take him far away, a new vision of azure appeared before my eyes" (T, 176–77).[27] And, as a moment earlier he prepares to enter the Guermantes courtyard, reflecting on the coldness and sterility of intelligence, reason, and clarity, he anticipates the magical moments about to come: "But sometimes it is just when everything seems to be lost that we experience a presentiment that may save us; one has knocked on all the doors which lead nowhere, and then, unwittingly, one pushes against the only one through which one may enter and for which one would have searched in vain for a hundred years, and it opens" (174). Though implicit, the allusion is unmistakable; it is the redemptive Intimation (the "presentiment that may save us") cast metaphorically as the "Open Sesame" of the Ali Baba story, that which unlocks the door to salvation by abolishing "intellectual doubt . . . lifted as if by enchantment" (175).

In Le Temps retrouvé the narrator says of his projected work that "[i]t would be a book as long as the Arabian Nights perhaps, but quite different" (335). Proust's novel is certainly very different, in ways that scarcely need specifying. On the other hand, probably no book haunted his imagination more, and among the many things it gave him was a formula for a narrative architecture defined as a collection of strategically intervening djinns and Open Sesames. The latter also came to Proust via Ruskin. In the notes to his translation of Sesame and Lilies, Proust distinguishes "the three meanings of the word Sesame, reading which opens the doors of wisdom, Ali Baba's magic word, and the enchanted grain."[28] A scene of reading, an oriental tale, and a life-giving substance converge on a conception of art notionally combining wisdom, magic, and enchantment. Is this therefore what it means to call Proust "a great writer of fairy tales"? The description is Michael Wood's, specifically in connection with the

---

[27] See also the "génie" in the violins at Mme de Sainte-Euverte's concert in "Un amour de Swann": "we think we hear a captive genie struggling deep inside the intelligent, bewitched and tremulous box" (349–50).

[28] Proust, On Reading Ruskin, 144.

above passage from *Le Temps retrouvé*, which invokes the door that suddenly and unexpectedly opens to save us "just when everything seems to be lost." As a figure for the artist's magic wand, "Open Sesame" is a handsome device. But it is, of course, a device straight out of the magician's box of tricks. As Wood also observes, these allegedly random occurrences *never* happen randomly in the *Recherche*; Proust is his own "organizer of chance"; "sometimes" means "always, within the story . . . what might not have happened but always does," while "never" means "when I need it" or "just when you thought it was too late."[29]

This is almost as good as it gets with skeptical exposure of the more cunning moves of the salvationist aesthetic. But even better is Proust himself. For in addition to the three meanings of "Sesame" enumerated in the Ruskin commentary, there is a fourth meaning or dimension that is diabolical and devastating. For Proust the "realist," there are two kinds of magic, or rather two negative fates that ultimately visit all exercises in magical thinking. The first entails a form of emptiness or emptying out, for example, the disintegrating fairy tale of the Name, as with the name of Madame de Guermantes at the beginning of *Le Côté de Guermantes*: "Sometimes, hidden deep in her name, the fairy is transformed by the needs of our imaginative activity through which she lives . . . However, the fairy wastes away when we come into contact with the actual person to whom her name corresponds, for the name then begins to reflect that person who contains nothing of the fairy" (9). We shall see in chapter 4 how, in respect of the place-name "Venice," evacuation of imaginary content can take the stronger form of a potential "vomiting." The second kind is the magic spell as evil spell, most notably in the psychopathological domain we call "love," for example, the delusional universe Swann builds around Odette, described as "some magical illusion, some evil spell" (*S*, 319). This is also the context for the fourth manifestation of the Open Sesame motif, where the spell turns destructively back on itself, opening the door that leads not to paradise but to hell.

There are two occasions when the narrator's psyche snaps open as if in obedience to an Open Sesame command. Both have to do with thoughts and memories centered on Albertine. The second instance, in *La Fugitive*, is perfunctory, a brief glimpse into a buried world of suffering, which

[29] "Other Eyes: Proust and the Myths of Photography," in *The Strange M. Proust*, ed. Benhaïm, 109. Wood has Proust himself, of course, know this. While the narrative and ideological structure of the *Recherche* rests on the chance encounter (articulated in the opening pages: "It depends on chance," *S*, 47), chance in the novel is never there just by chance. In a letter to Antoine Bibesco in 1912, Proust put the point in a delightfully paradoxical form: the contingent has a place in the novel only when necessary (to showing the contingent in life). *Corr.*, 2:235. In a sense, nearly the entire narrative is a sequence of Open Sesames; wherever the narrator goes, doors open, often incredibly (the welcome into the world of the Guermantes and the Verdurins, for example).

nevertheless remains buried mainly because the moment occurs both after Albertine's death and, more important, against the background of the narrator's acquired indifference to her memory. By contrast, the first occurrence, toward the end of *Sodome et Gomorrhe*, is shattering. The narrator is chatting idly with Albertine about the attractions of the Verdurin gatherings, in particular, the prospective pleasure of hearing some pieces by Vinteuil: "If I tell you that his name's Vinteuil, my sweet one, are you any the wiser?" What follows is the casual, unself-conscious delivery of the nominally anodyne yet annihilating revelation of Albertine's acquaintance with Mlle Vinteuil and her friend:

> But the words "That friend is Mlle Vinteuil" had been the "Open Sesame" that I would have been incapable of finding for myself, which had caused Albertine to penetrate deep into my lacerated heart. And I might have searched for a hundred years without knowing how the door might be reopened that had closed on her. (*SG*, 519)

The textual parallel is striking. In the euphoric moment of *Le Temps retrouvé* "unwittingly, one pushes against the only [door] through which one may enter and for which one would have searched in vain for a hundred years, and it opens." Similarly, where knowledge of Albertine is concerned, "I might have searched for a hundred years without knowing how the door might be reopened that had closed on her." But Albertine's inadvertent disclosure is less the blissful turning of a magic key than the firing of an arrow straight into an unprotected psyche, a mind that, because it has located its anxieties elsewhere, has no defenses in place with which to ward off the shock that unexpectedly erupts into it. It is without question the most rawly terrifying scene of the whole novel, a vision of a subject rent, fractured, and "bleeding," who undergoes an experience close to traumatic regression. The image of a psyche gashed and blood-stained gains a supporting context from the closing scene of *Sodome et Gomorrhe*, through association and contiguity with that ordinary and ordinarily greeted phenomenon of everyday life: sunrise.[30] The extract is a long one, but every reader entranced by the "poetic" effects of the sun-dazzled and the sun-dappled in Proust should pay very close attention to the way its beautifully cadenced syntax delivers one tremor after another, as it sweeps the reader into a dark night of the soul:

> The light of the sun, which was about to come up, by modifying the objects around me, made me once again, as if shifting my position for a moment in relation to it, aware, even more cruelly, of my pain. Never had I seen so beau-

---

[30]There is a marked contrast with the other Balbec sunrise viewed from within the arriving train, the narrator running from one side of the carriage to the other to catch the "intermittent fragments of my lovely, changeable red morning, so as to see it for once as a single lasting picture" (*JF*, 233–40).

tiful and so sorrowful a morning. Reflecting on all the indifferent landscapes that were about to be illuminated, and which, only yesterday, would have filled me only with the desire to visit them, I could not contain a sob, when, in a mechanically executed gesture of oblation seeming to symbolize for me the bloody sacrifice that I was about to have to make of all joy, each morning, until the end of my life, a renewal, solemnly celebrated at each dawning of my unhappiness and of the blood from my wound, the golden egg of the sun, as if propelled by the break in equilibrium produced at the moment of coagulation by a change of density, barbed with flames as in paintings, burst in one bound through the curtain behind which I had sensed it quivering for the past few moments, ready to enter on to the stage and to spring upwards, and whose mysterious, congealed purple it erased beneath floods of light. I could hear myself crying. (520)

The narrator's mother, having heard him grieving in the night, comes into his room:

catching sight of the rising sun, she gave a sad smile, thinking of her mother, and so that I should not lose the benefit of a spectacle that my grandmother regretted I never watched, she pointed to the window. But behind the beach of Balbec, the sea, and the sunrise, to which Mama was pointing, I could see, in a fit of despair that did not escape her, the room in Montjouvain where Albertine, pink, curled up in a ball like a big cat, with her mischievous nose, had taken the place of Mlle Vinteuil's friend and was saying, to peals of voluptuous laughter: "Oh well, if we're seen, that'll only make it better. Me, I wouldn't dare spit on that old ape!" This was the scene I could see behind that spread out in the window, which was nothing more than a mournful veil superimposed on the other like a reflection. It seemed itself indeed almost unreal, like a painted view. Facing us, where the Parville cliffs jutted out, the leafy tableau of the little wood where we had played hunt-the-ring sloped all the way down to the sea, beneath the still golden sheen of the water, as at that hour when often, at the day's end, I had gone to have a siesta there with Albertine, we had got to our feet on seeing the sun go down. In the disorder of the night mists that still hung in blue and pink shreds over waters littered with the pearly debris of the dawn, boats were passing, smiling at the oblique light that had turned their sails and the tips of their bowsprits yellow, as when they return home in the evening: an imaginary scene, shivering and deserted, a pure evocation of the sunset, which did not rest, like the dusk, on the procession of hours of the day that I was in the habit of seeing precede it, slender, interpolated, more insubstantial even than the horrible image of Montjouvain that it had not succeeded in cancelling out, in covering, in concealing—a vain and poetic image of the memory and the dream. (521–22)

This is an echo of the several occasions on which, from his hotel room in Balbec, the narrator frames a view by looking through a window.

Normally, the "spectacle" is pleasurable, whether in the terms of mother and grandmother (the greeting of the new day as life-affirming ritual) or in those of the Elstirian aesthetic (as in the view from the hotel window in *À l'ombre des jeunes filles en fleurs*).[31] Here the visible world becomes a screen on which land, sea, and sunrise appear as but a "reflection" super-imposed on another mentally visualized "scene" lying behind it (Mont-jouvain, imagined as having Albertine in it). It is "like a painted view," an "image" at once "poetic" and "vain." Proust's art of the image has become the image as frozen artifice, cold, garish, menacing, the image as scopic horror, with the viewer enthrall to what mutilates the psyche.[32] Many of the favorite Proustian colors are here—pink, gold, blue, yellow—but they are the dead colors of an inversion, as sunrise is hallucinated as a sunset. It is not the sunset of the natural diurnal cycle, one that "rests . . . on the procession of hours of the day that I was in the habit of seeing precede it," but an "imaginary scene, shivering and deserted," the sunset of a world out of joint, turned on its head, an inversion that is a conversion of the new day into the terms of the arriving night, the darkness of mourning ("a mournful veil") and the embrace of death. It is the darkened room in a new guise, the place of antimagic. While the power of the Open Sesame motif is restored one last time in *Le Temps retrouvé*, what otherwise re-mains of it in the novel is either the door that briefly opens before being slammed shut (the recollection of Albertine in *La Fugitive*) or, more sub-stantially, its comic desecration in the narrator's exchange with Jupien after witnessing Charlus's flagellation in Jupien's brothel. The narrator confesses to having initially misunderstood what was happening before his eyes, as if confusing two tales from *The Arabian Nights* (one the story of a rescue, the other the story of a beating). Jupien, "disconcerted . . . that I had seen the Baron being beaten," retrieves the situation with the following sally of "that refreshing wit" said to be typical of him:

> "You've mentioned several tales from the *Arabian Nights*," he said. "But I can think of one which I believe I have seen at the Baron's" (he was alluding to a translation of Ruskin's *Sesame and Lilies* which I had sent to M. de Charlus). "If you were ever curious, one evening to see, I shan't say forty, but a dozen thieves, you have only to come here; to know whether I'm in, you have only to look up at that window, I'll leave open a crack so that the light shows, mean-ing that I'm there and you may come in; it's my own private Sesame. Only Sesame, mind. Because if it's lilies you're looking for, I'd advise you to look elsewhere." (141)

---

[31] See chapter 5.

[32] There is a further instance (in *La Fugitive*) of dawn imaged as a knife cutting into the psyche: "the early light of dawn . . . had just drawn over my curtain its now funereal blade, whose cold, dense and implacable whiteness entered and struck me like a knife blow" (449).

III

What happens in Balbec at the end of *Sodome et Gomorrhe*, as the renewing promise of sunrise fades over an "indifferent landscape" shrouded in a "mournful veil," is but an intensely dramatic instance of the ways in which the world can appear to the narrator as lifeless matter, most notably at late or ending moments. One such is the walk through the Bois de Boulogne at the end of *Du côté de chez Swann*; another, even more telling, is the visit to Venice toward the end of *La Fugitive*.[33] At some indeterminate point in later life, the narrator decides to take a detour through the Bois in order to catch the pleasures afforded by that "May of leaves," which is the early fall. However, it is an autumn not just seasonal but also historical (at a great distance from the enchanted epoch of Odette de Crécy's appearances in the Bois). Separated from an epoch long gone, the narrator learns three things. First, that what we most cherish is a function of our desires: "One sensed that the Bois was not merely a wood, that it fulfilled a purpose foreign to the life of its trees, the exhilaration I was experiencing was not caused merely by an admiration for autumn, but by some desire" (426); second, that the projections of desire are responsible for "a fetishistic attachment to the old things which our belief once animated, as if it were in them and not in us that the divine resided" (428); third, that once desire no longer animates its objects, the Bois, like the "shivering and deserted" landscape perceived at Balbec, takes on an air of the "inhuman." The narrator finds himself no longer able to do with nature what throughout the novel, other than at moments such as these, he does over and over again—"compose" and frame a natural scene in his mind as a work of art (usually as the mental analogue of a painting):

> And I no longer had any belief to infuse into all these new elements of the spectacle, to give them substance, unity, life; they went past scattered before me life, randomly, without reality, containing in themselves no beauty that my eyes might have tried as they had in earlier times to form into a composition. (428)

Proust's tendency to "compose" nature in this way is often read as evincing the reflex of the late nineteenth-century aesthete, for whom nature is nothing and artifice everything, who can happily see the world only through a framing screen. But the episode in the Bois tells a somewhat

---

[33] Consider also the ending of *À l'ombre des jeunes filles en fleurs*, designed to coincide with the last days of the summer season. The morning ritual of Françoise drawing back the curtains to reveal a bright sunny day full of promise and desire (mainly focused on the young girls) abruptly changes focus. The girls have now left, and though the weather remains the same, summer is now experienced as dead ("as dead, mummified and immemorial as a mummy," 531).

different story, one that evokes a humanizing rather than an aestheticizing relation of the mind to reality (though the extent to which Proust succeeds in keeping them distinct is exactly one of the major questions raised by his belief in an art-based redemption of experience). What is lost in the late walk is the sense of what the narrator claims to have once had in the Bois, the sense of "living in a human atmosphere":

> Nature was resuming its rule over the Bois, from which the idea that it was the Elysian Garden of Woman had vanished; above the artificial mill the real sky was grey; the wind wrinkled the Grand Lac with little wavelets, like a lake; large birds swiftly crossed the Bois, like a wood . . . the tall oaks which . . . seemed to proclaim the inhuman emptiness of the disused forest. (429–30)

This is nature disenchanted, before which imagination is powerless and from which "charm" (a term used twice in the sequence, in the strong quasi-magical sense) has disappeared. The experience also involves a seizing up of the analogy-machine, as metaphor and simile turn into pure tautology: "the Grand Lac, like a lake . . . the Bois, like a wood."[34] This is analogy that loops back to its referential point of departure in a circular movement that is, however, quite unlike the circular trajectories of Proustian metaphor at its most creative, where the referential point of departure is not so much restored as dissolved into the terms of pure figure. In the closed circular form of a tautology, analogy becomes pseudoanalogy, a mere repetition devoid of *energeia*, of the dynamic properties of configuration and transfiguration at the heart of Aristotle's account of "living" metaphor.[35] Inert, without substance, it is an empty form.

The world loses its magic when no longer suffused by desire. But how exactly is this loss to be understood? Where is the lack or defect to be located: in the object or the subject, in the world perceived or the perceiving self? Is the removal of "charm" (of "poetry") from the Bois de Boulogne an unmasking of the world (the disclosure of its "truth" when seen in the cold light of day)? Or is it the description of a subjectivity stricken by imaginative impotence, which, from some local or contingent paralysis of sensibility, can no longer grasp the magic before its eyes? Proust's name for this condition was "indifference" (*L'Indifférent* is the title of a very early story), that affectless detachment from both wonder and suffering that is the natural ally of the anesthetizing force of Habit and the interring work of Forgetting. When in Venice the narrator receives a letter from his stockbroker, part of its phrasing ("I will take care of any sums to be carried forward") reminds him of the more suggestive words used

---

[34] In her translation Lydia Davis has "real lake" and "real wood," which is consistent with the preceding "real sky." But Proust does not preface either lake or sky in this way, presumably to highlight the sheer strangeness of his simile that isn't one.

[35] See Paul Ricoeur, *La Métaphore vive* (Paris: Seuil, 1975).

in respect of Albertine by the bathhouse girl at Balbec ("I took care of her personally"). The coincidence triggers the second Open Sesame moment: "these words, which I had never before recalled, had the effect of crying 'Open Sesame,' making the hinges of the dungeon spring open" (*F*, 605). However, whereas the first instance in *Sodome et Gomorrhe* inflicts a tear in the very fabric of being, here it is but a ripple on the ocean of oblivion in which the memory of Albertine and the pain associated with her have been drowned. Not only do we lose what we have or covet, we also lose our feelings of grief and anguish over those losses. That is the benefit of Indifference, but there is also a cost; *anaesthesis* (the comparison of Habit to an anesthetic is Proust's) is the death of *aesthesis*, the bodily ground of imaginative play and creative metamorphosis.

There is an issue here that calls for a decision to the extent that one is possible. In thinking about these moments of imaginative collapse in the *Recherche*, what do we identify as the relevant opposition, and what kind of values attach to it? Is it truth supplanting illusion or numbness annihilating aliveness; is the problem objective or subjective? The issue is exquisitely, and undecidably, posed in the conflicting perspectives brought to bear respectively by the narrator and Saint-Loup on the latter's mistress, Rachel. For the narrator (who has previously encountered her in a brothel), she is but a cheap tart who can be had for twenty francs; for Saint-Loup she is an "idol," the "essence of love . . . mysteriously enshrined in a body as in a tabernacle" (*CG*, 154). Saint-Loup's version is a product of what is called the "momentous" power of the imagination, whereas the narrator's version consists of those "miserable, worthless material elements" into which "something that was once the target of countless dreams might be decomposed if, on the contrary, it had been perceived in a quite different manner, by the most coarse sort of acquaintance." From this latter perspective Rachel is but a collection of mechanical parts, a sort of "clockwork toy" (155). By an accident of circumstance, Saint-Loup himself will shortly have a glimpse of this demystified Rachel, in a formulation that begins by equating "Rachel, the little tart" with "the real Rachel." Here Proust appears to adjudicate the "relativist" dilemma by staking a claim to a truth of the matter (in the sense of "accuracy") on the side of the narrator's perspective.

Yet, characteristically, there is an immediate qualification: "if it is true that Rachel the tart was more real than the other." The qualification is a hedging of bets or a suspension of judgment, whereby indifference is not to be unquestioningly aligned with lucidity, and where *droit de cité* is restored to the claims of the imagination. We cannot enlist the narrator in the cause of an objectivist epistemology, since it may well be not so much that, unillusioned, he can see reality clearly, as that from lack of imagination he is blind to its poetry. If a decision or a choice has to be made, perhaps Saint-Loup's way of seeing things is therefore the one to go for. We would be encouraged to do so by virtue of a further development in the episode with Saint-Loup that has a contextual or associative connection with the desolate scene of the Bois de Boulogne when stripped down to its own variety of "worthless material elements." The narrator, moved by his friend's suffering, turns away and directs his attention to the pear and cherry trees of a neighboring garden. Their effect is very different from the forlorn trees of the Bois de Boulogne (or the mute trees of Hudimesnil): "Guardians of the memories of the golden age, keepers of the promise that reality is not what we suppose, that the splendour of poetry, the magical light of innocence may shine in it and may be the reward which we strive to deserve, were they not, these great white creatures so magnificently stooped over the shade that invites us to rest, to fish, to read, were they not more like angels?" (157).

That looks emphatically like a vote cast for the party of imagination, poetry, and magic. This seems also to have been the spirit of what Proust envisaged as his last word on the meaning of the Bois episode. It is clear from a letter to Jacques Rivière in February 1914 that Proust was much exercised by how it would be (mis)interpreted by his readers. The letter is the only time Proust uses the expression "disenchanted scepticism" in connection with his larger artistic designs. But he uses it as if with distaste, no sooner deployed than on its way to the wastepaper basket, its dispatch assisted by a proleptic appeal to the affirmative program of *Le Temps retrouvé*:

> Only at the end of the book . . . will my position be revealed. The one I put forward at the end of the first volume, in that excursus on the Bois de Boulogne . . . is the *opposite* of my conclusion. It is just a step . . . on the way to the most objective and optimistic of conclusions. If someone were to infer from this that my attitude is a disenchanted scepticism, it would be exactly as though a spectator, having seen the end of the first act of *Parsifal* . . . imagined Wagner to be saying that purity of heart leads nowhere . . . I did not want to analyze this evolution of a belief system abstractly, but rather to recreate it, to bring it to life. I am therefore obliged to depict errors, without feeling compelled to say that I consider them to be errors; too bad for me if the reader believes that I take them for the truth.[36]

Too bad indeed, especially for this reader and the arguments of this book. The remarks to Rivière are a categorical rejection of the skeptical point of view embodied in the Bois de Boulogne excursus, in favor of the "optimistic" conclusions of *Le Temps retrouvé*. However, Proust writing to Rivière in 1914 is but Proust at a particular moment in the evolution

---

[36] *Corr.*, 13:99.

of his enterprise, but a "step," so to speak, in the long trajectory of what is compositionally yet to come, much of which in 1914 lay for Proust in the sphere of the unknown. Seen in the light of what is to come, the Bois de Boulogne episode reflects more than just a passing mood, a moment of dejection in which the magic of the world is temporarily lost to the subject. Rather, the episode hangs like a cloud or casts a shadow over the whole book, suggesting that the "optimistic" and the "objective" are not so much natural kin or mutually supportive neighbors as adversaries pulling in different directions. If the world seems a cold and inhuman place, it is not just because the imaginative powers and desiring energies of the subject have crashed; it is because this is the world as it is anyway,[37] how the world truly is and how it truly appears to us when vision is not distorted by the charm-conferring agency of desire. Just how long a shadow the episode casts is clear if we now go to what comes late, both narratively and compositionally, the Venice chapter in *La Fugitive*.[38]

Venice is relatedly the "magical" city and the "oriental" city, both terms appearing in the description of Venetian first impressions said to resemble, mutatis mutandis, those of Combray ("impressions analogous to those that I had so often felt previously in Combray, but transposed into an entirely different, richer mode," *F*, 588). The impressionistic patchwork is thickly patterned with motifs from *The Arabian Nights*. Gondolas negotiate the canals as if guided by a genie ("My gondola followed the side-canals, as if the mysterious hand of a genie were guiding me through the byways of this oriental city . . . like a magical guide holding a candle between his fingers to light my passage," 591). The narrator's night walks through the city are expeditions undertaken as if by a character from *The Arabian Nights* ("In the evenings I went out alone, surrounded by this enchanted city where I found myself in the middle of unknown neighborhoods like a character from *The Arabian Nights*," 614).[39] The streets lead to "one of those architectural ensembles" that "seemed to be deliberately hidden in a criss-cross of alleyways, like those palaces in Oriental tales

---

[37]The phrase "the world as it is anyway" is an expression of Bernard Williams's, in contradistinction to "the local perspectives or idiosyncracies of enquirers." *Descartes: The Project of Pure Enquiry* (London: Penguin, 1978), 64.

[38]Nathalie Mauriac Dyer reminds us that the "decomposition of Venice" was originally planned as the ending of *La Fugitive*. She also points to the thematic parallel with the ending of *Du côté de chez Swann* in the Bois de Boulogne: "This tableau of dereliction, placed at the conclusion of *Albertine disparue* . . . singularly echoes another tableau, also placed at the end of a volume: the disenchanted visit to the Bois de Boulogne." "Genesis of 'Ruine de Venise,'" in *Proust in Perspective*, ed. Mortimer and Kolb, 74.

[39]There is here an echo of Charlus describing himself to Jupien at the beginning of *Sodome et Gomorrhe* ("like the caliph who used to roam Baghdad mistaken for a simple merchant, I sometimes indeed condescend to follow some curious young person whose silhouette has amused me," 14).

where a character who was led there by night and taken back home before morning is unable to find the magical dwelling and finally believes that he saw it only in his dreams" (614–15).

Having seen it only in dreams would be one way of summarizing the story of Proust's Venice. With—and in part because of—the departure of his mother, the narrator's imaginative investment in the "magical" city shrinks and dies. Venice "petrifies," and its stones become just that, inanimate stone, pure matter, in the same way that its waters become mere chemical compounds: "The city I saw before me was still Venice. Its personality and its name appeared to me as mendacious fictions that I no longer had the heart to relate to its stones. The palaces appeared reduced to their congruent parts and their portions of indifferent marble, and the waters to a combination of nitrogen and hydrogen, eternal and blind . . . the Canal and the Rialto were bereft of the ideas that made them original and were dissolved into their crudely material elements" (616–17). What the narrator is left with is the subjective equivalent of the petrified city, the sensation of "cold numbness" (618). This is Venice as it might appear to science rather than to poetry, the atomistic object of chemistry rather than the transmuted creation of alchemy, without the pinch of magic sand that redeems the dust of reality, mere "indifferent marble."

Indifference, numbness, paralysis—these are also Baudelairian emotional registers (aspects of what he called *ennui*), and suggest a very different Proustian "filiation" with Baudelaire, one that ultimately scrambles any nineteenth-century literary geography based on the simple opposition of lyric and novel, poetry and prose. Baudelaire may have cast lyric in the mold of "sorcery," but he was also fully cognizant of the world's resistance to the reenchanting power of poetry. In *Les Fleurs du Mal* this is often represented as an experience of "petrification." In "La Beauté," Beauty is paradoxically personified as a speaker addressing a petrified humanity (in the sense of frightened), but as a speaker also petrified (in the sense of lapidified), projected as a glacially terrifying dream of pure stone ("Je suis belle, o mortels! comme un rêve de pierre" [I am beautiful, o mortals, like a dream of stone]).[40] In the protomodernist urban landscape of "Le Cygne," Haussmann's building site of a city (the makeover of Paris, which included the redesigned Bois de Boulogne through which Proust's narrator strolls), melancholia settles cripplingly on imagination, the sky turns "ironic" (*le ciel ironique*), and memory turns to stone and grows heavy and hard as rock: "Et mes chers souvenirs sont plus lourds que les rocs" (And my fond memories are heavier than rocks).[41] If, in terms of the legacy of the nineteenth century, Baudelaire is the key figure

---

[40] Baudelaire, *Œuvres complètes*, ed. Pichois, 1:21.
[41] Ibid., 1:86.

for Proust, then it is a Baudelaire who faces in two conflicting directions. Where they lead is where we must now go.

One road will take us back to Venice and its famous basilica. Another goes via the Balbec of *À l'ombre des jeunes filles en fleurs*, with consequences that matter for the ideological tenor of Proust's aesthetic, especially the posited relation in *Le Temps retrouvé* between art, truth, and epiphany. While in Balbec, but before he first meets Elstir, the narrator looks out over the sea and the sky as at a painting that offers a "revelation": "the violet sky, which seemed to have been branded by the rigid, geometrical, fleeting, flashing iron of the sun (as though in representation of some miraculous sign or mystical apparition), hung down over the sea at the juncture of the horizon like a religious canvas above a high altar" (*JF*, 383). Seeing the world framed as a painting prefaces the encounter with Elstir's art,[42] but it also recalls the abortive attempt to frame the Bois de Boulogne as "a composition." For here too there is a failure, another collapse from the enchanted into the disenchanted, in terms that, through the mix of aesthetic and religious vocabularies, also unmasks one of the faces of idolatry in Proust. The narrator's eye orders the relations of sky and sea on the axis of the horizon in a manner designed to evoke a religious canvas placed above an altar, as if inside nature as a church (reminiscent perhaps of Baudelaire's conversion of nature into a "temple" in one of the greatest of his magic-making poems, "Correspondances"), in which some "miracle" is about to be revealed or performed. The "miraculous sign," however, is but a "representation," an effect of artifice, mere image. And "some weeks later" (in narrative time), but just one page later in the text, we once more have the narrator viewing sea and sunset through a hugely elaborate skein of impressions, only for it all to fall away, in another unmasking: "I was surrounded on all sides by images. However, quite often they were nothing but images: I would forget that beneath the colour of them, there was the forlorn, empty shoreline" (384). The narrator's forgetting is one of Proust's ways of remembering, or rather of reminding us of how it is in reality.

[42] See chapter 5.

CHAPTER FOUR

Éblouissement

IN DRAMATIZING A FROZEN imagination and a sterilized world, Baudelaire's rocklike formations crush the life from any belief in the spellbinding or "reenchanting" capabilities of lyric. Subjectivity turned to stone has also been linked (most notably in the wake of Benjamin's reflections on Baudelaire) to another distinction—that between symbol and allegory in the aesthetics of poetic representation. In Baudelaire the petrified order of things signifies the death of the "symbol," understood as the quasi-animistic, "living," and embodying force of analogy and *correspondances*, and a fall back into the disjunctive, broken sphere of the allegorical, where matter is but the dead, "heavy" wrapper of meaning, and meaning but a ghostly trace flitting across the material ruins of the world. The symbol/allegory distinction is more a topic for the final chapter of this book. If I here anticipate that more extended discussion, it is because of a particular, and very unusual, reading of Proust that is directly relevant to the concerns of this chapter. Angelo Caranfa has written of the collapse of the traditional economy of the Symbol in *À la recherche*. The striking general feature of his reading is that it is conducted entirely within a framework shaped by religion and theology. Caranfa draws a contrast between *À la recherche* and Bonaventure's *The Soul's Journey into God*. The medieval religious thinker describes a spiritual odyssey based on the incarnate Word as the mediation of the human and the divine. Giotto's Padua frescoes are the translation of this thought into paint and figural representation; his art is properly "symbolic" insofar as it is an embodying art in which idea and materiality, heaven and earth, the human and the divine are united (Giotto's Charity, for example, is "an outer representation of the transfigured state of human beings, an actual manifestation of the spiritual world, the world of humanity's inner perfection, and of the unlike radiancy coming from having attained the summit of spiritual ecstasy, of seeing God in the human image of the incarnate Word."[1] In *À la recherche*, on the other hand, "Giotto's representations have no meaning beyond the purely mental construct of the artist . . . if symbols manifest any meaning at all now, they must testify to the subjective dimension of existence . . . meditation is synonymous with self-divinization; everything is stripped of its participation in divine life,

---

[1] Angelo Caranfa, *Proust: The Creative Silence* (Lewisburg, Pa.: Bucknell University Press, 1990), 130.

its correspondence to the image and its relation to the incarnate Word, the Image (Christ-Man). What exists is subjugated to the individual truth of the inner self, the mind's eye, the reserve, the spotless mirror of the artist as creator, the image of the artist's self-projection."[2] The darkened room (a motif of which Caranfa makes great play) becomes the private space of the "self-divinizing" artist, the laboratory of the alchemist extraordinaire, and, although Caranfa does not use the term, the shrine of the idolater.

It is rare to encounter a discussion of Proust from within the terms of Catholic theology. Proust was not a "religious" writer and the *Recherche* is not a "religious" book.[3] He wrote in and for a secular world long since forsaken by the gods. Indeed, François Mauriac saw Proust as one of the greatest enemies of religion that twentieth-century French literature had produced. Mauriac was, of course, an interested party to the relevant argument, and by "religion" he meant specifically Catholicism, seeing in Proust a categorical refusal of any version of the divine-human relation based on the transfiguring and redemptive power of (Christian) "love." When Proust wrote that there is no such thing as a bad choice in love because all the choices were by definition bad, this was more than just another flourish of Proustian *esprit*. It was a pithy way of formulating a point devastating to believers: if without love there is no reason for living and believing, it remains the case that love is always and only the impossible demand we make on it to soothe the pain of which it is itself the cause.[4] This holds even, perhaps above all, in connection with so-called disinterested love (the love of mother for son, Maman for narrator, Mary for Jesus), which is why Mauriac had good reason to deplore or fear Proust as one of the great blasphemers and defilers of modern literature.

Yet if Proust is not a religious writer, there can be little doubt that at a very deep level and after a certain fashion he wanted to be one.[5] The grandest of his big themes is, after all, Death and Resurrection, its articulation in *Le Temps retrouvé* moreover stamped by a terminology straight out of the mystico-metaphysical lexicon of religious thought, while the most uplifting moment of his commentary on *The Bible of Amiens*—the commentary on the small figurine lost in the massive porch

[2]Ibid., 141.

[3]"There is no sense of the sacred in Proust's thought, which is strictly atheistic." Compagnon, *Proust Between Two Centuries*, 157.

[4]Kristeva, *Time and Sense*, 224–25.

[5]"Although I have no faith, there is not one day of my life from which religious concerns are absent . . . But from there to certainty, even to Hope, there is a great distance. I have not yet bridged it. Will I ever bridge it?" *Corr.*, 14:218. Blanchot thought that Proust wanted to see his epiphanies of the timeless in the temporal in this fashion ("this is his faith and his religion," *Le Livre à venir*, 32). Descombes, quoting Blanchot, speaks of the attempt by Proust to convert a "literary experience" into a "variety of religious experience." *Proust: Philosophy of the Novel*, 292.

of the Booksellers on Rouen cathedral—is an impassioned meditation on the religious theme of the resurrection of the dead; it is one of Proust's most exalted bits of prose writing.[6] And if the narrative of *À la recherche* repeats in its own way the modern Balzacian saga of lost illusions in a disenchanted world, it also bears some resemblance to a pilgrim's progress, as the narration of a journey through a wasteland (the sense of "wasted" in "perdu") toward a final redemption, a cleansing of the soul as the initiate steps (stumbles, on the paving stones of the Guermantes courtyard) into the "radiance" of the transcendental. There are no references to Bunyan in Proust's commentaries and notes on Ruskin, though in the course of his readings he may well have come across, and taken note of, Ruskin's complex love-hate relation with his spiritually exacting predecessor.[7] But with or without Bunyan's title in mind, he retained the image or model of "pilgrimage" for the titles of some of his own articles on Ruskin. More generally, in the initial fervor of his Ruskinian moment, Proust maintained that Ruskin's approach to art (especially the architectural monuments of medieval Christendom) was driven by religion ("Religion . . . dominates and characterizes his aesthetics").[8] Proust would later revise this view, but at this early stage he made a claim that would doubtless have taken even Ruskin's breath away.

The claim emerges slowly from a long paragraph toward the end of the second part of the preface devoted to the lesson of Amiens. The passage begins cautiously: "the teaching that the men of the thirteenth-century came to seek at the cathedral" is for us a "teaching which, with a useless and bizarre luxury, it continues to offer in a kind of open book, written in a solemn language where each letter is a work of art, a language no longer understood." Proust thus acknowledges the existence of a gap, almost an incommensurability ("a language no longer understood"), between the two ages, the middle and the modern, such that Ruskin gives to the cathedral "a meaning less literally religious than during the Middle Ages or even an aesthetic meaning only." Yet even in this different, less literal form, Ruskin's example is apostrophized and saluted for having constructed a bridge between the spiritual world of the thirteenth-century and our own affective universe: "you have been able nevertheless to relate it to one of those feelings that appear to us as the true reality beyond our lives." This is the halfway house to what is affirmed in the last part of the paragraph: Ruskin "will make my spirit enter where it had

---

[6] Proust, *On Reading Ruskin*, 45–48.

[7] See Emma Mason, "The Victorians and Bunyan's Legacy," in *The Cambridge Companion to Bunyan*, ed. Anne Dunan-Page (Cambridge: Cambridge University Press, 2010), 155–56. Barbara Bucknall suggested a resemblance between *À la recherche* and *Pilgrim's Progress* (*The Religion of Art in Proust* [Urbana: University of Illinois Press, 1969], 172).

[8] Proust, *On Reading Ruskin*, 33.

no access, for he is the door. He will purify, for his inspiration is like the lily of the valley. He will intoxicate me and give me life, for he is the vine and the life. Indeed I have felt that the mystic perfume of the rose trees of Sharon has not vanished forever, since one still breathes it, at least in his words." Intoxication is, if in not quite the intended sense, the order of the day and leads to this stunning assertion: "And now indeed the stones of Amiens have acquired for me the dignity of the stones of Venice, and almost the grandeur the Bible had, when it was still truth in the hearts of men and solemn beauty in their work." There is still some sort of check on rhapsodic overdrive in the qualifying "almost," but it is obliterated in what follows: via Ruskin's work, Proust finds himself able to enter, from the vantage point of the early twentieth century, the religious world of the thirteenth century, not on the basis of scholarly historical understanding ("erudition"), but by reexperiencing it as a "lived" reality.[9]

This self-positioning vis-à-vis a thirteenth-century religious culture was nothing less than an act of stupendous self-delusion. Unless the belief systems are the same, there is no way of seeing (reliving) the past from the point of view of the past: the sophisticated Marcel Proust, habitué of smart Paris salons, educated reader of (among others) John Ruskin, could not possibly feel, think, and believe in the same manner as the faithful of medieval Amiens. This is fake empathy, the projections of the aesthete, and it masks what is actually going on in this mediated transaction between past and present. What is going on becomes clear if we unpack the following encomium from the closing pages of the "Post-Scriptum" to the preface: the reading of Ruskin on Amiens and Venice, claims Proust, brings us to "a state of grace in which all our faculties, our critical sense as well as all the others, are strengthened."[10] We have to make allowances here for literary protocol, for the have-it-all-ways, ecumenical rhetoric of peroration, Proust exiting his preface by formally genuflecting to the master he has just excoriated for idolatry (fairly hard to forget that just a few pages beforehand Proust has spoken of "the kind of trickery that a page of Ruskin is for each one of us").[11] But an account as severe with Proust as Proust has previously been with Ruskin might want to ask: What, in this context, would be the function of an accentuated "critical sense"? Presumably, it would be to tell the subject of the experience that whatever "state" he was in, it had little to do with the religious state of "grace" in either medieval Christian theology or everyday medieval Christian faith, and that one should be extremely wary of appropriating such a term for the pleasures and ecstasies that in the early twentieth century one might have before the stones of Amiens or Saint Mark's.

[9] Ibid., 27.
[10] Ibid., 60.
[11] Ibid., 51.

Fortunately, this critical sense was to survive (its importance already indicated by Proust's strictures on idolatry in the "Post-Scriptum"), and its survival was to prove crucial for the *Recherche*. In 1912 he wrote to Robert de Montesquiou that his love of Ruskin was also marked by "extreme skepticism,"[12] an attitude that, notwithstanding the 1914 letter to Rivière, he was to turn on himself. But here, in this rapturous moment, we might be forgiven for seeing the reference to the "critical sense" as little more than a token gesture. For we recall Proust's words to the effect that in the so-called state of grace, it is not only the critical sense, but *all* the senses (or "faculties") that are heightened, and there is good reason to believe that for Proust in this mood the skeptical knowledge made possible by the "critical sense" was unlikely to detract from the sheer aesthetico-sensuous bliss afforded by all the others.

We can thus say that Proust's sensibility and imagination were "religious" insofar as they were animated by the wish to intuit from a "feeling," a fleeting impression, a whole epiphanic structure within which the artistic vocation would find its meaning and confer meaning. But looked at from the point of view of more rigorously conceived religious belief and doctrine, the wish was pure folly, in many ways the blind alley of a writer whose natural subject matter was lost, decaying, and dying worlds, for whom religious faith was not a plausible option, but who was also indifferent to what had come to replace religion—the secular narratives of "progress" underpinning the Enlightenment project of "modernity." That Proust suspected it was folly is clear from his indictment of Ruskin (and, if less robustly, himself) with the charge of idolatry. Ruskin's enterprise was overtly didactic, a "teaching," the import of which was ethical, spiritual, and religious. As we have seen, Proust took this very seriously, but he also came to understand how the teaching had confused the religious and the aesthetic in the worship of the external forms of the beautiful. Ruskin's confusion was moreover potentially his reader's bewitchment; Ruskin too was a "trickster" ("trickery," we recall, is one of Proust's less endearing terms for Ruskin's prose), a magician before whose spellbinding powers we needed to be on our guard, and nowhere more so than in connection with Venice and its seductively gorgeous stones.

II

In *À la recherche* all roads, when not running to and from Combray, lead into and out of Venice, as a major switch-point in the multitrack geometric design of the novel. And so it is to Venice that we must once more return. It is Venice that provides the exemplary scenes of Proust's

[12] *Corr.*, 11:273.

own capture both of and by this Ruskinian confusion, above all as the "mixed" and "impure" pleasures experienced in that other darkened place, the penumbra of the baptistery of Saint Mark's. It was, of course, supposed to be otherwise, Ruskin as antidote to false gods. In a brief review of Mathilde Crémieux's translation of *The Stones of Venice* (1906), Proust remarks on the extent to which in contemporary French literary circles (the names cited include Barrès, Régnier, Mme de Noailles, Léon Daudet, and Jacques Vontade), "Venice" has become the object of a cult. Proust describes this image of Venice as tasteful, refined (*affinée*), and "a little passive." This is polite code for the Venice of the aesthetes and the connoisseurs, a Venice intelligently but lethargically enjoyed, source of a pleasure lightly perfumed with a whiff of decadence. Ruskin's Venice is a graver affair, ethically and intellectually more robust, our pleasure (*volupté, jouissance*) deepened by the "preachings" of a writer who, now speaking to us in French alongside his native English, is likened to "one of those apostles endowed with glossolalia that are figured in the baptistery of St Mark's." But a precious conceit devised merely to compliment Madame Crémieux for having made Ruskin available to French readers perhaps carries more than it was intended to bear. Allowing ourselves to be entranced by a speaker held in the charismatic trance is to expose oneself to the risk of the multitongued being the fork-tongued. Ruskin may bring us to a Venice designed to instruct the mind and uplift the spirit, but it is still Venice as a series of "enchantments," and the prose that transports us there an "enchanted ship."[13]

There are (at least) four Venices in the *Recherche*: the destination fantasized out of the proper name "Venise"; the "oriental-magical" Venice imagined as straight out of *The Arabian Nights*; the "dead" Venice of imaginative atrophy, reduced to meaningless chemistry; and the "sacred" Venice of the baptistery of Saint Mark's. It is with this last incarnation more than anywhere else that we might contemplate the possibility of a "Christianized" reading of Proust. Saint Mark's, we are told, "did not represent for me a mere monument, but as it were the terminus of a marine journey over springtime waters, with which St Mark's formed an indivisible, living whole." Entering the baptistery with his mother has something of the sacramental, the promise of a cleansing baptism, the waters of Venice evoking the gospel story of the baptism of Jesus by John in the river Jordan (the famous mosaics of the baptistery illustrate the story). It is also the place and the moment of a kind of benediction, in which the narrator's mother comes to resemble the protective figure of the Virgin Mary. The discourse shifts from the "then" of narrative to the "now" of narration, in a rhythmically crafted statement of filial piety:

---

[13] *Contre Sainte-Beuve*, ed. Clarac and Sandre, 520–23.

The time has now come for me when, on remembering the baptistery, facing the waters of the Jordan where St John immersed Christ while the gondola awaited us by the Piazzetta, I cannot remain indifferent to the fact that there was by my side in this cool twilight a woman clothed in mourning, whose respectful but enthusiastic fervour matched that of the elderly woman who can be seen in Venice in Carpaccio's *St Ursula*, and that nothing can ever again remove this red-cheeked, sad-eyed woman, in her black veils, from the softly lit sanctuary of St Mark's where I am certain to find her, because I have reserved a place there in perpetuity, alongside the mosaics, for her, for my mother. (*F*, 610)

In the embrace of memory by syntax (the solemnly deferred "for her, for my mother") to produce a moment of pure intimacy, this sentence may well qualify as the most reverential Proust ever composed, finding its place moreover in a passage that has been described as "one of the most important in the whole book."[14] But how important, and important in what way? The scene in the baptistery is cursory to a degree (less than a page) and surrounded on all sides by a complicating ambivalence. The mother-Madonna as also the mother incestuously desired is but one face of the "impure" and "mixed" nature of the pleasures afforded by Saint Mark's. More generally, the sparkling, bejeweled, and multicolored splendor of Venice is such that, even in its holy spaces, sacred and profane, sensuous and spiritual, worldly and otherworldly are never far apart; to be "charmed" (in the strong sense) by Venice was fatally to allow oneself to fall under the sway of what Ruskin called the *eidolon*. This is what Proust thought had happened to Ruskin himself in writing *The Stones of Venice*, and what had also happened to him as a result of reading Ruskin. Ruskin's descriptions of Venice do to Proust and his narrator what the city itself so often does: *dazzle*. Although part of a constellation that includes shine, gleam, sparkle, blaze, and scintillate, the term is far from being a casual synonym or cognate for the registering of light and color. It notably reappears in *Le Temps retrouvé* to characterize the inward explosion of light generated by the stumble on the uneven paving stones of the Guermantes courtyard: in a "vision" represented as "dazzling," the baptistery of Saint Mark's returns in memory as an unfocused bundle of "impressions of coolness and dazzling light" (175).[15]

---

[14]Tony Tanner, *Venice Desired* (Oxford: Blackwell, 1992), 258.

[15]The sketches for *La Fugitive* refer to "the dazzling descriptions" (*descriptions éblouissantes*) that Ruskin gives of Saint Mark's (*ARTP*, 4:693). Ruskin himself talks of being "dazzled by the brilliancy of Venice," in *The Stones of Venice*, in *The Complete Works of John Ruskin*, ed. E. T. Cook and Alexander Wedderburn (London: George Allen, 1903–12), 11:71. All further references to *The Stones of Venice* (vols. 9–11) and *Modern Painters* (vols. 3–7) are to this thirty-nine-volume edition. In terms of the Proustian aesthetic, we should also note the "dazzle-effect" of the Vinteuil septet in *La Prisonnière* (233).

For Julia Kristeva the vision, or more exactly the overpowering experience of inner illumination, is Proust's version of the Christian epiphany, dazzling light as revelation.[16] But we should bear in mind here a more immediate context, the extent to which *éblouissement* was a term of art for the fin de siècle aesthetes and designated the mix of intensity and refinement that the exquisitely calibrated literary temperament could bring to the contemplation of Simple Things, the latter more often than not exotic objects, luxury articles, or collectors' items (the more expensive end of Japanese porcelain a favorite). Proust's friend, Anna de Noailles used the term in the plural (*Les Éblouissements*) as the title for a collection of verse that Proust reviewed in 1907. The review is best passed over in silence; it is basically a pretty trip into a pretty poetic world, where appreciation is indistinguishable from flattery, leavened by a touch of Faubourg *mondanité* (the beauty of the verse is matched only by the beauty of their author).[17] But if this is little more than Proust delivering a literary calling card, he above all others understood the affectations and delusions that could go with cultivating the *éblouissant*, especially in that obligatory port of call for the late nineteenth-century aesthete, Venice. A compliment elegantly bestowed on Mme de Noailles costs little, but it was another matter altogether when it came to doubts in respect of the notionally more exacting example of Ruskin and the ambiguous or "mixed" pleasures of that page from *The Stones of Venice* on the basilica read by Proust in the basilica.

This was the confession Proust made in the "Post-Scriptum." The "joys" of reading Ruskin on Saint Mark's in the baptistery itself were "mixed" mainly because of Ruskin's dubious display of biblical "erudition," construed as a manifestation of intellectual pride ("a sort of egotistical self-evaluation"), the cultivated mind slipping into self-conscious ostentation (a form of what Proust understood by "snobbery"). Seen within a broader history of modern self-consciousness, it was also an index of the derivative and mediated inner life, its refraction by representations, as opposed to the nonreflective, spontaneous response to the meanings embodied in the great Christian cathedrals that Proust attributed to the community of medieval believers. But there is also something in this

[16] Kristeva, *Time and Sense*, 105–7. In light of this full-fledged "Christic" reading, one wonders how Proust, lover of both dark and dazzle, might have responded to the sermon by Donne: "They shall awake as *Jacob* did, and say as *Jacob* said, *Surely the Lord is in this place*, and *this is no other but the house of God, and the gate of heaven*, And into that gate they shall enter, and in that house they shall dwell, where there shall be no Cloud nor Sun, no darknesse nor dazling, but one equall light, no noyse nor silence, but one equall musick, no fears nor hopes, but one equal possession, no foes nor friends, but an equall communion and Identity, no ends nor beginnings, but one equall eternity." John Donne, *Works* (London: Henry Alford, 1839), 5:629.

[17] "*Les Éblouissements* par la comtesse de Noailles," in *Contre Sainte-Beuve*, ed. Clarac and Sandre, 535–45.

analysis that is much closer to the regime of the *eidolon* as normally understood, namely, the "dazzling" beauty of Ruskin's style, "the mosaics of its style that dazzle in the shadows," after the manner of the reflecting surfaces of gold leaf in the baptistery's own mosaics:

> I remember having read it for the first time in St Mark's itself, during a dark and tempestuous hour, when the mosaics shone only by their own physical light and with an internal, ancient, and earthly gold to which the Venetian sun, which sets even the angels of the campanile ablaze, mingles nothing of its own; the emotion I felt, as I was reading this page, among all those angels which shone forth from the surrounding darkness, was great, and yet perhaps not very pure.[18]

Little explicit trace of this survives in the baptistery episode of *La Fugitive* (what remains of Ruskin is a low-key displacement, the narrator's fetching of "the exercise books in which I would take notes for the study of Ruskin I was engaged in" from his hotel room before setting out for Saint Mark's, 609). It has been suggested that this reflects the cooling of Proust's enthusiasm for the Sage of Coniston and relatedly his surmounting of the idolatrous temptation. However, the secular attractions of the *éblouissant* still press heavily on Proust's narrative, and if the moment of solemn devotion in the baptistery is brief, this is in part because another Venice beckons, or rather because this other Venice is in many ways materially continuous with the physical and aesthetic fabric of Saint Mark's itself: "In Venice," writes Paul Hills, "Christian devotion is framed and coloured by the visual experience of San Marco: in the emergence of a Venetian aesthetic the mercantile and the religious are entwined."[19] In Proust's text, the transition from one to the other goes by way of a double reference to the paintings of Carpaccio (along with Vermeer, the most important real-life painter in the *Recherche*). Still within the baptistery, the narrator's mother is compared to the old woman in Carpaccio's *St. Ursula*, but this serves as a bridge to another Carpaccio, with very different associations (which "almost revived my love for Albertine"). This is *The Patriarch of Grado* and its world of colors, palaces, trades, goods, and apparel: "the admirable carmine and violet sky," the "tall, inlaid chimneys" with their "waisted forms and red, tulip-like blooms" (that recall Whistler's Venice paintings), the "marble palaces decorated with gilded capitals," the Canal boats "steered by youths wearing pink doublets and caps topped with osprey feathers," and finally the quayside "which was teeming with scenes from the Venetian life of the time . . . the barber wiping his razor, the negro carrying his barrel, the Muslims in conversa-

[18]Proust, *On Reading Ruskin*, 53.

[19]Paul Hills, *Venetian Colour: Marble, Mosaic, Painting and Glass, 1250–1550* (New Haven: Yale University Press, 1999), 21.

tion, Venetian noblemen dressed in ample brocade or damask robes and cherry-coloured velvet caps" (611). On one of the Venetian nobles the narrator recognizes the origins of the coat designed by Fortuny that he had given to Albertine. Carpaccio's paintings are the source of Fortuny's inspiration, while the costumes in the paintings are in large measure made from materials and dyes that come from the bazaars of the East.

There is a chain here that takes us, by way of color, clothes, money, and sex, back into the world of *The Arabian Nights*, but as much into the souk, the sphere of exchange, of commodities, commerce, and coin, as into that of genies and spells (not to mention—Proust doesn't though Ruskin does—the spoils of conquest).[20] There is, however, mention of something else—share prices and stockbrokers' commissions—which fits seamlessly into the picture of Venice as a trading city and the narrator's own relation to it as a potential "trafficker" in commodities, art, and sex. The penultimate invoking of the Open Sesame mechanism in the novel (the door of memory that briefly opens onto Albertine) is prompted by a letter from the narrator's broker, an echo in turn of the conversation in the same hotel between Norpois and Madame de Villeparisis on the latter's holding of Suez stock. While the narrator's earlier extravagance in respect of Albertine means that, as the "owner of barely one-fifth" of his inherited wealth, he is now in a position of "relative ruin," this nevertheless proves no deterrent to the fantasy of purchasing power, which attaches to the Venetian shop girl—described as "dazzling"—whom he wants to "buy" and take back to Paris, as one buys a beautiful Titian: "The beauty of her seventeen years was so noble and radiant that she became a virtual Titian painting to be acquired before leaving" (604).[21]

III

Even when experienced in the architecture and decorative detail of its holy places, Venetian *éblouissement* in Proust is thoroughly this-worldly. Formed from its history of maritime commerce, power, and plunder, the public face of Venice was an endless feast for the eyes, its mix of exotic materials—veined porphyry, jasper, *verde antico*, fine enamel, rare jewels,

[20] "The ship of war brought home more marble in triumph than the merchant vessel in speculation; and the front of St Mark's became rather a shrine at which to dedicate the splendour of miscellaneous spoils than the organized expression of any fixed architectural law or religious emotion." Ruskin, *The Stones of Venice*, 11:97.

[21] Carpaccio is also invoked in connection with Charlus's sense of wartime Paris as a scene of endless sexual possibility (*T*, 71). In a letter to Gaston Gallimard explaining the later addition of the wartime episodes, Proust writes of Charlus benefiting from a Paris "teeming with soldiers like a city by Carpaccio." *Corr.*, 15:132.

millefiori glass—making it the "polychromatic" city above all others. The color schemes of Saint Mark's alone have been described as a "visual bricolage" of "Saracenic, oriental and Western sources," embodying the "alliance between material value and beauty as spiritual power that underlies Venetian attitudes to colour."[22] However, if there was one material that trumped the others, it was gold and its decorative uses as gilding and gold leaf (no accident that Saint Mark's was known as the *chiesa d'oro*). Venice, remarked the brother of one of the Byzantine emperors in 1438, is "that most wondrous of cities, so rich in colour and in accoutrements of gold."[23] The two qualities—richness of color and accoutrements of gold—went together on the spectrum of the city's visual splendor. But gold was, of course, also the precious metal that filled the city's coffers (including the closely guarded treasury of Saint Mark's), and, as signifier of wealth, gold was the *eidolon* incarnate, the universal fetish of idol worshippers, starting with the golden calf of the Hebrew Bible.

The Worship of the Golden Calf was the subject and title of one of Tintoretto's late works, a painting famous for its luminous hues, so deep and luscious as to suggest an effective, if unintended, complicity with the story it depicts (Tintoretto himself has been identified in the picture as the figure carrying the calf). Certainly, for both Ruskin and Proust, the Venetian painters—Bellini, Carpaccio, Tintoretto, Veronese, Giorgione, and Titian—were as important as the natural setting and material reality of the city itself for understanding Venice's unique relation to color. The traditional view, valuing *disegno* over *colore*, and the monochromatic over the polychromatic, looked askance at the so-called *colores floridi* of the Venetians. Reynolds, who stood for the superiority of the "simple and grave colours," wrote disapprovingly of the "florid eloquence" of Tintoretto and Veronese, their "comparatively sensual style" concerned only with "those parts of the Art that give pleasure to the eye or sense," claiming that "they seem more willing to dazzle than to affect" and that "the Student must take care not to be so much dazzled with this splendor."[24] *Éblouissement* is not an artistic category or an aesthetic effect that Reynolds, and those who think like him, admired. Proust does not appear to have been directly acquainted with Reynolds's *Discourses*, although he may have come across Ruskin's engagement with Reynolds in the preface to the second edition of the first volume of *Modern Painters*. Ruskin's conservative adversaries had invoked the authority of Reynolds as a counter to Ruskin's championing of Turner. Ruskin met the challenge by endorsing Reynolds's stress on the primacy of the intellectual, the noble,

---

[22] Hills, *Venetian Colour*, 21, 23.

[23] Cited in Hills, ibid., 74.

[24] Joshua Reynolds, "Fourth Discourse," in *The Discourses* (San Marino, Calif.: Huntington Library, 1959), 63–68.

and the elevated, but in a manner that assigned to vivid color a value in these terms that Reynolds could never have recognized or accepted. In the practice of the Venetian painters so frowned upon by Reynolds, the "great element of colour . . . is ennobling to all things, and is an abstract quality, equally great wherever it occurs"; the "right splendour of colour" is "purifying and cleansing, like fire." Yet even as he affirms the intellectual and moral virtues of color, Ruskin hesitates over a conundrum: it is, he concedes, "not possible" to distinguish clearly "right splendour" from "the appearance of Sensual character." The only solution—but it is no solution at all—is to place one's trust in the character and motives of the artist ("the work of good and spiritually-minded men").[25]

To assert, as did Ruskin in *Modern Painters*, that "colour is the most sacred element of all visible things"[26] was necessarily to risk worship of the profane in the name of the sacred, and at the heart of his hesitation over "right splendour" lay the worry shared also by Proust concerning the relation between love of beauty and idolatry. On the other hand, Proust seems to have had no interest in the debates about the merits of the Venetian school, and there is little reason to think that he saw color, in both nature and art, as anything other than a gloriously lavish gift to both eye and soul. Proust was a natural-born "chromophiliac," like Goethe instinctively drawn to color for its own sake, and seeing it not only as a feature of the world but as a force in it. The world becomes more interesting when the process of coloration takes hold of it, especially as polychromatic variation in time (Proust's literary equivalent of the impressionist "series," such as Monet's water lilies or Rouen cathedral painted at different times of the day and in different lights). He also followed the example of the impressionists in extending the polychromatic universe to include the "color" of shadows—for instance, the extraction of blue from the play of shadows on the marble of Saint Mark's Square to produce the image of "little blue flowers" on the "desert of the sunlit paving stones" (F, 589) and the "blue shadows" perceived by the narrator and painted by Elstir that flicker across rock and sea by the Creunier cliffs near Balbec (*JF*, 478–79).

For the narrator, Elstir's painting is "this magic picture" (Elstir is the one artist-figure in the *Recherche* whose way of seeing and composing attracts both the terms "magic" and "poetic"). The magic has something to do with the coloring of shadows: their depiction as "blue" but also, and more curiously, as "varnished" (*verni*). According to Michael Taussig's historical anthropology of chromophobia and chromophilia in modern Western culture, color at its most humanly meaningful is best understood

[25] Ruskin, *Modern Painters*, 4:305, 4:194–95.
[26] Ibid., 5:281.

as "polymorphous magical substance," fundamental to the enchanted relation between man and natural world.[27] Proust is one of the tiny band of writers with a major role in Taussig's story, and the metaphorical (but is it only metaphorical?) preoccupation with varnish-style applications is at the heart of that role. In a letter to Anna de Noailles, Proust wrote of aiming for an effect that would resemble the "Varnish of the Masters," and claimed to have found in her own novel *Le Visage émerveillé* something of this sort, in combination with a "dazzling freshness of colour."[28] We can discount the characterization of the novel as yet another instance of Proustian good manners, but as a shorthand summary of his own literary aims the phrase "the Varnish of the Masters" recalls Bergotte's last reflection on his own art before Vermeer's *View of Delft* ("I should have applied several layers of colour," *P,* 169). Vermeer's mixing of varnishes and pigments generated an effect of "light trapped and bent through transparent or semitransparent layers." Proust wanted to create something similar, "a diaphanous depth of colour itself," a form of buried luminosity, something hidden and yet "shining through," a deep gleam or radiance that is nothing less than *éblouissement* transformed by the promise of the epiphany.[29]

Color as "polymorphous magical substance" is Proust's "go-between" for the "miracle of transubstantiation" (as he put it in a famous letter to Lucien Daudet),[30] grasped as the process of "nature passing into artifice" or the "crossover" between nature and culture.[31] It was an equivalent of the magician's or shaman's way of restoring us to our "bodily unconscious," that "zone beyond the image and beyond conscious recall" that Walter Benjamin memorably imagined as the "weight" of the fisherman's "catch."[32] I know of no account of Proust from the point of view of magical thought more arresting than this. Yet even Taussig has to acknowledge the "trickster character" of the painter's varnishes.[33] The effect of buried luminosity is wondrous, but it is also an illusion, a false light, not unlike the luster of gold. We thus come back to the *chiesa d'oro* and the gold mosaics of Saint Mark's baptistery. In religious settings and representations, *aurum* is often a signifier of aura (in the sense of "halo"); Hills cites

[27]Taussig, *What Color Is the Sacred?*, 47.

[28]*Corr.,* 2:86.

[29]Taussig, *What Color Is the Sacred?*, 180, 208.

[30]*Corr.,* 12:343.

[31]Taussig, *What Color Is the Sacred?*, 180–81.

[32]Ibid., 197; "The Image of Proust," 210. The inspiration for Benjamin's analogy may have been Proust's gloss of "the inner book of unknown signs . . . which my attention, exploring my unconscious, cast around for, stumbled over, and traced the shapes of, like a diver feeling his way underwater" (*T,* 187).

[33]Taussig, *What Color Is the Sacred?*, 208.

Bellini's virgin and child panels as paradigmatic.[34] On the other hand, as the theologians and scholars of Byzantium often observed, the "light" emitted by gold and gilding in religious interiors was a "surrogate" for the resplendence of the sun.[35] Proust's Venice gives us both: a constant from the early sketches to *La Fugitive* has the narrator awakening on his first morning to the glorious blaze of the sun on the golden angel of the campanile. Inside the baptistery, on the other hand, Proust, while reading Ruskin, registers another kind of yellowish light, chthonic and telluric, out of the earth rather than from the sky, unlike the sunlight on Vermeer's yellow patch of wall in *View of Delft*: "the mosaics shone only by their own physical light and with an internal, ancient, and earthly gold to which the Venetian sun, which sets even the angels of the campanile ablaze, mingles nothing of its own."[36]

IV

Joys that are "mixed," an "emotion" felt to be "not very pure," a non-natural or substitute source of light, an "impure" color (in the technical sense of "mixed" rather than "primary," but with also the moral connotations that link both the metal and the color gold to the idolatrous)—these fit uneasily into the experience of the sacred and the rituals of spirituality, and can perhaps be read as so many signs of a mind scrutinizing the ambiguous grounds of its own pleasures. And if we are reluctant to see Proust's Venice in this way, he provides additional food for skeptical thought, along another axis of the pleasure-seeking sensorium—the gustatory rather than the visual—where it is "food" itself (in particular the more intricate arts of baking) that furnishes the paramount frame of reference. Bakery and church are literally contiguous in the remembered landscape of Combray, so intimately bound together that the church steeple assumes metaphorically the shape of a brioche (*S*, 108),[37] and, in the preface to the translation of *Sesame and Lilies*, the smells of the pastry cook's wares ("cakes in the shape of towers") and the church as "magic abode . . . of the blessed bread" seep metonymically and synesthetically into each other: the "lazy and sugary fragrance" of the former "mingled for me with the tolling of the bells for high mass and the gaiety

[34] Hills, *Venetian Colour*, 157.

[35] Ibid., 47.

[36] In the *Farbenlehre*, Goethe's discussion of the origin of color in light and darkness centers on two basic colors, yellow signifying light and blue darkness. See John Gage, *Colour and Meaning: Art, Science and Symbolism* (London: Sage, 1990), 172.

[37] The analogy is in fact the local curé's; whether it is also Proust's is a question that opens onto the discussion of metaphor in chapter 6.

of Sundays."[38] The gold mosaics of Saint Mark's ("made by sandwiching gold leaf between layers of glass"),[39] along with Bergotte's recipe for literature ("I should have applied several layers of colour"), may also be said to evoke the creations of the *pâtissier*, but have more in common formally with that stratified sugary confection known as the *feuilleté*.

The stammered thoughts of the dying Bergotte on the lesson of Vermeer for what his own art might have been are often taken to echo Proust's ideal conception of literary "style." Style could be analogically modeled as painting, but less as optical representation than as material "substance" (what Gérard Genette dubbed "l'idée d'un style-substance").[40] A stylistically created effect of "homogenous substance" was one of the things he found and admired in Flaubert, and in the letter to Noailles where he used the comparison with the "Varnish of the Masters," he also spoke of "a kind of blending" (*fondu*), a "transparent unity," where "all things" are "pierced through by the same light" and "seen one inside the other."[41] The commonplace trope of the writer's language as artist's palette is here semiliteralized; the dream is of words become matter like paint, to be mixed and blended (the sense of *fondu*). From there it is but a step to another association: of pigment and impasto with pastry and dough, and hence the positing of style as the kneading and molding of words into a consistent, pastelike thickness that can then be folded back, snakelike, on itself in superimposed formations or cut into slices and layered as a *feuilleté*.

Ross Chambers, taking his cue from some remarks of Deleuze and Guattari, gestures toward an aesthetic of the *feuilleté* or what he calls "flaky poeisis"; there are some literary texts (his own example is the city poetry of Baudelaire) "whose texture is like certain kinds of pastry (a croissant, say, or a baklava)."[42] In poems such as "Le Cygne," urban "jumble" is poetically represented as a loosely structured montage or palimpsest of sights, sensations, and memories. *À la recherche* is, of course, *all* palimpsest; and when in *La Fugitive* the narrator uses the expression "leafing through [*feuilletant*] our memory like a dossier of eye-witness accounts" (476), beyond the immediate context of the paranoid detective-lover ransacking memory for proofs of the betrayals of his beloved, we may find ourselves thinking of the layers of a cake as well as of the "leaves" of a book. Consider, for example, that locus of richly concentrated synesthetic memory resurrected by the taste of the mad-

---

[38] Proust, *On Reading Ruskin*, 109.

[39] Hills, *Venetian Colour*, 47.

[40] Gérard Genette, *Figures* (Paris: Seuil, 1966), 42.

[41] *Corr.*, 2:86.

[42] Ross Chambers, "Baudelaire's Paris," in *The Cambridge Companion to Baudelaire*, ed. Rosemary Lloyd (Cambridge: Cambridge University Press, 2005), 110.

eleine, the room adjoining Aunt Léonie's bedroom, where the syntax of description molds itself to the multilayered field of sensation described, beginning with "the sweetness of warm bread" and proceeding to the extraordinary construction: "the fire baked like a dough the appetizing smells with which the air of the room was all curdled and which had already been kneaded and made to 'rise' by the damp and sunny coolness of the morning, it flaked [*feuilletait*] them, gilded them, puckered them, puffed them, making them into an invisible, palpable country pastry [*gateau provincial*]" (*S*, 52–53).

Aunt Léonie's rooms are not just rooms (in the same way that for Proust in the *Recherche* an hour is not just an hour but a vessel). They supply the terms of *the* palimpsest, at once inaugural and foundational, of the *Recherche*. Their remembered smells are a layered structure built from the taste of tea and cake, which in turn sends the narrator toward a visual memory at the edge of vision, an obscure commotion in the depths of the bodily self, imaged as the "eddying of stirred-up colours" (*S*, 49). The stirred-up colors of the past and the remembered warmth of fresh bread and fire baking odors as if they were dough may in turn recall the primitive etymology linking *calor* and color.[43] The precedent of Baudelaire—virtually omnipresent where Proust's deepest artistic convictions are in play—is once again potentially relevant, namely, his speculations in the *Salon de 1846* on the calorific origins and values of color.[44] But it is more the sweetness of the warm bread and of the puffed and flaky country pastry that might here call Baudelaire to mind, or, more precisely, remind us of Proust quoting, in his essay on Baudelaire, the (unprepossessing) line from the discarded poem "La Voix": "the Earth is a cake full of sweetness [*douceur*]."[45] The poem can scarcely have counted for Proust, but sweetness certainly did. There are many sweet cakes in the novel. The most celebrated (and celebratory) is, of course, the madeleine, "grooved" or "pleated" rather than *feuilletée* in shape, but definitely sweet, a mouthful of which releases a spasm of delicious pleasure that spreads like an ineffable deliquescence through mind and body. There is also that teatime cornucopia of a cake platter served by the Verdurins at La Raspelière, which includes a *feuilleté normand*, along with *galettes*, "boat-shaped tarts filled with cherries, like coral pearls," and "diplomats" (*SG*, 396). More evocatively, there are the cakes of the cliff-top picnic with the young girls of *À l'ombre des jeunes filles en fleurs*. "The girls all preferred sandwiches and exclaimed at seeing me eat only

[43] Beckett relates them in connection with the image of the "vase" or "vessel" of memory ("filled with a certain perfume and a certain colour and raised to a certain temperature"). *Proust*, 55.

[44] Baudelaire, "De la couleur," in *Salon de 1846*, in *Œuvres complètes*, 11:422.

[45] "Sainte-Beuve and Baudelaire," in *Against Sainte-Beuve*, ed. Sturrock, 50.

a chocolate cake, with its Gothic architecture of icing, or an apricot tart." The narrator's preference derives not merely from the possession of a sweet tooth, but because "cakes were privy to much, and tarts were talkative." The knowledge of which they speak is, of course, knowledge of the past, "many things about Combray," which include "the illustrated *Arabian Nights* side-plates which had once afforded such a variety of entertainments to my Aunt Léonie" (*JF*, 481). Patisserie, plates, and Scheherazade come together on the Normandy coast.

Douceur, maintains Jean-Pierre Richard, is fundamental to "the Proustian mythology."[46] While phenomenologically anchored in the taste buds, it variously signifies the moral qualities of softness, kindness, and tenderness (the virtues of the sweet disposition), as well as an indefinable aesthetic quality, for example, "the grave sweetness" that marks "certain pages of *Lohengrin*, certain paintings by Carpaccio, and that explains why Baudelaire was able to apply to the sound of the trumpet the epithet delicious" (*S*, 178). By way of Carpaccio (in the company of Wagner and Baudelaire), sweetness thus returns us to Venice, in particular to Saint Mark's and another synesthetic superimposition, the yoking of *éblouissement* to *douceur*. One of the notes to the translation of the *Bible of Amiens* refers to "the baptistery of Saint Mark's, whose dazzling freshness is so sweet during Venice's burning afternoons" (91). And in *La Fugitive* the idea of sweetness is taken up as a figurative honey taste: the "wide arches" of the baptistery "lend the church an air of having been constructed from a soft and malleable material like the wax of giant honeycomb cells" (610).[47]

From layered pastry to giant honeycomb cells ("from the honeycombs of memory," observes Benjamin, "he built a house for the swarm of his thoughts"[48]). But in all this succulence there is a risk of the cloying, for instance, the "cloying creaminess" of the picnic cakes in *À l'ombre des jeunes filles en fleurs* and in the same volume the unpleasant "smells of the pastrycook kitchens" next door to the Balbec church that contribute to his disappointment on seeing the church for the first time (238). The *doux* can become the *doucereux*, repulsively sweet, just as the remembered olfactory ambience of Aunt Léonie's rooms eventually reduces to a composite sensation that includes the "sickly" and the "indigestible." If the dazzling can dull or blind the eye, excess intake of the richly saccharine can induce nausea. And that these are not simply incidental side effects is clear from Proust issuing, in the first part of the preface to his

---

[46] Jean-Pierre Richard, *Proust et le monde sensible* (Paris: Editions du Seuil, 1974), 22.

[47] The narrator also says of the gravestones in the Combray church cemetery "time had softened them and made them flow like honey beyond the bounds of their own square shapes" (*S*, 62).

[48] Benjamin, "The Image of Proust," 198.

translation of *Sesame and Lilies*, an indirect admonishment from within two of the privileged scenes of childhood life, the scene of reading and the ritual of the family meal.[49] These are among the most affecting pages outside the *Recherche* itself that Proust ever wrote. "Sweetness" is everywhere in them—the "sweet" safety of hiding places in meadow, park, and hedge; the tolling of the church bells, whose "sound reached but feebly and sweetly the end of the park"; above all, the "sweet memory" of reading, those incomparable moments of quiet solitude "during which the thousand sensations of poetry and of obscure well-being which take wing joyfully from the depth of good health come to compose around the reader's reverie a pleasure as sweet and golden as honey."[50] It is, however, a pleasure interrupted by the demands of that commonplace, everyday event: the family lunch. This ordinary occasion, rooted in the monotony of bourgeois country life, nevertheless becomes the site of an agon, a dispute in which it is precisely the pitting of what, in connection with Ruskin, Proust called the "critical sense" against an excessive taste for sweetness that is at stake.

It is a dispute or contest between the narrator's great-aunt and his grandfather over the preparation of strawberries. For the great-aunt, "on things whose rules and principles had been taught to her by her mother, on the way to prepare certain dishes, to play the Beethoven sonatas, and to entertain graciously, she was sure to have a precise idea of perfection . . . For these three things, moreover, perfection was almost the same: it was a kind of simplicity in the means, a kind of sobriety and charm."[51] These are the principles and values with which the grandfather's views on the appropriate relation between strawberries and sugar clash:

> My grandfather had so much self-respect that he would have liked all dishes to be a success, and he knew too little about cookery ever to know when they were a failure. He was willing to admit that sometimes, if very rarely, they were, but only by pure chance. My great-aunt's criticisms, always justified, implying on the contrary that the cook had not known how to prepare a given dish, could not fail to appear particularly intolerable to my grandfather. Often, to avoid arguments with him, my great-aunt, after having tasted gingerly, did not give her opinion, which would let us know immediately that it was unfavourable. She would say nothing, but we could read in her gentle eyes a firm and deliberate disapproval which had a way of infuriating my grandfather. He would ironically beg her to give her opinion, become impatient at her silence, press her with questions, lose his temper, but one felt she would have been led

[49] He also wrote to Anna de Noailles, in response to her gushing remarks about Proust's preface, that he feared that his writing was a "sort of indigestible nougat." *Corr.*, 5:232.

[50] Proust, *On Reading Ruskin*, 108; 99; 133–34.

[51] Ibid., 102.

to martyrdom rather than confess to the belief of my grandfather's: that the sweet dish did not have too much sugar.[52]

As Swann watches Odette prepare orangeade, anxiety turns into pleasure and even happiness, with everything bathed in "a sort of superabundant sweetness" (S, 302). But, like excess sugar, superabundant sweetness is bad for you, a surfeit that renders the mind as well as the body sluggish, lazy, and prone to self-delusion, as well as to self-indulgence. It can end by making you want to throw up. And so it is with the sumptuously sweet splendor of Venice, or rather with its anticipation via the Magic of the Name. If the experience of Venice ends as a sensation of "cold numbness" before a meaningless chemistry of material parts, it begins as an excitement of the organism so intense as to engender a "vague desire to vomit" (S, 397). This ejection of overload, of "foods" experienced as alien to the body, can be interpreted in a number of ways. For example, it can be read psychoanalytically as the symptomatic reflection of the solipsist temptation, that extreme form of the "skeptical attitude" that expresses itself as rejection or denial of the reality of "otherness." I shall briefly consider the connection between skepticism and bodily expulsion in the penultimate chapter. But the "vague desire to vomit" inspired by "Venice" is not the solipsist's refusal of the reality principle; if anything, it is the exact opposite, an instinctive rejection of those sweetly toxic substances that numb the rational mind and the critical faculty, encourage a surrender to infantile regression and the fantasy of the self's dominion over the world, in short, everything that halts the painful but necessary passage to adulthood and delays the long good-bye to fairy tale and magic. Naturally, the "sweetest" thing in the whole novel—serially represented as such[53]—is the mother's good-night kiss. It is "like a fruit that has turned sweet and bursts its skin" (S, 33), a sweetness desired, withheld, no sooner tasted than desired again, of which one can never have enough but which must be renounced, if only in the form of its desecration.

À la recherche is a novel about a lost (or hypothetical) enchanted garden and the fitful, sporadic promise of its blissful recovery. But it is also a novel about the necessity of leaving it. This will take many forms and occupy many thousands of pages. It will involve defilement of the cherished (as revenge for its loss), savage mockery of worldly relations, death and mourning, and imaginative disempowerment and bodily decrepitude before coming face-to-face with the ultimate test—extinction, where the "sweetness" of the world is dissolved in the perishability of all things, including that which was meant to hold and transfigure the sweetness: literature. When in Le Temps retrouvé, the narrator speaks of the "illu-

[52] Ibid., 102–3.
[53] See also S, 17, 26.

sory magic of literature" (163), he means a certain kind of literature, the false kind, the type of meretricious writing illustrated by the Goncourt journal, a semi-institutionalized, fashionable house style, a literature of notations that is all slick, witty, and glamorous surfaces. Proust's idea of "literature," the one that belongs with "the true life," is, of course, entirely different. But the difference is not necessarily quite the straight-forward opposition Proust or his narrator would have us believe, the difference, let us say, between illusory magic and efficacious magic. What for Proust counts as the superficiality of the Goncourts is such that the test that exposes it is an easy one to administer. The test that would challenge Proust's conception of "literature" is necessarily far more exacting, as well as being seriously unwelcome. But one thing is certain: Proust would not and did not allow himself to be bewitched, dazzled, or sweet-talked into simply ignoring the force of its questions.

CHAPTER FIVE

What's in a Comma?

MOST TRADITIONAL "SEARCH" narratives are traveling narratives, and in many the hero makes his way to the sea (often to a port as the departure point for either new adventure or a return to a known world). In these terms, the *Recherche* is committedly minimalist: it gets us to the Channel and the Adriatic at the level of narrative (courtesy of the trips to Balbec and Venice), but to the Mediterranean only on the back of an analogy, whose content moreover suggests it is not the best of places to go for sustaining a rational grip on reality. Swann "in love" (that is, ensnared by his own narcissism) resembles "a traveler arriving at the Mediterranean shores on a day of fine weather," who "allows his vision to be dazzled . . . by the rays of light emitted in his direction by the luminous, resistant azure of the waters" (*S*, 234). Here, on the Mediterranean beach, *éblouissement* becomes the agent of blindness, cause of the errors and delusions that make Swann's life pure torment. Proust, of course, has a dozen ways of making his point about Swann's self-deceiving follies. This particular imaging of them (blinding dazzle as an effect of sunlight and sea) is special in being an ironic harbinger of things to come, most immediately, in the next volume, the sun-drenched summer spent in the seaside resort at the other end of France. Balbec is where the young narrator will learn much about the relations between sun, sea, perception, and art in the form of an induction into dazzled and dazzling vision that is, however, held to be exemplary rather than dangerous.

This is the lesson that above all awaits him in Elstir's studio, the moral of which, drawn from looking both at Elstir's paintings and at the sea from his hotel window, is flaunted as simultaneously and connectedly seeing nature "poetically" and seeing nature "as she is." The poetry of the impression and the truth of nature are one and indivisible. The flaws in that forced conjunction of ways of seeing are what the following chapter—in an important sense this whole book—is about. The deceptive azure of the Mediterranean and the educative blue of the Normandy coast turn out to have much in common in laying traps for those who behold them. Arrival at the Balbec hotel is experienced as entry into a pure color zone, its dining room dissolving into "a yellow glow edged by the blue dazzle of the sea" (*JF*, 308). Many pages later, however, at afternoon tea, the narrator finds himself exposed to another, more unsettling kind of dazzle: a "sudden and intermittent sunlight, a dazzling and unreliable form of illumination." Dazzle now pairs conjunctively with unreliability, the skeptic's category in the field of perception and knowledge. What proves locally unreliable is the narrator's ability to distinguish between the different women who are taking tea in the Rivebelle restaurant (some "from the most fashionable society," some "of easy virtue"), such that they all blend in a marinelike color as so many aquatic specimens in a fish bowl (393). But the issue of unreliable perception stretches much further. After his first meetings with Saint-Loup, the narrator reflects: "Well, I thought, I've already misread the man once, I've been fooled by a mirage" (312). First (but also second) impressions can be untrustworthy or downright false impressions.[1] This is a jaunty way—almost another joke—with a theme that winds its way through the *Recherche* in numerous connections. One of the most important concerns the role of "first impressions" and "poetic seeing" in Elstir's paintings.

If the last part of *À l'ombre des jeunes filles en fleurs* ("Nom de pays: le pays") is a major chapter of the narrator's aesthetic education, a preparatory apprenticeship for the great revelations binding impression to memory in *Le Temps retrouvé*, it also embeds poetic seeing in a context of what is openly declared to be all "mirage" and "optical illusion." These are strange, epistemically disconcerting terms to come across in an account stressing the excitements of a way of seeing based on the instantaneous impression, the terms of a discourse that, even as its user rejoices in the immediacy of appearances, remains wary of the evidence of the senses after the fashion of the traditional skeptic. They point to another unreliability and raise a question, the most important of the skeptic's questions, not only in but *for* Proust's novel: Is poetic seeing also true seeing, and how can it be if poetic seeing is the seeing of a mirage? Proust's answer—not his formal answer, of course, but the answer given by the totality of his text in all its intricate contradictoriness—is double. The formal answer is yes, and has to be if the novel is to be more than just an extended impressionistic patchwork woven from the random and the inconsequential. On the other hand, the space in which the affirmative answer is delivered is also such as to give us everything the skeptic might need to answer the question in the negative, or at the very least to doubt what is otherwise so confidently affirmed.

In the beginning was the Impression—thus runs Proustian scripture, where "beginning" covers at least three dimensions of firstness, foundational as well as inaugural: what comes first when the impression is stripped of sedimented overlay and cut back to its originary root ("the root of our impression," CG, 417); "first" in the sense of the priority, both temporal and qualitative, granted to the impression over rational

---

[1] "[W]hen we have started out from a wrong assumption . . . it is possible, once we have discovered our mistake, to replace it not with the truth, but with another mistake" (*JF*, 525).

cognition or what Proust normally calls "intelligence"; and "first" in the chronological sense of first thoughts, Proust's early formulation of what his art might be about, already in place in the opening sentence of the "projected prefaces" to Contre Sainte-Beuve: "Daily, I attach less value to the intellect. Daily, I realize more clearly that only away from it can the writer repossess something of our past impressions, that is, attain to something of himself and to the one subject-matter of art." This was to be an art in which the bodily unconscious "speaks" in and through sensations attached to the "things through which we can retrieve any part of us that the reasoning mind, having no use for it, disdained."[2] However, if this is the Proustian orthodoxy (repeated almost ad nauseam in À la recherche), there is a paradoxical catch that Proust himself nicely identifies even in the aggressively polemical Contre Sainte-Beuve. The intellect may be the enemy of the impression, or at best its impaired poor relation, but it is also the eloquent, efficient, and indispensable instrument of its own demotion (nothing more intelligent than Proust's critique of intelligence): "But it is to the intellect we must look all the same to establish the inferiority of the intellect. The intellect may not deserve the supreme accolade, but it alone is capable of bestowing it. It may hold only second place in the hierarchy of virtues but only it is capable of proclaiming that instinct has to occupy the first."[3]

Folding a compliment into an insult—or, more exactly, making the latter the occasion of the former—is an impish form of devil's advocacy, but it is not merely an entertaining game with paradox for its own sake. Intelligence intelligently inspected, thereby reaffirming through its own self-critical practice what in theory is denied to it (importance, even indispensability), is table-turning in more ways than one. The formal paradox enunciated in Contre Sainte-Beuve reappears in À la recherche (with a slightly tired air),[4] but far more enlivening is the spectacle of Proust the quick-witted satirist declining to suffer fools gladly—on, naturally, the subject of "intelligence." Here he is on witheringly top form at the Verdurins:

> "It all depends on what you call intelligence," said Forcheville, who felt it was his turn to shine. "Now, Swann, what do you mean by intelligence?"
>
> "There you are!" exclaimed Odette. "That's the sort of subject I'm always asking him to talk about, but he never will."
>
> "But I do," protested Swann.

[2] Against Sainte-Beuve, ed. Sturrock, 3.

[3] Ibid., 8. For a helpful summary of the pros and cons of "intelligence" in Proust's thinking, see Roger Shattuck, Proust's Binoculars: A Study of Memory, Time and Recognition in "A la recherché du temps perdu" (New York: Random House, 1963).

[4] "And it is the intellect itself which, while recognizing their superiority, uses its reasoning in order to abdicate in their favour and accepts the role of collaborator and servant" (F, 391)

"What tripe!" said Odette.

"Tripe with onions?" asked the doctor. . . .

"There is," said Brichot, rapping out the syllables, "a very curious definition of intelligence in that gentle anarchist, Fénelon . . ." (S, 265)

Whatever the register, dogmatic or satiric, the signs of a mercurial and probing intelligence are to be found almost everywhere at work in the *Recherche*, even when, as here, its theme is intelligence as worthless social coin. What nevertheless surprises is finding the signs so actively and centrally present in the very place where in theory "intelligence" is relegated to at best a strictly secondary function. The narrator's meditation in *Le Temps retrouvé* on the work-to-come has the staple assertions of firstness (the primordial moment of the impression) and secondariness (the derivative elaborations of the intellect), a view rationalized in the (misleading) distinction between the working processes of literature and science: "An impression is for the writer what an experiment is for the scientist, except that for the scientist the work of the intelligence precedes it, and for the writer it comes afterwards" (T, 188). These are the terms that inform the narrator's account of the revelatory triplet (paving stone, napkin, and spoon). But, leaving to one side the spurious differentiation of literature and science (a period residue), the terms fail to make proper sense of the facts of Proust's own text. When Proust wrote that "intellect rules the world" (T, 269), he meant a species of misrule from which his kind of impressionistic art was to deliver us. Yet despite the manifest allegiance to contemporary forms of anti-intellectualism, Proust could go only so far with it, in part, perhaps, because anti-intellectualism was so often the natural ally of the irrationalist ethnonationalisms that erupted into public discourse around the Dreyfus affair.

It is certainly a noteworthy fact of *Le Temps retrouvé* that the sequence that so determinedly proclaims the virtues of the impression-based work of art is also the sequence where the standing and labor of the "intelligence" are most powerfully reinstated. It comes more and more to be seen as uniquely the source of explanations that are not just post hoc clarificatory supplements, dutiful yet inferior adjuncts to the all-encompassing authority of the impression, but as irreplaceably necessary to the project of making sense of impressionistic experience. It is as if a limit has been reached in the aesthetic of the impression, a discovery belatedly made, and a despised paradigm of inquiry restored to its rightful place. What the narrator could not see at the time of the madeleine, he can now grasp as essential—the "search" is, among other things, a search for reasons ("the objective reason") and causes ("the cause of this happiness"), without which the experiences (paving stone, napkin, spoon) will remain unintelligible: "This time, though, I had decided not to resign myself to not knowing the reason for it as I had done on the day I tasted the madeleine dipped in herb tea . . . I therefore forced myself to try to see as clearly and quickly as possible into the nature of the identical pleasures I had just experienced three times in a few minutes, and then to isolate the lesson I was to draw from it" (*T*, 175–77). The lesson is that the spontaneously generated impression does not spontaneously yield its meaning, and that brute sensation is "like those negatives which show nothing but blackness until they are held close to a lamp . . . one does not know what it is until it has been brought into contact with the intellect" (205). We are back in the Proustian darkroom, this time, however, with intelligence as the developer that brings the negative (the "obscure impressions," 186) into the sphere of visibility and understanding.

Only someone thinking in the language of a rationalist analytical tradition could write like this. Who else in the modern pantheon would assert within the work of fiction itself that "a piece of writing, even if it directs itself exclusively to subjects that are not intellectual, is still a work of the intelligence" (*CG*, 182)? It is not often said, but needs to be, that Proust is unique among the great modern novelists in being situated not just "between two centuries" (the later nineteenth and the early twentieth), but between several, including the seventeenth and the eighteenth, or what is sometimes called the Age of Reason. But if that wider historical context suggests that the relation between intelligence and impression in *À la recherche* is less that of servant to master than one of near-equals, we should not thereby conclude by drawing a picture of harmonious collaboration inside a stable division of labor parallel to, and even superimposed upon, a similar division of roles between the "prosaic" and the "poetic." As we saw in chapter 3, this makes little sense of the novel's tensions and struggles with literary idiom and heritage. In the same way, intelligence and impression are not best seen as peacefully coexisting neighbors, Proust's text moving freely from the embrace of one to that of the other as local needs dictate. It is more a case of it bouncing unsteadily back and forth from one to the other, as if unsure as to where its real "argument" lies. The narrator wants to believe, and wants us to believe, that all struggle on this front is finally and decisively resolved in favor of the impression and its stylistic correlate, the image, but the anxiously repeated appeals to a more analytical discourse suggest that the belief is perhaps not that securely held. And if confidence wavers here, it is then but a step to harboring a more general doubt as to the validity of a whole enterprise based on the alleged magical powers of the impression.

II

To a large extent this is a topic primarily of interest to the literary historian tracing the multiple influences that flowed into the making of a historically circumscribed aesthetic ideology. It is a useful exercise, especially for the production of a historicized Proust as a counter to cult-Proust. The sparring contest of intellect and impression runs deeper, however— into a question that, while also partaking of Proust's historical moment, belongs to a higher order of generality, namely, the question of "truth." There is no word more important in *À la recherche*, and yet that proves more elusive. As a bedrock term on which many of the other talismanic words (impression, memory, resurrection) rest and find their meaning, its interpretation nevertheless faces a twin difficulty. The first is figuring out what Proust meant by it. The quick (because obvious) answer is many things; "truth" in Proust is irreducibly plural. Yet this evident plurality of meaning does not always have as its corollary a happily relativistic pluralism; meanings indeed multiply across a vast range of narrative contexts and maxim-style utterances, but as a multiplicity that on closer examination often reveals conceptual divergence, and even collision. The second difficulty is methodological (I mention it partly as an advance health warning over much of what follows): the attempt to figure out what Proust could have coherently meant in situations of semantic or logical clash calls on that most un-Proustian of qualities, the heavy plod of the hairsplitting, necessary-and-sufficient conditions brigade. Wrapping this straitjacket around Proust's quicksilver mind is not a fetching prospect, something of a withered Anglo-Saxon embrace. On the other hand, if clumping through a set of analytical discriminations lacks appeal, indeed, in connection with Proust resembles a drearily implausible solecism, it is better, in the end more productive, than approaching the question in, so to speak, casually "impressionistic" fashion.

In the well-known letter to Jacques Rivière outlining his artistic aims in 1914, Proust placed "truth" at the center of the search: the novel is basically about the "search for Truth" or "what Truth consisted in for me."[5] Proust, alas, does not elaborate on the distinction he draws—between Truth, period, and Truth-for-me. Perhaps he did not think of his terms as constituting a distinction and saw them more as synonyms that denoted broadly the same idea twice over. But what is true-for-me and what is true irrespective of my point of view are evidently not the same thing. The former accommodates all the vagaries of subjectivity and point of view; on this account, truth is always and can be only the "unique inflection of a personality")[6] a reflection, in Proust's terms, of the "hundred universes" that "each of [us] sees, that each of [us] is" (*P*, 236). This is what most readers of Proust take his idea of truth to be, for good reason; it is the conception that informs the central meditation on "the book of unknown signs" that is the narrator's interior history and on the work of art that the creative "decipherment" of that book brings into being out

---

[5] *Corr.*, 13:99.
[6] Proust, *On Reading Ruskin*, 123.

of the "obscurity within . . . which can never be known by other people" (*T*, 188). But there is also the absolutist sense, the meaning of truth as that which is true anyway, whatever anyone happens to think. Let us return here to the famous proposition defining the nature of the "true life" (*la vraie vie*). When Proust writes that "life finally uncovered and clarified, the only life in consequence lived to the full, is literature," we are likely to understand this as a statement made in the spirit of what is true-for-me, a more emphatic expression of the view that it is "the lonely work of artistic creation" that takes us "towards an outcome of truth." Proustian truth would therefore be subject to the logic of a project (the "work of artistic creation") also described in the letter to Rivière as a literary "construction"; the "outcome" will be the outcome of a fictional making, "truth" as the layered and interconnected dimensions of a temporal existence caught and displayed through the layering and interconnecting dynamic of the literary work. But—here the plod, I'm afraid, gets particularly heavy—the propositional representation is also very general, a statement about the true life as such, not merely the true life for someone in particular (Proust's narrator). The view in question is more than just an opinion, but a view held to be categorically true. What the sentence actually claims is that it is true that this is the only true life. Is it? Certainly, it is a very odd claim when taken out of the historical context of aestheticist thinking and projected as a universal. Yet that is how it *is* projected; the form of discourse Proust uses necessarily commits him to a conception of truth that is more than just subjectivist truth-for-me.

Whatever the logical entailments of Proust's sentence, it is not at all obvious that this is the kind of thinking Proust wanted his book to encourage. It is where the work of "intelligence" formally described as "philosophy" might want to take us. Proust's objective, however, is to enter a space beyond the propositional universe of "intelligence," the space of the bodily unconscious opened up by "the discord between our impressions and their habitual expression" (*S*, 156). In the determination of what will count as "truth," priority is once more granted to the impression: "Whatever the ideas that may have been left in us by our life, their material outline, the trace of the impression they originally made on us, is always the indispensable warrant of their truth . . . Only the impression, however slight its material may seem, however elusive its trace, can be a criterion of truth" (*T*, 188). No surprises there, of course, but it brings in its wake a further question: If the only criterion of truth is the impression, what are the criteria, or attributes, of the criterion? What is it about the impression that qualifies it as the very essence of Proustian truth? The trudging legwork begins here, in a terminological thicket ring-fenced by, as foreground or dominant terms, "true impression" (*impression vraie*) and "genuine impression" (*impression véritable*), along with a set of outrider terms—"real impression" (*impression vraie*), "first impression" (*impression première*), "deep(est) impressions" (*impressions profondes*), and "original impression" (*impression initiale*).[7]

True, genuine, real, first, deep, original . . . How do the items of this textual cluster relate to one another, and how do they converge on what Proust calls the "important questions," in turn specified as "the question of the reality of Art, Reality itself" (*P*, 345–46)? That is some apposition. It recalls the linking of "artistic creation" to an "outcome of truth," but compacts too much to be of any real analytical help; between the paired terms "reality of Art" and "Reality itself" there is a gigantic ellipsis. One possible guide to what Proust appears to have meant is a view of truth based on a principle of "immediacy"; truth is what is to be found in the unmediated directness of the impression (for example, "the immediacy of his impression" that is singled out by the narrator as the defining characteristic of some of Elstir's watercolors (*CG*, 417). In this context, the true-for-me becomes the true-to, phenomenological truth or fidelity to appearances, sensations, and perceptions, things as they truly appear to the perceiving eye/"I," even if what appears is what Proust on several occasions unabashedly calls an "optical illusion" (an expression familiar to Cartesians but with little, if any, epistemological freight in the vocabulary of the phenomenological *epoché*). The intellectual rival of the true-to is the true-of, what is true of the thing independently of the observer, and which therefore cannot itself be an "illusion." The first case is perhaps best expressed by the term "genuine" or "authentic" (*l'impression véritable*), while the term "true" (*l'impression vraie*) is best reserved for the second case, that which accurately captures what an object or state of affairs inherently is, an epistemological yardstick that Proust never disclaims and whose authority is the very condition of being able to name the phenomenological event as an "illusion" at all. What then is going on in the movement of Proust's thought between the *vrai* and the *véritable*?

The distinction can be further clarified by way of a set of antonyms— "factitious" for "genuine" and "false" for "true." The *impression factice* is the dead impression, creature of habit, product of the "tedious and pointless duplication of what our eyes see and our intellect records." The living impression, on the other hand, is the origin of "our true life, our reality as we have experienced it" and the route to a "rediscovery [of] the reality, distant as it is from our daily lives, and growing more and more distant as the conventional knowledge we substitute for it becomes denser and

---

[7]See "true impression" (*T*, 205), "genuine impression" (*JF*, 415), "real impression" (*T*, 178), "first impression" (*CG*, 417), "deep(est) impressions" (*CG*, 547), and "original impression" (*P*, 345).

more impermeable, this reality which we run a real risk of dying without ever having known, and which is quite simply our life" (*T*, 204). "Life" is the affective charge of sensations and perceptions unmediated by the conscious mind, "the sense of existence as it may quiver in the depths of an animal" (*S*, 9). The confluence of the true, the real, and the lived, with which the argument of this book began, returns here in the terms of late nineteenth-century vitalism, the "quiver" as an instinctive alertness to what serves the interests of "life" in its endless war with the death-dealing embrace of habit (habit also serves life, not, however, by quickening its pulse, but by drugging it into the slumber of the mundanely habitable). The "true" in the expression "our true life" is thus understood as essentially the quality of an experience, the measure of which is supplied by the pleasure principle on a spectrum that runs from simple happiness to blissful transport, in at least three senses of the latter term ("transport" as the impromptu return, via involuntary memory, to another time and place, as a mythical journey back into Eden, and as ecstatic transport of mind and body). As ever, the madeleine episode is exemplary: the narrator is "invaded" by "a delicious pleasure," "a powerful joy," an experience characterized by the compressed epistemo-affective equation implied by yet another elliptical apposition, "its felicity, its truth" (*S*, 48). At the founding moment of the novel, the true and the blissful are syntactically positioned not merely as neighbors but as inseparable companions.[8] All the subsequent "privileged moments," whether partial or complete, conform to this pattern, variously attracting the terms "joy," "happiness," "delight," "bliss": the approach to Hudimesnil and its row of three trees "suddenly filled me with a feeling of profound bliss" (*JF*, 296); the sequence of paving stone, napkin, and spoon produces "an increasing sense of personal joy" (*T*, 184).[9] One name we might give to this

---

[8]The madeleine sequence hints at four aspects or models of Truth, which when placed alongside one another do not naturally harmonize: first, the romantic notion of truth as inwardness, primarily a truth of "self" ("the truth I am seeking is not in the drink but in me"); second, the idea of truth as a quality or intensity of felt experience ("its felicity, its truth"); third, truth cast in the classical mode as object of inquiry ("seeking") and potential knowledge ("The drink has awoken it in me but does not know that truth"); and fourth, the modernist sense of truth as a creation ("Seek? Not only that: create," coming "face-to-face with something that does not yet exist," which is therefore made rather than found). *S*, 48. Most of the issues bound up with how we are to understand "truth" in Proust are to be found here.

[9]There is, however, a bracing counterproposition to this view of the relation between art, life, and happiness, where we find Proust in seventeenth-century *moraliste* mode (a few pages back he has quoted La Bruyère): "As for happiness, almost its only useful quality is to make unhappiness possible. We need, during periods of happiness, to form particularly pleasant and powerful bonds of trust and affection in order that their destruction can cause us the precious laceration called unhappiness. If one had not been happy, even if only in expectation, unhappiness would be devoid of cruelty and consequently fruitless" (*T*, 216).

range of jubilatory sensation is a "sixth sense" that hovers over the five of the sensorium, something close perhaps to what Heller-Roazen calls the "inner touch," understood as the diffused and pleasurable consciousness of sheer sentience.[10]

Looked at from the point of view of Bernard Williams's anatomy of our truth-telling dispositions,[11] we might want to situate the "vitalist" conception as close to the virtues of "sincerity." A better term, however, might be that late nineteenth- and early twentieth-century consort of sincerity, "authenticity" ("a characteristically modern value," as Williams puts it). While an overlapping concept, authenticity nevertheless differs from sincerity in signifying less a conscious moral commitment to telling (to others) what we believe the truth (generally of ourselves) to be than the instinctive acknowledgment and expression of our deepest feelings, or, more exactly, what Williams calls the "deepest needs and impulses" that form the bedrock of "the real self."[12] In this very strong version, the doctrine of Authenticity was to have something of a murky career in several of its post-Nietzsche guises (in particular, its disreputable association with sheer mythmaking), none of which has any precise bearing on Proust's novel. The "heroic ideal of coinciding with oneself" in a state of aristocratic indifference to everyday ethical obligations,[13] or indeed to the requirements of Truth as normally conceived, does not seem a recognizably Proustian one. The term "authentic" could, however, stand as a further translation of the idea of the "genuine" (*l'impression véritable*) and thus serve as one way of representing a relation between art and truth that rests on being true to the primacy of the existential "quiver" and the vibrant impressionistic economy of self that it underlies.

The "authentic" as the opposite of "factitious" provides one set of terms for construing Proustian truth as "the truths that one has reached within oneself" (*T*, 206). In its alliance with the impression, it is informed by a type of experience that displays three general characteristics: spontaneous rather than willed at its point of origin; disruptive or transgressive (of the order of habit) in its basic operations; and in its effects a source of

---

[10]Daniel Heller-Roazen, *The Inner Touch: Archaeology of a Sensation* (Cambridge, Mass.: Zone, 2007). Heller-Roazen notes that Maine de Biran was the first thinker in France to use the expression the "inner touch" as an analogy for the "absolute sensation of existence." Maine de Biran's psychology influenced Bergson and may have indirectly filtered through to Proust.

[11]See chapter 1.

[12]Williams, *Truth and Truthfulness*, 183–85. Mapping Proustian values on the very different intellectual careers of the ideals of sincerity and authenticity is a fascinating prospect, but it is not for here. "We can be as pleased by what we belive to be the case and is not, as by what we know to be the case." Williams, "Pleasure and Belief," in *Philosophy as a Humanistic Discipline*, ed. A. W. Moore (Princeton: Princeton University Press, 2006), 34.

[13]Ibid., 184.

high excitement for the psyche. We shall shortly encounter all three characteristics in connection with the Elstir episode in À l'ombre des jeunes filles en fleurs. However, that heady moment, along with many others in the Recherche, has to cope with the intrusion of another pair of opposed terms, "true"/"false," and a corresponding view of "truth" in the more objective sense of apprehending the world as it is rather than for what about it excites or speaks to our more urgent needs and desires. Inside this frame of reference, the true impression is the impression that is true of something, engaging the principle of accuracy rather than the standard of authenticity. We should bear in mind that this was also an issue for the theory of impressionism generally. In 1874 Jules-Antoine Castagnary wrote what in many ways still stands as the canonical definition of the impressionists' aims: "They are impressionists in the sense that they render not the landscape, but the sensation produced by the landscape."[14] However, a true record of the sensation or impression is not necessarily the same thing as a true record of the landscape. An anxiety over the erasure of the latter by the thrill of the former entered the critical discourse and was bent on stressing that the new use of light, color, and shadow was "true to nature" because "derived from a nature directly observed, a nature that everyone could experience";[15] the impressionist "effect" was not just a trick played on the eye, but proposed a way of seeing differently that was also a way of seeing more truthfully.[16]

For at least some of the defenders of impressionism, an ideal of accuracy thus mattered. It seems to have mattered also for Proust. When the young narrator is taken to the theater to see La Berma play Phèdre, he looks at the stage first with the naked eye, then through his grandmother's opera glasses. He expresses doubts as to the worth of the latter perspective ("I felt it was not La Berma that I was seeing, but only an enlarged picture of her"), not so much with a view to rehabilitating the cognitive superiority of the naked eye over the optical instrument, but rather as the pretext for the posing of a question: "I put the glasses down—but what if the image received by the naked eye were no more accurate, given that it was an image reduced by distance? Which was the true Berma?" (JF, 23). At one level, this is the phenomenologist as relativist; the "image" of reality received by the eye is a function of the varying conditions of its perception by the subject (the determining condition here being relative "distance"). Yet Proust does not let his narrator simply relax into an easygoing "spectatorial" perspectivism. The form in which he asks his

[14]Cited in Richard Shiff, Cézanne and the End of Impressionism (Chicago: University of Chicago Press, 1984), 3.

[15]Ibid., 16.

[16]For example, Théodore Duret wrote that Pissarro saw his landscape painting as an "exact reproduction of a natural scene." Cited in Shiff, Cézanne, 22.

question implies a wish to know which of the two ways of seeing is the more "accurate." No answer is immediately forthcoming, and there are those who would argue, reasonably, that it is of the essence of Proust's enterprise that no answer of this type could ever be forthcoming.

The question ("Which was the true Berma?"[17]) has nevertheless been posed and must therefore count for something beyond the transitory moment of perplexity it represents for the young narrator on his first outing to the theater. What, however, is harder to determine is just how much this was more generally the kind of question that counted for Proust. He is more familiar to us as the writer for whom relativities of interpretation are ineluctable and nonadjudicable. Consider, for example, the narrator's self-revising reflections, at Madame de Villeparisis's afternoon reception in *Le Côté de Guermantes*, on how our words and actions are interpreted by others. They are basically a meditation on the topic of image and truth, beginning with an entirely conventional contrast: "the image other people form of our actions and exploits no more corresponds to our own than an inaccurate tracing does to the original drawing." Across the gap between how we picture ourselves and how others picture us, there is a distribution of error and truth where priority is granted to the interpretations performed by the self on itself. But then comes the first of two revisions. If, on the one hand, the image others have of us is inaccurate by virtue of not matching our own self-understanding (it is the inaccurate tracing of the original drawing), on the other hand, "the strange tracing which seems to bear so little resemblance to us has the same sort of truth about it—unflattering, certainly, but also profound and useful—as an X-ray photograph." This inverts the earlier hierarchy (X-rays go deeper than drawings), only, however, to be succeeded by a further turn of the screw. We know how important the trope of the X-ray was to Proust as an analogy for his own writing, yet here, even as it penetrates below the surface of things in the way the "drawing" cannot, a further revision intervenes to claim that it is not in fact necessarily any more authoritative than the original drawing: "Not that this is any reason why we should recognize ourselves in it" (268–69). All the points of view have merit, but none can definitively command our allegiance.

The medley of propositions, each a cancellation of its predecessor, is a prime instance of the restless Proustian text on the move, refusing to settle on or into any fixed position. But there is another, less buoyant way of reading Proust's self-amending tactics, as the reflection of an awkward struggle with the complex relations of truth, perception, and recognition, an awkwardness manifesting itself moreover where we might least expect it. If, as Proust wrote in the letter to Rivière, the Search is the "search for

---

[17]It is the same question as that posed in respect to Berma's rival, Rachel (see chapter 3).

Truth," we should expect a very high degree of self-confident clarity at the consummation of the search, namely, in the climactic triple revelation of *Le Temps retrouvé*. This indeed seems to be what we get or are about to get: "I therefore forced myself to try to see as clearly and quickly as possible into the nature of the identical pleasures I had just experienced three times in a few minutes, and then to isolate the lesson I was to draw from it." That is a ringing statement of the interpretive challenge that faces the narrator and of his readiness to meet it. But what we actually get, in what immediately follows, is an explanatory promise either deferred or abandoned in an intellectual cul-de-sac. The passage continues:

> On the enormous difference between the true impression [*l'impression vraie*] *we have had of a thing* and the artificial impression [*l'impression factice*] we gave ourselves of it when we try by an act of will to represent it to ourselves, I did not pause. (177, emphasis added)

I add the emphasis in order to bring out the peculiar character of Proust's phrasing in this decisive formulation of his aims. The italicized portion is ambiguous. The presence of the "artificial impression" as the opposing term would suggest that "true impression" is intended in the phenomenological-vitalist sense of "genuine" or "authentic" (the freshly spontaneous, perceptual event). But the qualification of "true impression" as "the true impression we have had of a thing" invokes the other sense of "true" as true-of, the impression as a true image of the object that causes it, accuracy of perception rather than intensity of sensation. In this context, the artificial or factitious can be the antonym of "true" only if in addition to the meaning of "lifeless" it also has the meaning of "false." Since one does not automatically go with the other (few things are livelier or more enlivening than our desires), this is potentially confusing (to put it mildly). Two utterly different ideas bleed into each other at a narrative and textual crux, but—the blind alley—it is a crux in which Proust's narrator chooses not to dwell. He has raised a question by which he does not propose to be detained (over the differences and distinctions in question "I did not pause"). Why this speedy retreat and casual dispatch? One reason, perhaps, is that the question simply bores him (as I have already said or implied more than once, it is manifestly absurd to judge Proust from the point of view of the concerns and procedures of analytical philosophy). It may, however, be more a case of Proust brushing the issues under the carpet by virtue of the tension of wanting it all ways while knowing he can't have it all ways, at least not without having to confront a potential conflict of meanings and loyalties. Discretion may then be the better part of valor here; best just to bypass the question, even if the consequence is to leave both writer and reader stranded in a kind of intellectual no-man's-land.

We have already seen much of Proust's marked liking for blocking out the world in the darkened room of the solitary, owl-like creature, where ego is sovereign; with eyes shut, the private imagination enjoys virtually limitless powers of transposition unconstrained by any consideration of whether or not the imaginings or transpositions correspond to the world as it really is: "lying in bed with my eyes shut, I would say to myself that everything can be transposed" (P, 73). But when the eyes open in the full glare of the daylight world we have in common with others, a limit is necessarily placed on the empire of the ego. In the early drafts of the opening to *Sodome et Gomorrhe*, Proust spoke of "that little disk of the eye's pupil, through which we look at the world and in which our desire is engraved."[18] Like "desirous thinking," purely desirous seeing, while it can intoxicate, is full of traps. From the point of view of an account of "truth," it is rarely a trustworthy source of true knowledge, and is often its mortal enemy. It may be that "our slightest desire, although striking its own, unique chord, contains within it the fundamental notes on which our whole lives are based" and that the "natural accompaniment" of "our deepest impressions" is "a joy, the joy that springs from the life of creative people" (CG, 547), but that can hardly be the basis of a reliable epistemology; as Williams so aptly put it: "We can be as pleased by what we believe to be the case and is not, as by what we know to be the case."[19]

This is pure late nineteenth-century vitalism, a direct echo of the philosophers of Instinct, such as Nietzsche, bent on defining and celebrating the "authentic" life as a joyous, creative making. It is also consistent with the unbreakable link Proust made in the Ruskin commentaries between aesthetic pleasure and the discovery of truth.[20] The marriage of pleasure and truth forged by the emancipating impression was to be later glossed, at the revelatory moment of *Le Temps retrouvé*, as a form of the shock experience ("the shock to my senses," T, 180). But, as we have already seen, shock can ravage as well as delight, disclosing or hinting at truths of which the mind would prefer to know nothing at all, the Open Sesame that is best interrupted and the key buried deep in forgetfulness and indifference. Proust also knew that, along with its capacity to appall and terrify, "shock" can produce "impressions so vivid as to make all that has gone before seem pallid, and on which, because of their intensity, we fasten with the fleeting exaltation of a drunkard" (SG, 429). It is no surprise that this less flattering reflection on the intoxicated state reminds the narrator of the Rivebelle restaurant in which he is wined and dined by Saint-Loup (and where indeed he gets drunk).[21] In *Les Paradis*

---

[18] *ARTP*, 3:924.
[19] Williams, "Pleasure and Belief," in *Philosophy as a Humanistic Discipline*, 34.
[20] Proust, *On Reading Ruskin*, 53.
[21] See chapter 6.

artificiels Baudelaire warned against confusing the intoxicating joy of the imaginative epiphany with the cognitively delusional elations created by the use of stimulants. Similar thoughts seem, if less systematically, to have crossed Proust's mind, in connection not only with the effects of alcohol on the mind (compared with Baudelaire's investigations, Proust is, so to speak relatively small beer), but also with the hallucinogenic properties of the datura-based pharmacopeia Proust was in the habit of using on a daily basis.[22]

III

Choosing not to dwell in a crux of his own making gives all manner of hostages to fortune, especially when situated alongside another, over which we cannot simply refuse to "pause." While looking at the Elstir watercolors in the Guermantes collection, the narrator interprets the painter's aim of capturing "the immediacy of his impression" as the attempt "to undo the various mental assumptions we impose upon the visual process" (*CG*, 417). This is what impressionism (or, more broadly, modernism) sought to do, and it is the principle underlying the artistic radicalism (in the literal sense of contact with the "root") of the seascape paintings before which the narrator earlier marvels in the painter's Balbec studio (elsewhere Elstir is termed an "impressionist painter," *SG*, 408–9).[23] Mental assumptions undone is also the intended effect of Proust's novel, in its unrelenting crusade against that other form of misrule, the hegemony of habit. But the implications of the undoing are far-reaching and cannot always be contained by the bravura of an affirmed artistic program. Suppose the form of seeing is akin to the narrator's excited but frustrated attempt to extract from the three trees at Hudimesnil "a pattern I knew I had seen somewhere before," creating something "rather like the feeling I had once had from things such as the steeples of Martinville" (*JF*, 296). The attempt fails, and the narrator's disappointment at the resistance of the landscape to his appropriative wishes comes out as a worry: that perhaps what he thought he "saw" was "only an impairment

---

[22]Proust inhaled an infused datura powder as part of his asthma-relieving rituals, while in the novel it shows up rather as a sleep-inducing drug (*CG*, 11, 385–86). Luckhurst, while reminding us that the datura is sometimes known as "the tree of paradise" and the flower of "sorcerers," posits it as the antithesis of the ecstasy-triggering lime blossom tea ("the negative counterpart of the *tilleul*"). Its effects included "intellectual excitation resulting in sensory hallucinations, a disorientation in time and space, euphoria or attacks of anxiety and depression, dilation of the pupils, disturbing vision, an abnormally rapid heartbeat, loss of muscular strength, and dizziness leading to loss of muscular coordination." Luckhurst, *Science and Structure*, 219–20.

[23]For those so disposed, Elstir is a near anagram of Whistler.

of my eyesight, making me see double in time as one can see double in space" (298).[24] These are the salutary and instructive second thoughts of a mind skeptically curbing an initial enthusiasm. No such explicit worry or doubt appears to attend what, in the description of Elstir's pictorial practice, is nevertheless explicitly identified as an "optical illusion," and the fact that this is what, repeatedly, it is called necessarily focuses attention on an issue that will not go away: namely, however thrillingly radical in freeing "visual process" from this or that "mental assumption," what possible relation can there be between an optical illusion and what Proust understands by truth?

Elstir's studio is billed as "a laboratory" in which the artist forges a "new creation of the world." The narrator first enters it "in half-darkness," with shadow ("the blinds being down on most sides") played off against the "one part where daylight's fleeting decoration dazzled the wall" (*JF*, 414). The chiaroscuro effect makes the studio appear less a laboratory than another instance of the darkened room, a sort of Aladdin's cave in which the artist works his magic, the "enchantment" of his portraits and seascapes, above all that "unreal and mystic picture" (416), which the narrator will describe at great length, *Harbour at Carquethuit*. It is a picture in which elements and dimensions are reordered as so many identity-switches (far as close, water as earth, steeples as masts, fisherwomen as sea nymphs). The ground of the reordering is phenomenological, anchored in what the narrator calls the "genuine impression." This is the impression delivered by "first sight," and by virtue of which Elstir is said to paint only what he sees, not what he knows ("not to show things as he knew them to be, but in accordance with the optical illusions that our first sight of things is made of," 418). The illusion (or "mirage") is of a certain kind, one that transgresses the law of identity and difference in the form of a chiastic reversal, painting the land as if it were the sea and vice versa; the human equivalent is the *Miss Sacripant* portrait, its sitter ambiguously positioned between genders, the narrator at first seeing a young woman, and then a young man). Borrowing a term from literary art (but, in Proust, it is the term of terms), the narrator characterizes Elstir's pictorial art as "metaphorical," by which he means a practice of (re)naming things, the studio-laboratory thus the place of an experimental catachresis in the medium of paint:

> Almost all the works I could see about me in the studio were, of course, seascapes done recently here in Balbec. But I could see that their charm lay in a kind of metamorphosis of the things depicted, analogous to the poetical device

[24]Given that Monet is one of the sources for the creation of Elstir, one might wish to bear in mind that the extraordinary color worlds of Monet's late paintings derived in part from severely cataracted vision.

known as metaphor, and that, if God the Father had created things by nam-ing them, Elstir recreated them by removing their names, or by giving them another name . . . One of the metaphors which recurred most often in the sea-pictures which surrounded him was one which compares the land to the sea, blurring all distinction between them . . . It was to a metaphor of this sort—in a painting showing the harbour of Carquethuit, which he had finished only a few days before . . . that Elstir had alerted the mind of the spectator by using marine terminology to show the little town, and urban terms for the sea . . . On the beach in the foreground, the painter had accustomed the eye to dis-tinguish no clear frontier, no line of demarcation between the land and the ocean. (415–16)

In this world renamed by the artistic equivalent of God the Father, "truth" is a variant of the true-for-me, a "truth of the spirit" (442), or, in the more conventional trope the narrator uses, a truth of "genius" (430, 439). Does the whole question then come down to the cliché of romantic genius decked out in impressionist clothing, truth as uniquely the prop-erty of the private and privileged vision of the Artist? There can be no doubt that much of Proust's thinking runs along these lines, at its least original in touting a well-worn celebration of "originality." On the other hand, Elstir is not alone, and thus not unique, in seeing the world in this chiastically reordering fashion. The young narrator gazes at the sea from his hotel window and momentarily confuses water and land:

At the hotel in Balbec, there had been mornings when Françoise unpinned the blankets keeping out the light, or evenings when I was waiting for it to be time to go out with Saint-Loup, when an effect of sunlight at my bedroom window had made me see a darker area of the sea as a distant coastline, or filled me with joy at the sight of a zone of liquid blue which it was impossible to say was either sea or sky. The mind quickly redistributed the elements into the categories which the impression had abolished. (415)

With the commonplace act of looking out of a bedroom window, there is a shift of context from the artistic to the nonartistic, from the spe-cialized world of the artist's studio to the everyday reality of the tourist hotel (though as an "everyday" universe in which the order of habit is turned upside down). The two moments—in the studio and in the hotel—institute a dual-track set of mutual confirmations: the view from the hotel window confirms what the narrator has previously seen in Elstir's un-usual seascapes; Elstir's pictures authenticate the value of the narrator's own perceptions. In both cases, the mind's habitual mode of perception is not merely disturbed but inverted. A further shared feature is the trans-formation of "effect" (the impressionist effect of light on water) into "af-fect," acute forms of pleasure represented in both cases by the term "joy." Elstir's painting is a "rich" source of "joys," while the view from the hotel window "filled me with joy." The parallel between the everyday and the aesthetic, life and art, is further elaborated a few pages later, where "life" becomes "the unconscious well-being" that is "drawn from the summer's day," which in turn "helped to swell, like a tributary, the joy I had taken in seeing *Harbour at Carquethuit*" (422).

Thus are joined, in art and in life, the shock impression and the pleasure principle. But there is also something else that Elstir's pictorial method and the narrator's visual experience allegedly share: a way of seeing that, it would seem, grants access to nothing less than the truth of nature: "Those infrequent moments when we perceive nature as it is, poetically, were what Elstir's work was made of" (415). This sentence, unobtrusively tucked away in the middle of the paragraph detailing the view from the hotel window, is a ground-shifting sentence, one that truly sets the cat among the pigeons and guarantees to disturb the contemplative equanimity of Proust the night owl. By virtue of being optical illusions, what Elstir paints and the narrator "sees" fall by definition into the category of error. This is of no consequence for the version of Proustian truth that is bound to the pleasure principle ("truth" as designating the authenticity of a lived experience). But now we are being invited to endorse the version tied to the principle of accuracy rather than authenticity, no longer a view of truth as indifferent to error but as the opposite of error; what painter and narrator "see" is "nature as it is."

The aspects of this notionally modest yet astounding sentence that call for special comment are the adverb "poetically" and the comma that precedes it. There is no evidence in the manuscript material to suggest that the presence of the comma was anything other than fully intended. To grasp why this matters, consider how the sentence might be parsed if the comma were omitted, that is, let us play off the actual sentence Proust composed with a fictitious one. This is not just a heuristic device. The sentence is in fact occasionally quoted with the comma left out, as if, therefore, it were the sentence Proust himself wrote (for example, in—of all places—a study of Proust's attitudes to painting and painters).[25] Remove the comma and one has a different structure of grammatical relation: with the comma, the adverb "poetically" modifies the verb "sees," whereas without the comma the adverb modifies the verb "is." From a strictly grammatical point of view, the second relation is irregular, even illicit, in that the forms of the stative or copula verb "to be" are not adverbially modifiable (one can say that nature is poetic, but not that nature is poetically). However, this is unlikely to deter anyone other than the severest grammarian (one way of making it acceptable, at least to the less

---

[25] "Mais les rares moments où l'on voit la nature telle qu'elle est poétiquement, c'était de ceux-là qu'était faite l'œuvre d'Elstir." Juliette Monnin-Hornung, *Proust et la peinture* (Geneva: Droz, 1951), 46. It is worth noting that none of the English translations rewrites the original in this manner.

exacting speakers most of us are, would be to transform "poetically" into the phrase "when poetic": thus, seeing "nature as she is when poetic," or "nature when seen in her poetic aspect."

What, then, is in a comma, or at least in this one?[26] The old adage according to which professors read sentences and people read books might spring to mind here as a deterrent to further inquiry. But, as one of the dread band of pedants, I take comfort from citing once again Charlus's observation: "I have always respected those who defend grammar and logic. We realize, fifty years later, that they averted serious dangers." For if the fastidious parsing of adverb and comma is pure plod, it also pinpoints a theoretical clash at the very core of the Elstirian-Proustian aesthetic. The actual sentence with the comma and the hypothetical sentence without it express two very different arguments. If Proust had left the comma out, his meaning would have been "the rare moments when we see the poetic aspect of nature as it [the poetic aspect] truly is" and his main claim would therefore have been that Elstir's magical paintings direct the eye and the mind to what is true of the poetic dimension of nature, as distinct from what is true of her other dimensions (for example, the scientifically law-bound). But that is a fruitless speculation. Proust did not leave the comma out, and, while we cannot know just how alert Proust was to its general implications, in the absence of any indication suggesting a slip of the pen, a printer's error, and so forth, it must be allowed to say what in fact it does say. The presence of the comma makes the sentence deliver a very large claim indeed: it is only in those rare moments when we see nature poetically that we see nature as she truly is. Instead of the relativity of different ways of seeing, of which the poetic is but one, free to traffic in "illusions" for the purpose of procuring certain kinds of life-affirming pleasures, we now have the absolutist claim whereby one way of seeing—the poetic—is affirmed as superior to all others in revealing nothing less than the truth of nature.[27]

---

[26] Genette calls the sentence "the quintessential formula of the Proustian enterprise." Genette also glosses the formula as belonging to a modified aesthetic in which an original interest in "essences" gives way to an interest in "mirages" (*Figures*, 49). This is not quite right; the point about the sentence is that mirages masquerade *as* essences. That commentator superlatively attentive to language, Karl Kraus, once remarked on "the rhetorical and semantic" disaster produced by a "missing comma." Cited in Stanley Corngold and Benno Wagner, *Franz Kafka: The Ghosts in the Machine* (Evanston, Ill.: Northwestern University Press, 2011), 99.

[27] Even the superlatively attentive Descombes slips here, quoting the sentence with the comma, but to mount an interpretation that makes sense only if the comma is removed: "Elstir shows nature 'as she is, poetically,' which means: as she is when she accords us the favour of fantastic phenomena, here seen as belonging to the realm of the 'poetic'" (*Philosophy of the Novel*, 269). This can only mean that Elstir shows nature as she is poetically (without the comma).

In itself the affirmation could be seen as consistent with a long romantic and postromantic ontologizing of the poetic. What would not be consistent with that tradition is Proust having also identified Elstir's way of seeing as based on an "optical illusion" or a "mirage." In short, he has put us in an intellectually uninhabitable place. Elstir paints one of the rare moments when we see nature as she really is, yet what he paints is not nature as she really is but nature through the prism of an illusion. How can this be? Elstir is not a dupe, nor does he seek to dupe. He knows that he does not paint what he knows, and the viewer of his paintings, including the narrator, knows that what he sees is not what he knows; knowledge of the suspension of (customary) knowledge is part of the point. In neither intention nor effect are we dealing with a trompe l'oeil (although interestingly the latter term is used in the account of the sequence of triple revelation in *Le Temps retrouvé*). Elstir does not seek to deceive the eye but to record an impression on the basis of a willed state of ignorance or forgetting ("the effort . . . to rid himself of all the ideas the mind contains, to make himself ignorant so as to paint, to forget everything for the sake of his own integrity," 419). In fact, Proust's own terms here are misleading (the original French: *se faisait ignorant, oubliant tout par probité*).[28] Elstir cannot simply render himself "ignorant" (knowledge acquired can be bracketed but cannot be undone); nor does he obey some ethical imperative to "forget" what he knows (in Proust "forgetting" is not a willed, ethically driven process). Elstir does not paint reality in the blissful condition of a conjured amnesia; he does not forget, he disregards or deliberately sets to one side. On the other hand, the narrator's account of Elstir's enterprise does not suggest that it is also one of his aims self-consciously to paint the illusion as illusion. His "subject" is not the tricks our senses can play on us. That is not his purpose at all, and not what the narrator finds and admires in his work. Elstir paints an illusion but does not issue an invitation to the spectator to see it as illusion. On the contrary, he paints land as if it really is sea. And in the narrator's gloss, this is a reflection not just of how Elstir chooses to do things (exercising the rights of "genius" and all the rest of the romantic business), but also of how things are in nature.

Proust has thus mobilized the prestige of "poetic seeing" to advance an impossible set of claims. If poetic seeing gives us access to nature as she really is, then what is seen cannot also be an optical illusion, unless we here reinterpret the notion of "illusion" as itself illusory. Perhaps Proust meant something like this. In connection with Elstir's work, he refers to poetic seeing in terms of the pleasure principle, but also in terms of cognition, as a form of poetic knowing (*connaissance poétique*), specifically, knowledge

---

[28] *ARTP*, 2:196.

"of many forms I had hitherto never distinguished in reality's composite spectacle" (414). The knowledge in question may be of a different kind from that secured by the work of reason, but it is still knowledge, an epistemologically sanctioned way of apprehending the world. But if we press harder on exactly what this knowledge looks like, Proust's text remains as blurred as the impressionist blur it describes. On the one hand, and notwithstanding the polemical opposition of artist and scientist, there is what appears to be a fitful gesture toward the models of the "new" science. In the drafts, Proust toyed with, but dropped, the idea of Elstir's studio as an artistic "laboratory" in which Elstir explores the physics of invisible "electrical waves."[29] In the text itself, this time in connection with the *Miss Sacripant* portrait, chemistry is the model, Elstir's mode of portraiture described as a high-temperature chemical process of decomposition and recomposition in which the customary order of nature is inverted: "An artist's genius functions like the extremely high temperatures which can dissociate combinations of atoms and reshape them into a totally opposite order, one which corresponds to a different pattern" (439).[30] Alternatively, perhaps the thought is that there is no pattern other than one arbitrarily imposed by the intelligence—the real "illusion" is less one of Cartesian optics (the deceptive appearance of the twig bent in water) than the veil of Maya fashioned by the rational mind and cast over the phenomenal world to mask the truth of nature as the "chaos made of all things we see" (414).

[29] Ibid., 3:1268. Cited in Luckhurst, *Science and Structure*, 62. Elsewhere Elstir is seen in terms of "the process of creating some effect of perspective independently of the notions of physics he might use in other circumstances" (*CG*, 567). This is ambiguous: either "perspective" and "physics" are separate realms or perspective embodies another kind of physics different from what "he might use" for the purposes of routine understanding of the material world.

[30] The emphasis on relativity and indeterminacy in the new physics and mathematics seems to correlate naturally with Proust's literary endeavors (as a version of the "uncertainty principle" writ large), and, indeed, in Proust's own time comparisons with Einstein in particular were commonplace. Proust was interested in the comparison with Einstein, but only vaguely, and from time to time saw it as little more than a joke. More generally, the "rhetoric of scientific justification" in the *Recherche* "seems curiously indifferent to the spectacular developments of the early part of the twentieth century" and is based more on an invocation of the natural sciences—whether it be chemistry, biology, or physics—in their more traditional guise of the lawlike (Luckhurst, *Science and Structure*, 51–53). In our own time, an analogy has been run with Schrödinger's quantum physics and its implied replacement of the classical logic of either/or with the aporetic paradoxes of both/and (for example, Bowie's attempt to run Proust's method of "superimposition" across a conceptual grid defined by the example of the notorious cat, which, under the relevant experimental hypothesis in quantum physics, is both alive and dead. "Reading Proust Between the Lines," in *The Strange M. Proust*, ed. Benhaïm, 131. The analogy is attractive, but that is all it is, and fails to deliver anything in connection with Elstir's painting, which is not about something being in two contradictory states at the same time (the cat both alive and dead) but about one thing being taken for another (land as sea).

Here we might catch an echo of the metaphysics of Schopenhauer and early Nietzsche, being as the Dionysian flux of becoming, movement without limit in time and space, where there are no fixed boundaries or identities; the "blur" corresponds to how things really are and is not just an accident of our perceptual apparatus. "Our error," proclaims the narrator, "stems from believing that things habitually appear to us as they are in reality . . . But in fact reality is not at all what we usually perceive" (*F*, 538). An example is provided elsewhere, and it is not any old example: "Theoretically we are aware that the earth is spinning, but in reality we do not notice it: the ground on which we walk seems to be stationary and gives no cause for alarm. The same happens with Time" (*JF*, 57). What Proust does for time in his novel, Elstir does for space in his paintings. Elstir is thus exemplary in showing us that the ground on which we walk (or the sea on which we sail) is far from stationary, and in that endeavor is fully prepared to give cause for alarm (in his pictorial relocation of the things of seascape to the domain of landscape "it was alarming to see a ship steeply climbing the dry slope, like a carriage shaking water as it rattles up from a river-ford," 417).

Turner's naval companion isn't going to like this, and those who think like him may reasonably point out that such a view of the nature of being is not helpful in preventing shipwrecks, and not just of the mind. But perhaps this is where our gruffly commonsensical seafarer has to bow out. The great complication is that, however reluctantly, Proust and his narrator might have to bow out with him. For whatever he says, over and over, on the subject of habit, perception, and reality, Proust does not once disavow or even modify his use of the term "optical illusion." The latter implies error; it's not just that land appears where sea normally is; it is rather that the narrator mistakes sea for land and that Elstir gives the world less a new name than a wrong name.[31]

---

[31] See Michael Wood, "Noises in the Street: Proust and the Errors of Perception," unpublished paper presented to the Princeton Society of Fellows, October 2006. There is a third way of construing the operation: what we are invited to see is neither a mirage nor a representation of nature as she is but the creation of a new object without any kind of presumptive referential extension, positive (true) or negative (illusory) relation to the world. This ambition would be consistent with the modernist project of making it new as well as making it strange. Thus, Elstir does not depict land as sea and vice versa but creates a pure color zone (a "liquid azure"), which is an aesthetic object in its own right (echoed later by the view of Venice as a zone of "liquid sapphire," *F*, 588). There are many other examples of this in the *Recherche*, the most famous the "patch of yellow" in Vermeer's *View of Delft*. However, what is often overlooked is that Proust never once refers solely to an autonomous "patch of yellow"; it is always a "patch of yellow *wall*." What Bergotte repeatedly stammers, as at his death he discovers in Vermeer's picture the basis for an art consisting of "an entirely self-sufficient beauty," is "little patch of yellow wall" (*P*, 169). Even here a relation of reference to a familiar world is maintained.

There is all the difference in the world between painting only what you see (where what you see is incomplete or blurred) and painting what you see as if it were something else.[32] The first is indeed the record of an impression, but the second is the production of a chimera, a case not so much of the eye liberated from the tyranny of reason as tricked and bewitched by a deceptive manipulation of appearances. To be sure, as already remarked, Elstir does not intend a trompe l'oeil.[33] He knows that he is not painting what he knows; otherwise, we would have to conclude that he was either a madman or a con-artist. Nevertheless, the risk of representing reality through the prism of optical illusions is some form of cognitive suspension or disorder, seeing become seeing-as, in a manner that generates misperceptions and category mistakes. There is a telling, contrastive example supplied by the narrative, when, in *Le Côté de Guermantes*, the protective carapace of the habitual (the reassuring image the narrator has of his grandmother) is pierced by the shock experience of being suddenly forced into confronting the ugly reality of a broken and dying woman. This is a very clear instance of defamiliarization and true cognition working together. Superficially, it resembles the Elstir moment, itself a defamiliarization, illustrative, so the narrator suggests, of a class of "unfamiliar images of a familiar thing, an image that is different from the ones we are in the habit of noticing, unusual yet true, and which for that reason seems doubly striking, since it surprises us and shakes us out of our habits, while at the same time it turns us in on ourselves by recalling an impression" (*JF*, 417–18). In developing this thought, Proust lights on the analogy of the photograph, one that "will illustrate a law of perspective by showing a cathedral . . . taken from a point of view chosen so as to make it appear thirty times higher than the houses and jutting out beside the river, whereas it is nowhere near it." In Paris, as his grandmother struggles with the final symptoms of a mortal disease, he looks past his customary perception of her as the permanent and indestructible embodiment of loving tenderness to see her as a stranger in a snapshot portrait taken by a professional photographer, old, sick, hollowed out, and slightly deranged.[34]

While they have certain things in common, one could hardly imagine two such utterly different moments in the novel, one an occasion of high aesthetic animation, the other a scene of crippling anguish. It is worth pursuing further the differences and the similarities. Both are indeed defamiliarizations, but as reverse mirror images of the same process, and

---

[32] See Descombes, *Proust: Philosophy of the Novel*, 248.

[33] On the other hand, the triple revelations in *Le Temps retrouvé* are glossed as giving rise to a "trompe l'oeil." Patterson translates this as "optical illusion" (181).

[34] Several of the implications of this moment have been discussed by Michael Wood in "Other Eyes," in *The Strange M. Proust*, ed. Benhaïm, 107–10.

not just in terms of their respective affective values (one a source of pain, the other a source of pleasure). More important to the present argument is the different relation in each of habit and illusion, and thus how each stands to the real nub of the comparative exercise, the formula "unusual yet true." In the case of the grandmother, the narrator finds shelter from the truth for so long as the "usual," the regime of habit, can keep in place the comforting picture of the eternal fairy godmother; the "optical illusion" consists in screening out the visible signs of aging and illness. With Elstir, on the other hand, it is precisely the other way around; the illusion is not the habitual but what replaces the habitual. In both instances, the shock experience is therefore what shatters habit, but in the grandmother episode it is also what shatters (rather than produces) the illusion, the narrator brought face-to-face with a knowledge that the mind would prefer to ignore. The perception of the grandmother is "unusual yet true"; Elstir's perception of the Carquethuit harbor is also unusual, but it is false.

In short, despite what manifestly links the two moments, the differences are more fundamental. The episode with the grandmother is entirely consistent with the practice of narrative realism, the procedure of subjecting an error to the test of an unwanted but unavoidable "recognition." What the narrator discovers in Elstir's studio and from his hotel window does not belong in a recognition-scene of this type, the basic structure of which Proust inherits from the nineteenth-century novel. Rather, it embraces misrecognition as the price of the pleasures to be had from embarking on the mental adventures of impressionistic "firstness," even when that involves an error of perception. At the same time, however, alongside the willingness to pay that price, there is also the wish that the "rare moments" in question satisfy the kind of truth-claims so disturbingly yet uncomplicatedly satisfied by the spectacle of his dying grandmother ("nature as she really is"). We saw earlier that this was the kind of muddle Proust's narrator prefers to sidestep (over which "I did not pause"). But here, with Elstir's transformative painting, sidestepping is possible only if we disregard that beguiling yet hostage-taking comma, or come up with some evidence—of which there is none—to show that the comma itself was a "mistake" (as an oversight with all the unintended consequences of its unintended inclusion). The comma is not just a syntactic device, marking the place where parts of speech are divided. It also marks the divide, or more precisely the clash, of two conceptions. On the one hand, insofar as their poetic character offers us an insight into nature, Elstir's paintings redraw the cognitive map, pushing further and deeper toward "an outcome of truth." On the other hand, they forsake the cognitive map altogether in favor of the visual delights of the optical illusion.

There are those who see Proust's novel as embodying "a 'Copernican turn,' a revolution in the way we approach cognition."[35] But this is not the lesson Proust himself actually draws, most notably in the later return to Elstir's pictures in the Guermantes collection. This is the passage in which the narrator defines Elstir's project as seeking "to undo the various mental assumptions we impose upon the visual process." It is an aim motivated by "a sincere desire to return to the root of our impression" as the ground on which "we represent one thing by the other for which, in an initial flash of illusion, we mistook it." This is another restatement of the impressionistic aesthetic, now in explicit association with the principle of "sincerity." But it is emphatically not a bid for revolutionizing the paradigms of cognition. On the contrary, part of the point of Elstir's radical practice is that it confirms rather than usurps the normal workings of our cognitive life; "the initial flash of illusion" shows us that without the intervention of reason to reprogram the "first impression" and thus to distinguish object-identities, no true cognition is possible: "Among these pictures, several of the ones that society people found most absurd interested me more than the rest because they recreated the optical illusions which make it clear that we should never be able to identify objects if we did not have some recourse to reasoning" (*CG*, 417). The ride with Elstir may be visually liberating, but an overturning of our epistemological frames is not what the ride either offers or delivers. It teaches us that "surfaces and volumes" can be momentarily detached from "the names which our memory imposes on things once we have recognized them," but never proposes that the severance be made permanent in the name of a higher knowledge.

In the closing pages of the novel, Proust returns one last time to the painter's way with "illusion," to "what painters have done so often when they have depicted, very close or very far away, depending on how the laws of perspective, the intensity of colour and our first illusory glance make them appear to us, a sail or a peak which the rational mind will then relocate, sometimes across enormous distance" (*T*, 355). One of Proust's points is to declare once again the solidarity of his own literary art with this version of the painter's art ("by doing everything I could to give the most exact transcription" of the sequence in which he perceives and recalls things, 354). But there is also another governing thought that runs in the opposite direction, an assertion linking the claims of the "rational mind" to the operations of Proust's own narrative as a system that not only knows how to distinguish the "illusory" and the "real," the true and the false, but whose task, consistently performed throughout the long unfolding of its manifold episodes, has been to validate and enact

[35]Landy, *Philosophy as Fiction*, 51.

that distinction: "There are of course many other errors of the senses, and we have seen how various episodes of this narrative had proved this to me, which falsify our perception of the real appearance of the world" (354). In respect of the kinds of aesthetic perception illustrated by Elstir's *Harbour at Carquethuit*, in chapter 6 we will see some of the mechanisms used, after having been "dazzled" by it, to adjust the "mirage" to a more accurate picture of reality. But since it is above all by the sea and in seascape that the blurring takes place, let us return to Venice with Ruskin, in a passage that also speaks of "doubt" over where the lines separating land and water, reality and reflection end, and in which it is not only a question of "mirages" but also of "ghosts" (of which in Proust there remains much more to see). It is a beautiful passage at the beginning of *The Stones of Venice*, which steals quietly upon us, very different from Ruskin's more overbearing manner. Proust nowhere comments on it, but it is hard to believe it did not catch his eye. Ruskin looks out over the lagoon and registers "a ghost upon the sands of the sea—so quiet, so bereft of all but her loveliness, that we might well doubt, as we watched her faint reflection in the mirage of the lagoon, which was City, and which was the Shadow."[36]

[36] Ruskin, *The Stones of Venice*, 3:17.

CHAPTER SIX

Walking on Stilts

WHAT HAPPENS TO THE narrator in Elstir's studio is one of the novel's richer peripeteia, at once adventure, turning point, and discovery, but the episode is not just a way station on the long, stately procession of the *Recherche* toward the ultimate enunciation of an aesthetic in which the delectation of private sensations is made to carry a whole ontology.[1] It is rather a crucible in which the Proustian conception of truth is woven as a tangled knot of competing demands, unresolved contradictions, and unanswered questions. If we try to disentangle the knot, we can pick out three major threads, each corresponding to a particular need or wish that, when combined, prove to be incompatible. There is the need for the "illusion," for its life-enhancing or life-protecting properties. The illusion is superior to knowledge because of its power to release the imagination into creative metamorphosis, remaking the world, playing with its forms like "God the Father," reminiscent perhaps of Nietzsche's god-artist in *The Birth of Tragedy* who plays freely with the world as plastic substance and shape. But there is also a need for the recognition that it is illusion; just as Elstir knows that what he brackets is in fact the case, so Proust acknowledges that when his narrator perceives a stretch of sea as a distant coastline, he is not seeing the world as it really is. And if the two needs diverge, calling on different resources and capacities of the mind, there is always a point where "truth" in the sense of the facts of the matter prevails over illusion, usually in the manner of a correction: "the mind quickly redistributed the elements into the categories which the impression had abolished" (*JF*, 415).

However, the two strains can perfectly well coexist, if a trifle tensely (Intelligence wagging a reproachful finger at Impression); one can legitimately enjoy the pleasures of the illusion while remaining aware that this is what it is. One name given to the sphere in which these pleasures can be had without epistemological blowback is "fantasy." This is the sphere in which godlike playing with the world can be more modestly represented as playing a rule-governed game that acknowledges the rights of the imagination to roam freely. An example is a minor digression embedded in the account of the view from the Balbec hotel window, in which

---

[1] One thinks of Kristeva's astonishing formulation: "Proust savours his *sensations* as if they were the *essence* of objects." *Time and Sense*, 211 (emphasis in original).

the narrator returns in memory to an earlier time in Paris: "in my rooms in Paris I heard squabbling, almost rioting in the streets." The rectification comes swiftly: what the narrator actually heard were the "rumbling" sounds of a vehicle. On the other hand, while identifying the true cause of what he "thought" he heard, the narrator persists in maintaining that this is literally what "my ear had really heard," a set of sounds that nevertheless "my mind knew is not made by wheels" (415). As such the formulation is incoherent, impossibly facing all which ways (what I had really heard as what I had in fact not heard). The point, however, is that while it is the auditory equivalent of the optical illusion, nothing hangs by it; it appears as an aside, only to fade instantly from view as the text moves on elsewhere.

There is a very great deal of this sort of thing in *À la recherche*. It is, simply put, Proust having fun, reveling in the freshness and wildness of special "effects" for their own sake—hearing a quarrel where there are no quarreling humans, finding the sea in the sky, watching ships "cantering across sunlit fields," or desks taking off "at high speed." Michael Wood boldly terms this the "Disney" side of Proust, where fantasy assumes full, unimpeded charge of the impression.[2] Censorious highbrows should beware here: Proust the lover of magic lantern shows would doubtless have been a fan of the more inventive Disney productions. Let's call it Proust's baroque side, artful games played with the rhetorical conceit.[3] The modalities can vary: elision ("I heard a quarrel" instead of "I thought I heard a quarrel"), or substitution (Elstir's "renaming" of ship as carriage). The effect is obtained by literalizing the conceit (the catachresis, in the other example, of desks having "legs" or "feet" with which they can "take off," S, 187). But literalizing is not the same as taking literally; it is a pretend literalness, itself a conceit. The whole business is safely ensconced inside a rule-bound literary universe, without consequences beyond the game. No one inside the game will actually be alarmed by the "alarming" sight of the ship locomoting up the slope in Elstir's picture (although Turner's navy man might well view the game he has been invited to join as merely silly, beneath the dignity of commonsensical and practical men).

But this agreeable position, at once undemanding and sophisticated, in which we can pleasurably suspend judgments of knowledge without renouncing them, unravels in the third thread of the tangled weave, where Proust appears to want the fantasy and the truth, not as separable domains of discourse and discovery, but as one and the same. Asserting that something is true while knowing it isn't is all very well if the assertion occurs in a make-believe game (the fantasy known to all children as "let's

[2] Wood, "Noises in the Street," 10.

[3] Leriche refers to "the baroque manner so dear to Proust." "Proust, an 'Art Nouveau' Writer?," 198.

pretend"). But in contexts unconstrained by an understood and shared set of ludic rules, asserting something as true while knowing it isn't is either a lie or a symptom of dissociation; if not circumscribed by the acknowledged conventions of fantasy, and unable to satisfy either the conditions of the "sincerity" or the "accuracy" tests, truth in this context is doomed to being the casualty of an impossibly demanding aesthetic. And it is perhaps because of that impossibility that Proust buries a worm in the apple, working quietly to weaken the more precariously outlandish commitments of his text, in particular to the flash perceptual event as the basis for a violation of the law of identity and difference (e.g., the "renaming" of sea as land) that lays claim to reflecting a truth of nature.

The escape route the text offers, its way of backing off from these violations, is one that itself goes back, from the captured "effect" to the explanatory cause, a reversal of the order first articulated in the narrator's remarks on what he calls the "Dostoyevsky side of Mme de Sévigné." At the beginning of part 11 of *À l'ombre des jeunes filles en fleurs*, the narrator treats the reader to a short lecture on the strange affinities between the seventeenth-century French writer and the nineteenth-century Russian writer; both have a tendency to put cause-and-effect sequences back to front. He also compares her to Elstir: "Mme de Sévigné is a great artist of the same family as a painter I was to meet at Balbec, Elstir, who was to have a profound influence on my way of seeing things. I realized at Balbec that her way of depicting things is the same as his, that is, she presents them in the order in which we perceive them, instead of explaining them by their causes" (232). However, where, by virtue of the sequential character of writing, both Mme de Sévigné and Dostoyevsky have the option—often exercised—of restoring the order in which cause precedes effect, this cannot be an option for the nontemporal pictorial art of Elstir. It is, however, adopted by the narrator's own account of that art, in the form of a naturalizing description whose purpose is to highlight the external accidents and contingencies of both locale and viewpoint that causally explain the internal pictorial effects of *Harbour at Carquethuit*.[4]

---

[4]In her study of the changes from draft version (in *Cahier* 28) to published version, Ariane Eissen argues that where the former is through and through "impressionist," focused entirely on the "effect," the latter is more concerned with the distinction between illusion and truth reflected in the prioritizing of "cause" over "effect." "Les marines d'Elstir," in *Art et littérature: Actes du congrès de la Société française de littérature générale et comparée* (Aix-en-Provence: Université de Provence, 1988), 219–27. But to claim that in the later version Proust simply *reverses* the cause-effect relation by stating the cause first, a move thus "totally in contradiction with Proust's theory, which consists in presenting first the sensation, then its cause" is to operate far too neat a reversal. It implies a view of Proust not as exploring, hesitating, and modifying but as simply and unambiguously changing his mind without reservation. Proust's text does not lend itself to such a view.

The fabulous imaginings and constellations that make up the "unreal and mystic picture"—masts as chimneys or steeples, churches standing in water, sails as sleeping butterflies, shrimping women as the denizens of an underwater grotto—are shown to have their origin in the scrupulously listed topographical particularities of the setting, the list itself inaugurated by the causal conjunction "because": if land and sea get confused, one with the other, it is "because inlets of sea indented the land," a detail augmented by "irregularities of coastline," "a beach that dipped down to the level of the sea at the two points closest to the land, a bend in the course of a river, the apparent contiguity of the cliffs bounding a bay, a recess of the coastline"—all so many facets of a landscape that both require and enable a perfectly "natural" explanation of what the narrator terms "eclipses of perspective" (415–16). There are many such naturalizations in the novel. For example, the "little brown dots" that the narrator sees high up in the sky at dusk in wartime Paris "might have been taken, in the blue evening, for gnats or birds. Similarly, a mountain seen from far away can be taken for a cloud." One notices the tentative and conditional status of these identifications—the conditional perfect of "might have been taken" and the material circumstance that explains the hypothetical perception (the little brown dots identifiable as gnats or birds only because seen from a distance, in the same way that "a mountain seen from far away can be taken for a cloud"). This is a case of an optical "effect" that is at once "unsettling" (Proust's term) and held in check by a countervailing knowledge—"the knowledge that each brown dot in the summer sky was neither a gnat nor a bird, but an aeroplane crewed by men who were watching over Paris" (*T*, 41). Appearances, in short, however quirkily interesting to the avant-garde eye, must not be taken for reality.

Causal explanation by reference to material contingencies and contiguities takes the "effect" out of the realm of the metaphorical (the figural name-giving of God the Father) and into the realm of the metonymic. Much has been written about the role of metonymy in *À la recherche* as an unobtrusively constraining force on the more intrepid moves of Proustian metaphor. The Carquethuit sequence, emphatic in its disregard for the unobtrusive, demonstratively brings the metonymic into the foreground. The description yields to a takeover by those elements of the text on which readers entranced by the unreal and mystic picture tend not to dwell. It is, however, the place where Proust leaves his skeptical calling card that invites a different sort of reading. Shortly before his first encounter with Elstir, the narrator watches the sun go down, confuses "a broad band of sky" with the sea ("which I thought was the sea") and imagines the scene "as though in an Impressionist painting" (Whistler is mentioned). He espies a ship on the horizon, so "absorbed and liquefied" by the latter that it "appears" to be the same color and for that reason "seems" to be made of "the same material" (*JF*, 385). Visual experience is thus dragged toward the domain of the ontological, as boat and horizon are felt to partake of the same material stuff. But the verbs "appear" and "seem" are stop signs placed in the path of ontologizing the phenomenological, and remind us that the perceptions in question are all about transient states of mind in equally transient states of the weather;[5] dependent on this and that variable, a change in both is always just around the corner (by the end of the season Balbec in summertime is seen as a mix of desert and ghost town).

There is something else too—the functional closeness of the verbs "appear" and "seem" to the preposition "like," the grammatical agent of simile, the less audacious cousin of metaphor. It brings us to another kind of contingency, internal and psychological (the subjectivity of comparison), and to another form of weakened commitment (the object not, boldly and brazenly, as something else, but, more modestly, as it appeared to me, provisionally, at this particular place at this particular time), and bearing in its train a further question: what it means to think Truth in terms of the "truths written with the aid of figures."

II

For a writer who appears to invest all in metaphor, as both capturing and preserving an extratemporal "essence" of things, Proust's text, including its more "theoretical" portions, is not only somewhat parsimonious in its use of the term "metaphor";[6] it can also be intriguingly relaxed over purely ad hoc uses of this quasi-sacred term of art, especially its uses as metaphor or analogy for something else. It is an even odder fact that the two prime examples of these uses are to be found at two capital moments in the enunciation of the Proustian aesthetic. One instance takes us back to the Elstir episode where, if we reread the relevant passage more carefully, we see that the word "metaphor" functions not as the classificatory term for a rhetorical operation but as an example of the operation itself. Elstir's art, we recall, is described as "metaphorical"; it names or renames by transporting the attributes of one thing to another across the logical

---

[5] For the role of weather (specifically of summer sunlight on water) in blurring the boundary between land and water, see also that most "Proustian" of novels, W. G. Sebald's *Austerlitz*: "But on bright summer days, in particular, so evenly disposed a luster lay over the whole of Barmouth Bay that the separate surfaces of sand and water, sea and land, earth and sky could no longer be distinguished" (London: Hamish Hamilton, 2001), 135.

[6] There are but twelve mentions of the term in the entire *Recherche*. In the narrator's meditation on literature in *Le Temps retrouvé*, there is but one mention, and just two in connection with Elstir's art.

space of identity structured according to the law that everything in the world is either p or not-p. The description, however, is at once more precise and more tentative than this audaciously modernist way with the doctrine of *ut pictura poesis*. Elstir's paintings are less metaphorical than akin ("analogous") to the metaphorical; the "charm" of his pictures "lay in a kind of metamorphosis of the things depicted, analogous to the poetical device known as metaphor." A literary term—"metaphor"—thus serves as itself a metaphor for a pictorial practice, and in this analogical appropriation of the figure of analogy we may already detect a degree of intellectual reserve; it is not that Elstir's work is something, categorically stated, but that it is merely like something, characterized by an affirmed resemblance to the canonical literary trope of resemblance.

The explicit comparison of Elstir's painting to poetic metaphor also serves to suggest an unstated similarity to, or tacit mise en abyme of, Proust's own writing. The analogical track is a two-way one, a self-confirming circle in which poetic metaphor furnishes an analogue for Elstir's painterly art, while the latter in turn stands as an analogue of Proust's literary art. The latter is, of course, arguably the most spectacularly elaborate tessellation of resemblances literary language has ever contrived, and in the meditative aftermath of the three successive involuntary memories that occur while the narrator is on his way to the Guermantes *matinée*, the momentous place of metaphor in the grand scheme of things is not only stated but enacted (it is our second capital moment), in and by a very famous sentence, governed by a rhythm of deferral and crescendo that delivers the word "metaphor" as the crowning glory of a whole aesthetic.

> One can list indefinitely in a description all the objects that figured in the place described, but the truth will begin only when the writer takes two different objects, establishes their relationship, the analogue in the world of art of the unique relation created in the world of science by the laws of causality, and encloses them within the necessary armature of a beautiful style [*les anneaux nécessaires d'un beau style*]. Indeed, just as in life, it begins at the moment when, by bringing together a quality shared by two sensations, he draws out their common essence by uniting them with each other, in order to protect them from the contingencies of time, in a metaphor. (*T*, 198)

If there is an account of what Proust means by "truths written with the aid of figures," it is here, in this orotund declaration of purpose, the project in which the "thread of life" will be spun as a unified metaphorical fabric, a network of similitudes and analogies resembling one vast sentence. The rhetorical conception also maps onto the "vitalist" conception. The "thread of life," we have seen, is Proust's own figure for his version of the Family Plot, the complex of "alliances" forged by marriage and offspring (Gilberte's daughter as the critical juncture at which the "ways" meet). Another of Proust's terms for metaphor is "alliance de mots,"[7] and what metaphors and families, rhetoric and biology have in common is the "coupling" of difference: "After all," the narrator reflects, "the coupling of opposites is the law of life, the principle of fertilization" (P, 95). But an even profounder law of life (as of art) is what lies outside the sanction of law, in the "illicit couplings" that are not only biologically fruitful in embroidering and diversifying the "thread" of kinship, but are also, in certain traditions of rhetorical commentary, what metaphor thrives on as the transgressive coupling of terms that do not belong in the same semantic "family": [8] "Relationships not sanctioned by the law can give rise to family connections no less varied and complex, only more solid, than those created by marriage" (P, 240); Gilberte herself is a case in point; while the text is not fully clear, it seems she is born before Swann and Odette marry.[9]

Yet if we look again at the imposing sentence, we see that there is a dissonant note in the tightly wrought and beautifully modulated hymn to the power and the glory of metaphor. Even as syntactic deferral makes of the word "metaphor" itself the object of an oracular unveiling (a "revelation" in its own right), we notice en route to the postponed declarative moment the sideways reach not just for a rationalizing "analogy," but curiously for the most opportunistically imaginable one: literary metaphor is "the analogue in the world of art of the unique relation created in the world of science by the laws of causality." The thought appears to be that where Elstir's painting is "like" metaphor in literature, metaphor in literature is "like" (an analogue of) causality in science. But this flies in the face of everything Proust has to say about the fundamental difference between literature and science, and the relative unimportance of "causes" when set alongside "effects." Whatever metaphorical representation is or resembles, the one thing that it is not "like" is causal explanation; and even if, as in connection with the description of Carquethuit, the causal can in practice come to usurp the metaphoric, in the Proustian ideology of art, which the sentence so splendidly affirms and confirms, the meta-

---

[7] In a draft version of the famous passage on metaphor in Le Temps retrouvé, what was to become "les anneaux nécessaires d'un beau style" in the published text was first formulated as "le lien indestructible d'une alliance de mots." ARTP, 4:1265.

[8] The two kinds of "coupling"—the sexual and the figurative—are elatedly joined in the Charlus-Jupien pickup scene: the juxtaposition of the "coupling" of orchid and bee with that of Charlus and Jupien provides the terms of an analogy that in turn "couples" the two events.

[9] Odette badgers Swann, especially in light of the example of one of her friends who marries her lover "although she did not even have a child with him" (JF, 42). More straightforwardly, "the purpose of Swann's marrying Odette was to introduce her and Gilberte . . . to the Duchesse de Guermantes" (45).

phoric, as medium for the translation of the impression, is always posited as the superior alternative to the causal, that which puts the "effect" first (in all the senses of "firstness" we have previously considered). Why then did Proust appear to feel the need for something with which to fortify the justification of metaphor, and why for the expression of that need did he choose such a transparently implausible analogy, the one more than any other likely to discredit intellectually the very principle he sought to defend?

That question becomes all the more pressing when we put this grand sentence back into relation with the incidents of which it is supposed to be the resounding explication, the sudden revelations in the Guermantes courtyard and library. It explains what the narrator-artist thinks he has to do with what has just happened to him—capture, from the repetition of the past in the present, a "common essence" understood as "a quality shared by two sensations" in a "metaphorical" structure that is home to a set of deciphered "meanings" (187–91). But if this is what the narrator prescribes for his experiences in the courtyard and the library, in what Proust's writing actually does with them—in the account of "the image each evoked"—there are, properly speaking (as it were), virtually no metaphors at all, other than banal or atrophied ones (dead images of Venice in the dead metaphor of "snapshots of memory"; the vision of azure that "intoxicated my eyes"; the feeling of happiness that "flooded over me," 177). These are just tokens, inert nominal and verbal carriers of the real action, which lies with a series of images that are intense, immediate, and synesthetically charged (from touch to color to scent to taste). But the images are not metaphors in the definition of the latter as the (re) naming of something as something else. They are the Open Sesames of the memory-box, reviving and liberating what is otherwise condemned to lie dead in the mind, but they do not involve giving either new or wrong names to things. The images are not substitutions, one thing represented as another, but repetitions, the same thing staged twice across a wide span of time separating them: the touch of a napkin in the Guermantes house sets in motion a spontaneous recollection of the touch of a napkin in the Balbec hotel, which then exfoliates by lateral association onto a whole world of recollected sensation that is metonymically driven and ingathered (namely, the vision of azure arising from the contiguous relation of the Balbec setting to the blue sea and sky). To call this metaphorical is, again, to use "metaphor" metaphorically; it is another analogy. In fact, the closest these richly concentrated two pages get to metaphor in the classical sense of the term is the expansion of the "vision of azure" into the multicolored plumage of a peacock ("the plumage of an ocean green and blue as a peacock tail"). But this is less metaphor as substitutive identity-switch than a version of simile (to the narrator's mind the superimposition of remembered colors on the spread and folds of the napkin bring him to see it as being "like" a peacock's tail).

There are strange happenings and nonhappenings here. The "theoretical" sentence states, amazingly albeit parenthetically, that metaphor possesses something "like" the explanatory properties of scientific causality, and yet when referred back to the sequence from which it emerges and which it is designed to explicate, we find it "explains" or interprets virtually nothing, precisely because the sequence itself contains no exemplifying or illustrative instances of what the sentence is supposed to explain. What then is so miraculous about the proclaimed "miracle of an analogy," akin to the "heavenly food" of the Eucharist and announcing the moment of a spiritual rebirth ("the being which had been reborn in me," 180–81)? This is a modernist testament to analogy in terms reminiscent of the medieval theology of the *figura*.[10] But perhaps we are more likely to end by describing analogy as "miraculous" only in the loosely casual (analogical) manner in which the term is often used in everyday discourse to denote chance events of the mind,[11] what the narrator calls "a simple chance of association of thoughts" (*S*, 89), or the product of "fugitive and fortuitous impressions" (*CG*, 88).[12] A celebrant before the altar of the form-giving powers of metaphorical construction, Proust also knows that belief in miracles is another instance of magical thinking,[13] and that the truth of the matter is that "[w]e have only formless, fragmented visions of the world which we fill out with arbitrary associations of ideas, creating dangerous suggestions," *F*, 538). None is more dangerous than the idea that "alliances" are necessary and permanent by virtue of being

---

[10] Proust encountered the medieval *figura* in Ruskin's investigations of the Gothic cathedral as the embodiment of a "typological" language that was to be "read at the four levels of the literal, the figural, the moral and the anagogical." Diane R. Leonard, "Proust and Ruskin 2000: 'Ces étoiles éteintes dont la lumière nous arrive encore,'" in *Proust in Perspective*, ed. Mortimer and Kolb, 214.

[11] Nearly all the instances of the term "miracle" in the *Recherche* have to do with chance and probability (for example, the narrator hoping for the "miracle" of Swann and Gilberte appearing on the Champs-Elysées, or the Charlus-Jupien encounter as a "miracle" in the same way that the bee lighting on that particular orchid is a matter of pure chance).

[12] Paul de Man characterized the entire structure of Proust's metaphorical language as "a figural play in which contingent figures of chance masquerade deceptively as figures of necessity," but where the mask keeps slipping, the true face of the figural revealed in the wayward and the aleatory moves of the mind. *Allegories of Reading*, 67. As previously noted, de Man's account is premised on a general view of language as preprogrammed to run on a one-way track, from construction to deconstruction; perversely, the force of the aleatory has all the authority of a cast-iron law of discourse. The whole argument of this book has been that Proust's way is multitrack, and that it is Proust, not some anonymous "agent," that travels it.

[13] One of the other "miracles" in the novel is the narrator hearing his grandmother on the telephone, also described as a form of "magic" (*CG*, 130).

providentially foreordained; even when, as in the manuscript sketches, described as "indestructible," alliances (whether of people or words) are optional, fragile, and can always be broken.

III

It remains nevertheless a truth widely acknowledged that metaphor in Proust is a serious business. In particular, failure to distinguish the figural and the literal is no joke, and requires in extremis medical intervention for those who stubbornly and foolishly insist on making it a laughing matter: one of the causes of Cottard having to reset Madame Verdurin's dislocated jaw after "laughing too much" is "her habit of taking literally the figurative expressions of the emotions she was feeling" (S, 192). But Madame Verdurin is not alone in her bad habit. Cottard may be adept at setting Madame Verdurin's jaw straight, but her hysterical theatrics are more than matched by his irritatingly "insatiable passion for figures of speech." Cottard's passion, however, has less to do with emotional theater than more with a childlike marveling before the extraordinary fact that words can actually signify beyond their literal sense (a "miracle" in its original sense of object of wonderment): "he wanted to know exactly what was meant by those [expressions] he had heard used most often: the bloom of youth, blue blood, a fast life, the hour of reckoning, to be a prince of refinement, to give carte blanche, to be nonplussed, etc." (203). The "etc." is a very nice finishing touch to the rudiments of a cliché-catalog that could clearly go on forever. Proust himself rounds it off (for now, the theme will reemerge later) with Madame Verdurin inviting Cottard to join her and her husband at a performance by Sarah Bernhardt. "'Sarah Bernhardt—she is in fact the Golden Voice, isn't she? And they often write that she sets the stage on fire. That's an odd expression, isn't it?' in the hope of commentaries that were not forthcoming" (204).

Commentary may—mercifully—be unforthcoming, but there is commentary aplenty elsewhere in the novel on the nature and significance of the figurative expression, most notably from the narrator in his guise as an amateur historian of language. There are his scattered thoughts on the prelapsarian beginnings of language as hieroglyph and ideogram before it falls under the regime of abstraction and the "arbitrariness" of the sign ("those peoples who adopt a phonetic script only after having used characters as symbols," P, 77), along with the aching counterfactual speculation while listening to the Vinteuil septet as to what human communication might have been if music rather than language had been its medium ("I wondered whether music were not the sole example of the form which might have served—had language, the form of words, the possibility of analyzing ideas, never been invented—for the communication of souls," 237). These, however, are more nostalgic and fanciful musings than historical observations. The two contexts for the latter are etymology (of which we shall see something in chapter 8) and tropology.

There are many reflections in *À la recherche* on the fate of the trope in time and history, largely as the tale of an original freshness and a subsequent fatigue, as figure loses its original force in direct proportion to acquiring a second-nature literalness. The pleasurable recovery of something of that original vitality is one facet of the more general project of recovering Time Lost. An early example is the way the young boy's imagination is seized by the style of *François le Champi*, in particular the charm of "the old ways of speaking in which we see a metaphor that is obliterated in our language, by the abrasion of habit . . . like an old piece of furniture, full of expressions that had fallen into disuse and turned figurative again" (*S*, 44). An example of the converse process is the effect of routinized sexual relations on the expression "make cattleyas," used by Swann and Odette in the first moments of their affair as a "metaphor" in a private code of intimacy that eventually is emptied of all personal color to become "a simple utterance they used without thinking about it when they wanted to signify the act of physical possession" (237).

These are, however, but passing remarks, made while on the narrative move. Where the narrator pauses for his lengthiest comment on the cultural and historical fortunes of the figurative within given speech-communities is during his discussion of the prose of the writer-mentor, Bergotte, in both its written and conversational forms:

> as anything new must first do away with the stereotype we are so used to that we have come to see it as reality itself, any new style of conversation, just like any originality in painting or music, will always seem convoluted and wearisome. We find its structuring figures so unwonted that the talker seems to be nothing more than a metaphor-monger, which wearies the ear and hints at a lack of truthfulness. (Of course, the earlier speech-forms themselves were once images, which a listener unfamiliar with the world they described had difficulty in grasping. But they have long since come to be taken as the real world, the reliable world.) (*JF*, 127–28)

The passage addresses several Proustian concerns, but it is basically a set of observations on the function of linguistic originality, likened, in yet another analogical elaboration of Analogy, to "originality in painting or music." Figures of speech redescribe reality in a challenge to the inertia of the "stereotype we are so used to that we have come to see it as reality itself." "Like" avant-garde art (Elstir's painting, Vinteuil's music), metaphor denaturalizes and defamiliarizes, and is for that reason experienced by most members of the speech community as "convoluted" and "wearisome" relative to the taken-for-grantedness of everyday idiom. But what its speakers have forgotten is that much in a socially naturalized idiom was itself once new, fresh, and "difficult," and comes to seem natural only when drained of figural energy. The narrator's point is that what we take for the literal often originates as a metaphor that is no longer perceived to be such once the work of time and habit has emptied it of its original liveliness (the process whereby the "legs" of a table or a desk are understood solely as inanimate and inert supports). It is only in reactivating the dead metaphorical content that we see "legs" as involving notions of locomotion (the table can walk, like Proust's desks "taking off").

As already pointed out, this crossing of semantic frontiers is harmless when confined to a game whose rules are known to all its players. Madame Verdurin appears to have forgotten the rules and gets into trouble as a consequence. Cottard's confusions (both active and passive) are, however, of a different kind. The distinctive feature of Cottard's "passion" is his sense of astonishment and consternation before a dead metaphor, and his ardently necrophiliac ransacking of the linguistic tomb in the ill-understood but in some ways admirable attempt to bring it back to life. On Odette's relations with Swann he ruminates: "'you mean she is on the most intimate footing with him, she has given him the key to her city,' asked the doctor, cautiously testing the meaning of the expressions" (S, 230); and even when much later, having acquired a belief in his own mastery of the art of the trope, he throws caution to the winds, taunting the inept "Cancan" (M. de Cambremer) for his use of the "'ready-made' expression" and bombarding him with a litany of examples designed to show his newly acquired social sophistication, he merely confirms the grip of his original obsession: "Why 'dull as ditchwater'? Do you think ditchwater is duller than anything else? You say 'forty winks.' But why forty particularly? Why 'sleep like a log'? Why 'go west'? Why 'paint the town red'? (SG, 320).

À la recherche is, of course, a novel that surveys most of the vices, foibles, and absurdities of the human comedy, but this one in particular seems to belong in a special class. However ridiculous (and ridiculed), in his own clumsy way Cottard is, along with the booming Prince de Foix, an incomparable educator. Where, in his hearty fashion, the prince unwittingly sheds light on a narrative structure governed by losing and finding, Cottard's naive questions and exclamations illuminate the strange complexity of the literal/figural relation that comes to light when tropes are brought back from the dead and the shroud of habit is removed from the erstwhile corpse. He spots that what lies buried in the dead metaphor is the very thing that contributes to its animation when "alive," namely, its literal content, the transfer to something (the town) of a set of predicates (painted red) that do not belong with it but that are essential to the way the expression's "novelty" works on the mind of its receiver. No wonder that he has a question, even if his social superiors—and a certain class of Proust's readers—would see it as the equivalent of the village idiot's question.

When the narrator speaks of the "truths written with the aid of figures," he adds "the meaning of which I was trying to find in my head." The Search is thus also the search for ("trying to find") the meanings of metaphors assumed to be "hidden" and accessible to the seeker only when subjected to an activity of "decipherment." There is, however, a lesson for the questing narrator's obsession with concealed meanings in the linguistic gawking of Cottard. If he wonders about the true sense of the "fast life," this is because he is trying to imagine a form of life literally unfolding at high speed, like a vehicle motoring fast. This, unbelievably, makes of Cottard a sort of unconscious Davidsonian.[14] The Davidson school of thought has taught us to be wary of a theory of metaphor based on the view that metaphor has any "hidden" or secondary meaning at all. According to Davidson, the meaning of a metaphor is simply what the words that compose it actually say, their literal content.[15] The meaning of "he is a lion" is not that he is unusually strong or fearless, but that he is a lion. Naturally, that way madness lies, a semantic version of the optical illusion pushing on the hallucinatory, and certainly a much graver condition than Mme Verdurin's dislocated jaw. But this unhappy outcome arises only if the literal meaning brings us to take the expression for reality itself (having "legs," the desk really can walk). This is to misunderstand the actual purpose of metaphor, which is less to convey a meaning than to act as a pragmatic indicator (of a perceived or imagined resemblance). In the Davidsonian scheme, metaphor, as a pointer to an alleged resemblance between two things, is in effect a compressed simile. Unbeknownst to him, Cottard's slow-witted learning curve in the fast lane turns out improbably to be a minor tutorial in the philosophy of rhetoric.

IV

Formally, metaphor proposes an identification, either as a substitution of identities (renaming x as y) or as a conjunction of identities (Proust's "alliance de mots," typically the synesthetic splicing of a noun and an adjective, which effects a transfer of sensory predicates from one sphere

[14] "Sort of" covers a multitude of intellectual sins (analogy gone mad, we might say), but the general idea should be clear.

[15] Donald Davidson, "What Metaphors Mean," in *Inquiries into Truth and Interpretation* (Oxford: Oxford University Press, 2001).

to another).[16] Simile, on the other hand, proposes a comparison mediated syntactically by "as" or "like" or by verbs such as "appear" and "seem."[17] The substitutive has total courage of its commitments. The comparative differs from the substitutive in that it openly advertises the rhetorical nature and subjective origins of the comparison. While the modalities of the figural in Proust are multiple (such that classifying them can come out sounding like Polonius), by far and away the commonest form is the more tentative simile, one of its functions indeed being to decompress and thus relativize the more absolutist character of "pure" metaphorical substitution. Quite often in the *Recherche* we find simile folded "inside" metaphor (as an explanatory parenthesis), or placed before it as a frame that serves to remind us of the comparative beginnings of the metaphorical representation, however bold the forms taken by the latter. Consider two sky-views, one from the first volume, one from the last. In the Bois de Boulogne the sunlight "thickens" the leaves of the chestnut trees and "cements" them against the sky, but the sentence in which these powerfully artisanal, metaphorical verbs appear qualifies and moderates that power by the quasi-parenthetical insertion of similes between the two verbs: the sunlight thickens the leaves "like bricks" and cements them "like a piece of yellow Persian masonry patterned in blue" (*S*, 425–26). In the second example, the narrator looks at the twilight sky over wartime Paris, in particular "that part of the city dominated by the towers of the Trocadéro": "the sky looked like a vast turquoise-coloured sea on the ebb." The comparison undergoes both a change of visual terms (from horizontal water to vertical icebergs) and a change of rhetorical form

---

[16] For example, the "golden" quality of the sound of the Combray bell or the "dark coolness" of the narrator's Combray room. The latter example is the one deployed by Paul de Man in his claim that "[t]he crossing of sensory attributes in synaesthesia is only a special case of a more general pattern of substitution that all tropes have in common" (*Allegories of Reading*, 62). In Proust the synesthetic image is not just a "special case" in the sense of a particular class of the figural, but special, period, a fundamental mechanism of the associative fabric of recollection from which whole worlds are exfoliated. The analogy-spinning of synesthetic perception is, however, notoriously vulnerable to the charge of arbitrariness and bad faith (the masking of an aesthetic convention as if it were a fact of nature). At its worst, in, for example, some of the minor symbolists to whom the young Proust was drawn, it degenerates into fake, mannered preciosity. Anatole France mocked it by focusing on the purely arbitrary relations between vowel sounds and color values: "M René Ghil says that O is blue and M. Rimbaud says that O is orange" (cited in Emeric Fiser, *La théorie du symbole littéraire et Marcel Proust* [Geneva: M. E. Slatkine, 1992], 198).

[17] In many of the standard accounts, simile is but a subset of the more general class of metaphor. Nevertheless, to say something is something else and to say something is like something else are two very different propositions. That difference is crucial for the argument here. Ellison notes Ruskin's stated preference for simile ("the clarity and explicitness of simile to the melted significant unity of metaphor"). David Ellison, *The Reading of Proust* (Baltimore: Johns Hopkins University Press, 1984), 59.

(from simile to metaphor); seized with a kind of "vertigo," the narrator perceives it as "no longer a level sea but a vertical progression of glaciers" (*T*, 70–71). Inside a semihallucinatory metaphor of this type, the reader may well be inclined to share the narrator's sense of vertigo, but can do so only up to a point, since our response has already been shaped by the more makeshift "looked like"; the vertiginous metaphor is but an extension in elliptical form of an original and governing simile.

In this connection, let us return to the seascapes of Carquethuit, this time in order to compare and contrast them with the steeples of Martinville. The juxtaposition furnishes a prism through which we can see Proust experimenting with his deepest stylistic interests as if on a revolving axis of uncertainties and second thoughts. Martinville is one of the obligatory stopping-off points for Proust criticism, the equivalent of the disciple's pilgrimage to Illiers-Combray, though it is certainly not the case that all go to Martinville simply to worship at a shrine. Martinville is nevertheless special not just by virtue of its "modernist" dedication to mobile perspective in which the object-world forms, dissolves, and reforms according to the shifting positions of the viewer, but also because of the dual or reflexively self-mirroring structure of the same scene written twice, first in the narrative (the narrator's account of his impressions on the carriage ride with Dr. Percepied) and then their translation into the "little prose poem." In this duplicated form, Martinville resembles Carquethuit: in both cases there is a movement or transfer from artwork to surrounding description, albeit as reverse trajectories (from Elstir's painting to narrator's description with Carquethuit, from narrator's description to his sketch of a prose poem with Martinville). Both cases, however, involve a shuttling between metaphor and simile.

The changing views of the steeples from Dr. Percepied's carriage are almost uniformly controlled by the verbs of "appearance" and the syntax of "as if": the two steeples of Martinville are shown as "appearing to change position with motion of our carriage and the windings of the road"; the steeple of Vieuxvicq, which, though at some distance from the Martinville steeples, "seemed to be right next to them"; on the approach to Martinville "the steeples appeared so distant and we seemed to approach them so slowly, that I was surprised when we stopped a few moments later in front of the Martinville church"; in the fading light "their lines and sunlit surfaces split apart as if they were a sort of bark." The draft of the prose poem, however, removes most (but not all) of the phenomenological markers of "seeming" and "appearing," as well as the comparative prepositions "like" and "as." In their place, we have full-fledged anthropomorphic verbs of agency involving transfer of the effect on perception created by the transitory movements of the carriage ride to the properties of the objects observed from the carriage; the represented entity *becomes*, as if a matter of fact, what it is represented as being or doing. The steeples of Martinville "ascended towards the sky"; they are joined by the "laggard" Vieuxvicq steeple "wheeling around boldly to position itself opposite them"; the Martinville steeples are "illuminated by the sun which I saw playing and smiling"; the steeples "flung themselves . . . roughly in front of us"; the carriage moves farther away, and "lingering alone on the horizon" all three steeples "watch us flee . . . waving good-bye with their sunlit tops"; one steeple "would draw aside so that the other two could glimpse us again"; a farther bend in the road and "they swung round"; finally figured as three girls, the narrator sees them "timidly seek their way . . . press against one another, slip behind one another . . . and fade away into the night" (*S*, 180–82).

There are as many interpretive readings of the two versions of the steeples of Martinville as there are views of the steeples in the text itself, but the variations reduce to a basic either/or polarity: Which of the two accounts is a truer reflection of Proust's artistic aims, the surrounding narrative or the little prose poem? There are those who read the prose poem as a mise en abyme of the integrating metaphorical dynamic of the whole work, an anticipatory microcosm of the centripetal force field *À la recherche* aspires to be. On the other side of the argument, there are those who see the prose poem as a very "Proustian" and yet ultimately abortive experiment, a failed "detour" that fails by virtue of surrender to the centrifugal dynamic of purely serial metaphor and slapdash, uncoordinated associations.[18] It is the one-off and never-repeated effort of the artist as a *very* young man, the product of a youthful mind that, entranced by the newfound resources of metaphorical naming and renaming (steeples as, in rapid succession, flowers, birds, girls, etc.), is "seized by a sort of drunkenness."

I have already suggested some reasons why it is not sensible to take the little prose poem as a proleptic mirror image of the whole work.[19] The relation of the former to the latter is rather that of a might-have-been, a possibility considered and then discarded, another in the list of prelapsarian counterfactuals. What is far closer to the general character of Proust's text is the surrounding narrative in which the prose poem is embedded; through its constant reminders of the contingency of appearance and the subjectivity of comparison, it "lowers the aesthetic temperature" of the high-octane metamorphoses effected by the prose poem.[20] And in any case, even the prose poem retains a certain discretion before all-out figural anthropomorphism, by pulling back into the verbs of "seeming" and

[18] See the interesting study by Peter Collier and J. D. Whitely, "Proust's Blank Page," *Modern Language Review* 79, 3 (1984): 570–78.

[19] See chapter 2.

[20] Collier and Whitely, "Proust's Blank Page," 574.

the preposition "like," some of which indeed frame the wilder personifications (at the poem's point of departure), such that no matter how extended the metaphorical flight, the text and its reading remain anchored, in the same way as the view of the Trocadéro, to an origin in simile: "appearing lost in the open country"; "like three birds poised on the plain"; "swung round in the light, like three golden pivots"; "seeming now no more than three flowers, painted on the sky." Finally, the narrator's entire literary effort, the transposition of visual impression into the language of prose poetry, is prefaced by another "analogy": "Without saying to myself that what was hidden behind the steeples of Martinville had to be something analogous to a pretty sentence . . . I asked the doctor for a pencil and some paper."

Here we have a sentence, pretty or otherwise, that speaks of the "pretty sentence" (*jolie phrase*) as an unconscious "analogy" for a set of visual experiences, in a manner reminiscent of "metaphor" as analogy for Elstir's way of painting Carquethuit ("analogous to the poetical device known as metaphor"). And however radical Elstir's chiastic pictorial metaphors, the narrator's own descriptions of both the painting and its objects consistently marry the naturalistic topography we have already considered (with its focus on physical and perspectival contingencies) to the language of subjectively grounded "appearances": "masts rose above roofs, like chimneys or steeples [echo of Martinville here?] as though making citified things of the ships . . . an illusion enhanced by other boats lying alongside the pier"; "the churches of Criquebec, which seemed to be standing in water"; "[m]en pushing boats out moved in the tide as on the sand, which, being wet, reflected the hulls as though it were water"; ships "seemed to be sailing in the thick of buildings"; shrimpers looked "as though they were in an under-sea grotto"; the sea heaves "as though it were a swift and spirited animal"; a "yawl" that is "shaken about like a farm-cart" and "controlled as though with reins."

Nearly all of Proust's translations of natural or social scenes into watery worlds are rhetorically constructed in this manner, where metaphor is an outcrop or derivative of simile. When taken by Saint-Loup to the restaurant at Rivebelle, the narrator views the dining room and its occupants as if he were looking into a fishbowl (*JF*, 393): "the place looked like a tank or a creel which a fisherman has filled with his shiny catch, some of the fish being half out of water, their sheen glinting and changing under glossy lights." But the scene in the Rivebelle restaurant also contains a lesson on the conditions under which some things can come to look "like" others. For it is here that the narrator gets drunk (imbibing "an amount of beer, let alone of champagne, which I would not have wanted to drink in a week at Balbec," *JF*, 390) and boasts of the heightened power granted by the state of intoxication to compare one thing with another, in an echo—

literal rather than figurative—of the narrator being moved to jot down the little prose poem while "seized by a sort of drunkenness": "I could see the round tables, a countless constellation of them filling the restaurant like so many planets" (391). Unlike the poor, benighted diners who remain trapped and lost in the mundane, the narrator who reaches for the stars is aided by "the harmony of these astral tables." The extraterrestrial trip becomes an occasion for self-congratulatory condescension: "I felt rather sorry for the diners, because I sensed that for them the tables were not planets, and that they were unpractised in the art of cross-sectioning things so as to rid them of their customary appearance and enable us to see analogies." The figurative "drunkenness" of Martinville thus becomes literal at Rivebelle, while, as analogy-generating condition, remaining a prodigal source or cause of the figurative. But it is surely a case of pitying the pitier here. The spectacle gives—and is presumably designed to give—("unlicensed") metaphor-making a bad name; it is not an especially fine advertisement for Proust among the stars.

V

Someone whom we have seen as highly practiced in astral imaginings is the narrator's restaurant companion. But since Saint-Loup's representations of Rachel as having "an astral quality, even something quite vatic" are felt to be absurd because produced by the intoxicating and madness-inducing rush of desire, it seems reasonable to infer that in the restaurant episode Proust is tarring his narrator with the same brush when he in turn takes an alcohol-fueled trip to the stars. Is, then, Proustian comedy marching here into territory notionally secured against satirical incursion? Nothing in Proust, of course, ever marches anywhere, certainly not in a straight line, above all when under the influence of the aroused imagination ("seeking happiness through satisfying my inner desires was as naive an undertaking to reach the horizon by simply walking forward in a straight line," *F*, 417). In principle analogy is untouchable. The narrator describes it as "miraculous" and the use—his use—of figures as "sacred." But the same uncritical reverence is not extended to others, and, as we shall see shortly, the narrator will become perplexed, edgy, or censorious when hearing or overhearing acquaintances speaking in the same way as himself. Is there then another kind of "dangerous intimacy" here, another context for the form of Proustian comedy in which his characters are used to expose something amiss in the ideals and passions of his narrator, in this particular case, the worship of tropes? We can, of course, discount those who, from the purely philistine point of view, mock or disapprove of the narrator's literary hopes and endeavors; the joke is on them. These include the Duc de Guermantes, commenting on the narrator's article in *Le Figaro*: "He regretted the somewhat hackneyed form of my style, which was 'as inflated and metaphorical as Chateaubriand's outmoded prose' " (*F*, 553). That the Duc de Guermantes would take a view on literary matters, and especially on the character and standing of Chateaubriand's prose, is itself something of a minor event in the drama of narrative oxymoron. Norpois also takes a dim view of the narrator's literary ambitions; the tremulous young hero shyly shows his little prose poem to the diplomat who, after reading it, "handed it back to me without a word" (*JF*, 29). The "word" comes indirectly a page later, with Norpois's remarks on "a certain politician known for preposterous utterances larded with mixed metaphors" (32). "Be warned" is the clear implication. But a warning from the cliché-monger, who makes of dead metaphor a cadaverous art form in its own right, is not one to which we are likely to pay the slightest heed.

There are, however, other voices that might catch our attention in rather unusual ways. Mme de Villeparisis is amused by her niece's remark about the queen of Sweden ("I was just telling these gentlemen that you thought she looked like a frog"). " 'It's purely arbitrary, all the same,' replied Mme de Guermantes" (*CG*, 207). This is in principle noteworthy, especially when we recall that in the course of the novel Proustian humanity is effortlessly compared to all manner of beast, fowl, and fish (looking like a frog is the least of it). Yet while the thought of Oriane holding forth with a quasi-Saussurian view of the "arbitrary" nature of the figurative sign and a quasi-Humean view of the aleatory (mental) association is truly impressive, her own intention is to impress for a different reason and in a different way, by imitating the speech of her witty friend and habitué, Charles Swann ("emphasizing her choice of adjective as Swann would have done"). The way Swann would have done it, or in fact actually does it, is a further source of laughter, this time from Oriane herself. In the company of Madame de Sainte-Euverte, Swann compliments Oriane on her hat by playing figuratively with the artificial fruits that decorate it: "Swann, who was accustomed, when he was in the company of a woman whom he kept up the habit of addressing in gallant language, to say things so delicately nuanced that many society people could not understand them, did not condescend to explain to Mme de Sainte-Euverte that he had been speaking metaphorically. As for the Princesse, she began laughing" (*S*, 343).

Talking in metaphor here is talking in code, the social code of "wit" where metaphor is manipulated for worldly ends, as a finely wrought compliment but also as the put-down designed to leave Madame de Sainte-Euverte baffled and humiliated. Oriane laughs to show her complicitous understanding of the language game as a mark of rank and a manifestation of social power. Similarly, her relative, Charlus, ever intent on the display of social caste, issues a rebuke to Jupien in the famous seduction scene at the beginning of *Sodome et Gomorrhe*: "I can see you have no ear for metaphors" (16). There are other class-bound ways of not having an ear appropriately attuned for metaphor, for example, the liftboy's in the Balbec hotel, which so irritates the fastidiously patronizing young narrator: "I found it hard to forgive him also for employing certain terms of his trade, which would for that reason have been perfectly suitable if used literally, only in a figurative sense, which lent them a somewhat puerile pretension to wit" (*SG*, 193). There is, it would seem, figure and figure, wit and wit. But this hostility to the mix of figural and literal usages by the lower orders ("trade") will rebound on the narrator later, in connection with Albertine's speech and in terms that suggest that it is very much part of Proust's explicit intention that it be seen rebounding.

Figures of speech are thus assumed to possess a certain cachet. There are those who command the discourse as an instrument of social authority, and those who wish to master it as a sign of acceptance or advancement. Cottard is one of the latter, if also redeemed by his infectious and unconsciously probing curiosity. Perhaps even more revealing of Proust's critical and satirical purpose is the wretched Prince von Faffenheim, the ambassador anxious to please in smart Parisian circles and desperate to be elected a member of the Institut. In the Guermantes salon he attempts a literary flourish when the conversation turns to Rachel and Saint-Loup: "'I run into her occasionally in the morning on the Champs-Elysées. She's rather flighty, as you put it, what you call *loose*, a kind of "Dame aux Camélias," figuratively speaking of course.' These words were addressed to me by Prince Von, with that desire of his to appear conversant with French literature and the refinements of Paris" (*SG*, 508). The truly priceless Faffenheim moment, however, comes in his protracted efforts to secure Norpois's support for nomination to the Institut. In his calculation of what he might offer Norpois in exchange for that support, he uses the "system of inference as he had used it in his diplomatic career, the same method of reading beneath superimposed symbols" (*CG*, 257). This is almost too good to be true; "superposition" is a Proustian *mot-clef*, a keystone of the novel's metaphorical architecture.[21] The slyly inquiring and ingratiating diplomat "reads" his opposite number in the palimpsest-like way we are supposed to read Proust's novel, layer upon layer!

But the speech mode that most uncannily resembles the Proustian manner, as its parodic negative, is that which adopts the rhetorical style precisely as "manner," in the less flattering sense of the term. "Manner" and "mannerism" are the stains imprinted on figurative language by

---

[21] Bowie, "Reading Proust Between the Lines," 126.

misuse, and many in the *Recherche* stand accused.[22] Swann's verbal embroidery of Mme de Sainte-Euverte's hat is pure preciosity. Saint-Loup's passion corrupts his normally intelligent conversation ("steeped in certain of the mannerisms current in the literary circles in which the lady moved"). And there is "the Bergotte manner" (*JF*, 126), generally understood and admired by the narrator as an example of a truly original "style" whose sheer novelty captivates him; what he seeks in Bergotte's written and spoken language is an equivalent of what he will find in Elstir ("I wanted to possess . . . a metaphor of his, for everything in the world"; and in particular for "certain seascapes," *S*, 97). There is, however, also a less appealing aspect of the style, where "the manner" comes across as affectation. Bergotte shows off his knowledge of the linguistically arcane by referring to Cottard as that "ludion" (128). The French term has a history; as a technical term, it is the name of a scientific experiment known in English as the "Cartesian diver" or "devil" (an experiment where a small tube inside a flexible container filled with liquid goes down when pressure is applied and up when pressure is released). Its figurative meaning designates someone who is indecisive, the passive victim of external influences. Poor Cottard thus gets it in the neck again, although, had he been within earshot, excitement would doubtless have won out over humiliation; as a man of science he would know the original experimental meaning, but probably not its figurative extension, to signify what he himself, in Bergotte's view, is supposed to be. The term "ludion" is cited as an example of the narrator's thesis on the figure as taxingly unfamiliar, but it makes just as much sense to see it as one of the many instances of the *recherché* in the *Recherche*, tinged moreover with something of the cruelty of Swann's performance.

There is just too much going on in this collection of speech styles and speakers, dispersed across the cast of Proust's characters, for us to fail to take note of how a certain idea of literary "style" can get contaminated by extraliterary desires and interests. The prize for "manner," however, goes to Legrandin, at once aspirant poet and yearning arriviste, like Swann a summer inhabitant of Combray but unlike Swann not received in the social worlds he dreams of entering. He is highly regarded by the narrator's family, with, however, an important reservation: "[m]y grandmother reproached him only for speaking a little too well, a little too much like a book" (*S*, 70). That is polite understatement. Here he is on the banks of the Vivonne, floridly floral on the subject of the sky while talking of Balbec: "you will see blooming in the space of a few instants celestial bouquets of blue and pink" (131), and a few moments later on the sub-

---

[22] In *Jean Santeuil* it is the hero who stands accused of "affectation," by his teacher, Beulier, who reproaches him: "You must take care to get rid of all these metaphors, all these images." Cited in Compagnon, *Proust Between Two Centuries*, 176.

ject of trees: "I have friends wherever there are clusters of trees, wounded but not vanquished, which huddle together with touching obstinacy to implore an inclement and pitiless sky" (132). The reader's guffaw comes easily, but may suddenly choke with the realization that there is someone else in the novel who talks about trees in a not entirely dissimilar way.[23] Moreover, it does not stop with trees. "I had dinner with Legrandin on his terrace; the moon was shining," the narrator reports. Legrandin expatiates to his dinner guest: "a novelist whom you will read later asserts that the only fit companions are shadow and silence . . . when our ears cannot listen to any other music but that which is played by the moonlight on the flute of silence" (S, 128).[24] The novelist alluded to is Balzac (the epigraph from his novel, Le Médecin de campagne), but in another possible world—one in which the character might be acquainted with his author (we have already seen how Proust is open to such possibilities)—it could easily have been Proust, whose narrator, we will recall, reminds us over and over of the unique virtues of shadow and silence.

And so it is that, as if by an effect of delayed contagion, in Sodome et Gomorrhe, while conversing with Mme de Cambremer on the "seaview" at Balbec, the narrator confesses to the following: "I began instinctively to talk to Mme de Cambremer, née Legrandin, in the manner in which her brother might have done. 'They have,' I said, referring to the gulls, 'the whiteness and stillness of water lilies.'" He then proceeds to elaborate the echo of Legrandin's manner, not, however, for Mme de Cambremer but for us: "And indeed they appeared to be offering an inert target to the little waves that were rocking them" (SG, 209). The narrator mimics Legrandin, but it is unclear whether as intentional mockery or as unconscious compliment.[25] For here he is again, two pages later, in full flow himself on gulls as water lilies: "The sun was just then getting lower, the seagulls were now yellow, like the water-lilies in another canvas of that same series by Monet" (211). This is no longer citation of Legrandin but the narrator speaking in his own voice. If, therefore, this is parody, what is object and what is instrument? We are not helped in getting an unambiguous answer to that question by the added intervention of the elderly dowager, Mme de Cambremer's mother-in-law:

[23] "Like the narrator in Combray or Balbec, Legrandin finds his inspiration in trees." Descombes, Proust: Philosophy of the Novel, 210. There is also very possibly a half-submerged quotation of Baudelaire's poem, "Correspondances," with its reference in the first quatrain to trees as familiar friends.

[24] Swann's descent into excruciating banality as a consequence of his marriage to Odette is caught in his comparison of Odette's piano rendition of the Vinteuil sonata as capturing "the whole static quality of moonlight, which is moonlight's most basic quality" (JF, 108).

[25] Compagnon sees the passage as governed by "the logic of pastiche." Compagnon, Proust Between Two Centuries, 181.

Whenever she talked aesthetics, her salivary glands, like those of certain animals in the rutting season, entered on a phase of hypersecretion such that the old lady's toothless mouth allowed a few droplets whose rightful place this was not to come from the corners of her faintly moustachioed lips. She would at once swallow them down again with a deep sigh, like someone recovering their breath.

It is not the best of prospectuses for aesthetics, although once again the perspective is altered as the elderly lady switches the conversation to the topic of the sea, when viewed through the foliage at La Raspelière, and compares its "ravishing" quality to a "fan" (the fan another Monet motif). The narrator is struck by the sincerity of the remark despite the revolting adventures of the salivary glands: "I sensed, from a deep breath intended to catch the saliva and dry the moustache, that the compliment was genuine." The ambivalent value of a whole language of impressionistic visual description is in play across these various speaking positions, making it difficult to distinguish what is genuine and what is fake and correspondingly difficult to place the narrator (and Proust himself) safely beyond the reach of Proust's comic vision. "There are very lovely violets and blues in the clouds this evening . . . a blue, especially, more flowery than airy, the blue of a cineraria, which is surprising in the sky. And that little pink cloud, too, has it not the tint of some flower, a sweet William or hydrangea" (S, 31). This is, of course, Legrandin again, discoursing by the Vivonne. But who is it who speaks of "a prism in which the colours of the light from outside were dispersed, a hive in which all the heady nectars of the day awaiting me were still separate and ungathered but already visible, a garden of hopes shimmering with shafts of silver and rose petals" (JF, 283)? It is the narrator looking out of the window in his grandmother's room at the Balbec hotel. It could have been Legrandin on a good day.[26]

It is also while in Balbec for the second time that the narrator is brought face-to-face with a more disconcerting speech-echo. Albertine, fretting at the first signs of the narrator's attempts to hold her prisoner, yields to a fit of exasperated petulance: "I'm beginning to get fed up with Infreville and all these little places the colour of spinach" (SG, 201). If the narrator can compare church steeples to yellow wheat sheaves, then why not places resembling the color of spinach (he also refers to the figure of Gilbert the Bad in the stained-glass window of the Combray church as

---

[26] "In À la recherche he seems to be mocking his own early tendency towards preciosity when he puts into the mouth of the ridiculous Legrandin exactly the sort of image he would himself have used earlier." May Slater, Humour in the Works of Proust (Oxford: Oxford University Press, 1979), 82. The point, however, is that the tendency is not just an "early" one.

"cabbage green," *S*, 172)? It is, in fact, a rather genially inventive image, capturing not just a particular hue of green but also, through its sheer oddness, the witheringly impatient contempt it is designed to convey (a place incongruously held to resemble spinach may not be one you would wish to visit, unless you happened to share André Breton's passion for all varieties of the color green). But it is in the next volume, on the subject of ice cream rather than spinach, that Albertine goes straight to the top of the class in baroque metaphor-making:

> As for ices (and I hope you will order me only the old-fashioned sort, moulded into every kind of improbable architecture), every time I eat one, the temples, the churches, obelisks and rocks are like a picturesque geographical tableau that I study first, before changing its raspberry or vanilla monuments into a cool sensation in my mouth.

This is merely a rhetorical appetizer (or a form of verbal foreplay), but already the narrator is a trifle perturbed ("I thought this was a little too elegantly phrased"). Albertine, however, thinks the opposite ("she sensed that I did find it well phrased, and went on, stopping for a moment to laugh when she felt she had drawn an effective comparison" (but at precisely what does she laugh?). She goes on as follows:

> "Oh dear, I'm afraid that at the Ritz hotel you will find Vendôme Columns of ice, chocolate or raspberry ice, and then you will have to buy several so that they can look like votive columns or an avenue of pylons raised to the glory of Cold. They make raspberry obelisks too, which can stand here and there in the burning desert of my thirst until they melt their pink granite in the back of my throat and they cool it better than an oasis" (and here she laughed deep in her throat, whether impressed by her own eloquence, or mused by her ability to sustain such a lengthy metaphor, or, alas, from the physical sensation of imagining something so delicious, so cool in her mouth, which gave her an almost sexual pleasure). "Those ice mountains that you get at the Ritz sometimes look like the Monte Rosa, but when the ice is lemon-flavoured I don't mind if it doesn't have a monumental shape; it can be a bit irregular, with cliffs, like one of Elstir's mountains. In that case, it shouldn't be too white, more yellowish, with that look of dirty, bleak snow that he gives to his mountains. It needn't be a big one, a half-ice if you like, but those lemon ices are always like miniature mountains, tiny ones, but your imagination puts everything in scale, like those tiny dwarf trees from Japan that you can see are really oak trees or cedars or upas trees, so that if I put some next to a little trickle of water, in my room, I could have a huge forest sloping down to a river, where little children could get lost. So, at the foot of my yellowy lemon half-ice, I can see postilions, travelers, post-chaises on whom my tongue brings down icy avalanches to swallow them up" (the cruel pleasure with which she said this aroused my

jealousy); "then," she added, "I use my lips to demolish, pillar by pillar, those Venetian porphyry churches that are made of strawberry ice-cream and bring down what I don't swallow on the heads of the faithful." (115–16)

Whew! There are many reasons why the narrator (and we with him) might feel bulldozed by this mighty figurative romp—thematically glacial but psychically hot—through monuments, mountains, and forests. For the anxious narrator, it is partly a sexual matter, from the provocative laughter to the allusions to the pleasures of oral sex. But there are other ways of playing on the narrator's jealousy, and none requires this kind of manic performance with outlandish trope. It is not just a provocation but also an emulation. This too disturbs the narrator, on grounds to do with what he sees as the appropriate use of linguistic and rhetorical expressions. Albertine is "impressed by her own eloquence"; the narrator is simply stunned ("What a change from Balbec, where I would defy even Elstir himself to have spotted in Albertine such a rich potential for poetry"), and even seeks consolation in the thought of his own influence "as a sign of my power over her, a proof that she loved me." The influence, however, is double-edged, and strays irreverently onto hallowed ground; as Michael Riffaterre puts it, "Albertine parodies the narrator and speaks her phantasm the way he would have written it. The text authors its author in turn, as it were . . . Evidently this far-reaching metaphorization on so prosaic a subject represents the most extreme form of catachresis."[27]

Albertine is "amused by her ability to sustain such a lengthy metaphor" (in its crazed hypotactic rhythm a mélange of Marcel Proust and Mistress Quickly), but the narrator, while amazed, is none too happy with this mimesis of his own manner ("her pains to use such 'written' images, which I felt should be put to another, more sacred use"). However, if he doesn't like this echo of his own speech, he has only himself to blame: "I should never speak like that, of course, myself, but, still, without me she would never have spoken in that way." Thus, try as the narrator might to distinguish Albertine's ludicrous speech from his own written use of figures (a "more sacred use"), with the injection of Elstir into her discourse ("like one of Elstir's mountains"), the dividing line has been irretrievably compromised. Albertine has been schooled by the narrator (the "dirty, bleak snow" an especially inventive touch), but in the mirror image sent back from pupil to teacher, comedy intervenes, with Proust as its impresario, standing between the two of them, looking both ways at once, wearing the gravitas appropriate to the "sacred" while joining in the laughter more suited to a sense of the comically profane. Moreover, made from ice cream, the monumentalizing architectural structures

[27] Michael Riffaterre, "The Intertextual Unconscious," *Critical Inquiry* 13, 2 (1987): 384.

are transient, destined for a thaw. The pink granite "melts" in the back of the throat, post-chaises dissolve in "icy avalanches."[28] And so too do the words themselves, as the tropes trope their own destiny in the back of the mouth, where the *pêle-mêle* accumulation rushes headlong toward collapse, as tottering and tumbling forms, like clowns falling off stilts.

VI

This is where it ends. With the last extended metaphor—part of the novel's more general finale—the text wanders foursquare into the world of circus (as well as the world of fairy tale). It begins by dizzily spatializing the theme of a life in time. The narrator recalls the tinkling of the garden bell, which in "Combray" would announce Swann's visits, and then proceeds to measure the vast expanse of time separating the present moment in the Guermantes salon from that childhood past: "perched on its vertiginous summit . . . I felt giddy at the sight of so many years below me, yet within me, as if I were miles high" (357). In the next and closing paragraph of the novel, the image of heights is transferred to the aged Duc de Guermantes, figured as walking on living stilts from which one must inevitably fall:

> I finally understood why the Duc de Guermantes . . . had, the moment he rose and tried to stand upright, wavered on trembling legs . . . and could not move forward without shaking like a leaf, on the scarcely manageable summit of his eighty-three years, as if all men were perched on top of living stilts which never stop growing, sometimes becoming taller than church steeples, until eventually they make walking difficult and dangerous, and down from which, all of a sudden, they fall. (357)[29]

This is very different from the near-fall occasioned by the stumble in the Guermantes courtyard. While that is outwardly comical to the onlookers, for the narrator (and the reader) it also sparks a revelation.[30]

[28] As Nathalie Mauriac Dyer points out, there is also an anticipatory echo here of the disintegration of the "stones of Venice" in *La Fugitive* as an embodiment of the Beautiful that becomes mere "atoms." Dyer draws our attention to an earlier draft in which Albertine says, "I call each of those temples to melt in my mouth 'the temple of Taste.'" Dyer glosses this as a willful "parody and mockery of the categories of Aesthetics," in "Genesis of Proust's 'Ruines de Venise,'" 79.

[29] Did Proust perchance see the 1905 silent film, "Sidney, le clown aux échasses"? In the Cecchio d'Amico and Visconti screenplay, the debauched clients of Jupien's brothel were sketched as "sad clowns." Cited in Martine Beuquet and Marion Schmid, *Proust at the Movies* (London: Blackwell, 2005), 72.

[30] "[T]he hero's unsteady gait in the Guermantes courtyard" is "like Charlie Chaplin dressed in black with hat and cane." Compagnon, *Proust Between Two Centuries*, 6.

The metaphor of stilts is subject to no such distinction between the social and the private. It is straightforwardly a clownish transformation of the metaphor of altitude (so highly prized by the narrator in connection with the narrative and affective world of Stendhal, *P*, 348). But the comedy here has perhaps more than just thematic value, in the implied contrast between youth (Stendhal's heroes) and age (Proust's gallery of decrepit buffoons). It is also arguably an implied parody of metaphor *tout court*, the prop that holds the whole thing up. Walking is one of the foundational topoi of the *Recherche*, above all, the family walks along the two ways in Combray, which in childhood the narrator thinks of as unconnected but which in late life he discovers as joined, thus describing the shape of a circle; the two ways and the two walks are the novel's privileged metaphor, the one that resumes the nonlinear system of connections that is the form of significant Proustian life ("the true life"). In the great last gathering, the *bal des têtes*, walking has become something almost unrecognizable, along with the identities of those who now crawl toward death: "With others whose faces were still intact, the only thing that seemed to worry them was having to walk" (242). They struggle, but can head in one direction only, for a fall: they "could not stand up, bent as they were, head lowered, in a curve which echoed their current descent between life and death, awaiting the final fall" (246).

Roger Shattuck called the reference to stilts "one of the most remarkable images in all of Proust" and traced its provenance back into various sources, including Boileau, Saint-Simon, Voltaire, and, above all, Montaigne. He reminds us that stilts as metaphor, specifically as dead metaphor in the expression "monté sur des échasses" has since the sixteenth century signified what in English we call "stilted," a form of affectation applying to both style and behavior. Montaigne's example matters here, in particular, the famous use of the stilts image in yet another final moment, the last of the *Essais*, to articulate the folly of overarching aspiration and the need to keep our feet firmly planted on the ground. Shattuck comments that Montaigne uses the metaphor of stilts "to suggest an affectation that destroys the just proportion of life."[31] As the last term indicates, the context here is Montaigne's commonsense, plain-man's life philosophy. But as well as being a plea on behalf of plain living, it could also extend to the notion of plain writing or what, in certain quarters, is known as plain language.

To associate the style of Marcel Proust with what is normally understood as plain language would be like trying to align his artistic ideals with Jeremy Bentham's view that ideas and beliefs other than pragmatic

---

[31] Roger Shattuck, "Proust's Stilts," *Yale French Studies* 4 (1965): 95.

utilitarian ones are but "nonsense on stilts."[32] I am struck nevertheless by Shattuck's use, in connection with Montaigne, of the expression "just proportion." For the notion of just proportionality is one of the great running themes in the theory of metaphor from Aristotle to modernism. In his essay "L'Image," Pierre Reverdy, for example, once defined poetic metaphor as a set of relations at once "lointains et justes" (distant and proportionate):[33] "lointains" carries the strong modernist stress on maximal semantic distance between the terms of the comparison, and hence on strangeness, the place of the arresting image in the project of making-it-strange. But we must also note, from this protosurrealist, the constraining force of the term "justes," the view, as it were, that for metaphor, so to speak, to stand up, there are limiting conditions of plausibility that must govern its construction. Am I then myself paradoxically violating the law of "justesse" in imagining the metaphorical stilts as a reminder (a metaphorical reminder) of this constraint, the metaphorical stilts as metaphor *on* stilts, unable to walk properly and, in its more stretched forms, destined for a fall? The text of *À la recherche* ends by taking the image of walking on stilts into that of giants straddling time ("like giants immersed in the years"); it is the fairy-tale element of the novel's finale. I confess I have never really understood this analogy,[34] but it may have something to do with the operations of metaphor, the sheer brio of metaphor; like giants striding across land, metaphor reaches across space (as well as time), gathering in what otherwise may be remote, so remote as to be otherwise irrecoverable. But if walking on stilts reminds us of the superhuman energies and the legendary reach of the giant, they also evoke the comic routines of the clown, always precarious, vulnerable, and likely to come crashing to the ground, which is precisely why we watch. Albertine is Proust's/the narrator's trick pony, and we almost hold our breath until her performance is over (will she make it to the other side?). Proust is ultimately still the juggler, keeping all six balls in motion (and sharing a joke with us at the same time, to not take this literary style too seriously, if, after all, a pony can learn it).

In her study of the "associative" nature of Proust's analogies, Christie McDonald remarks that the whole structure is held together by "the feeling of form" and adds that if this is removed or damaged, then the edifice

[32]Jeremy Bentham, *Anarchical Fallacies*, in *The Works of Jeremy Bentham*, ed. John Bowring (Edinburgh: William Tait, 1843), 2:501. Bentham used the expression specifically to characterize the Declaration of the Rights of Man and the Citizen, a subject in which Proust showed no interest whatsoever.

[33]Pierre Reverdy, "L'Image," in *Œuvres complètes* (Paris: Flammarion, 1975), 73.

[34]Northrop Frye saw it in these terms: "In Proust the stupid giants are the habit-lives of his characters; they recur, in a non-gigantic form, in Beckett's clowns." "The Third Notebook," in *The Notebooks, 1964–1972* (Toronto: University of Toronto Press, 2002), 290.

"totters."[35] Tottering is what the Duc de Guermantes ends up doing. And, as, with the Duc de Guermantes, we totter through that last long sentence, landing for the last time on the word "Time," we would do well to proceed immediately to a text by the poet Tom Raworth, where we can start again, not only by going from end to beginning but also from bottom to top (in terms of its layout on the page). The text is called "Proust from the Bottom Up," in a collection of poems with the appositive title, *Tottering State*. It takes (from the Kilmartin/Enright translation) the key passage about literature as the deciphering of the "book of unknown signs" and rewrites it, cheekily and literally, from bottom to top, while at the same time redistributing its elements in willful disregard of normal syntax and sense (beginning with "not traced by us is the only book that really belongs to us" and ending with "if i tried to read them no-one could help me with").[36] We make of this splintered Proust what we will. To the extent that Raworth's poem works with disarticulated and discoordinated parts of speech, it may also remind us of the fate of body parts. Proust's image is overdetermined. It involves not only the stilts but also the body perched on them, the decayed, geriatric structure that is now the Duc de Guermantes. This image of an aged body figuratively locomoting on a rickety contraption, the image, so to speak, of a body on its last legs, conjoins, in the register of the grotesque, two things that often go together in nineteenth-century aesthetic and literary theory: namely, metaphor and the body. There was a metaphysical dimension to the conjunction, the notion, based on what we might now term a somewhat rickety romantic-pantheist reading of Spinoza, of the metaphoric unity of the world whereby God is revealed in Nature, the divine fused with matter, the spiritual with the corporeal. In short, metaphor in this sort of context was no longer purely rhetorical, the representation of something by something else, but rather the embodiment of something *in* something else. In relocating from the sphere of representation to that of embodiment, metaphor becomes a conceptual variant of that central category of romantic aesthetic thinking, the Symbol.[37] And this set of relations between body (specifically the body of the word or, in another medium, the body of paint), embodiment, and the symbol opens onto the principal topic of chapter 7, that counterfigure of the disembodied, the Proustian specter and the various kinds of ghostly return staged by the novel.

[35] Christie McDonald, *The Proustian Fabric: Associations of Memory* (Lincoln: University of Nebraska Press, 1991), 16.

[36] Tom Raworth, *Tottering State: Selected Poems, 1963–1987* (London: Paladin, 1988), 184.

[37] As Tzvetan Todorov has shown, the association of metaphor and symbol is especially strong in German romantic theory, especially in the writings of Creuzer. *Theories of the Symbol* (Oxford: Oxford University Press, 1982), 216–21.

The dominant kind are those spectral returns from the dead that are reawakenings from time lost. In this novel about time, its scheme self-divides and self-organizes in time as a set of multiple temporal units. There is the split second (the moment of epiphanic inrush); there is the hour (which is not only an hour but "a vessel full of perfumes," *T*, 197). And there are the days and the years. As Proust's novel charts the grainy microstructures of the smaller units, it also rolls them up across the narrative into the accumulated tally of years, folding them into the great arc of Time to which its narrator turns in one last metaphorical flourish by invoking giants and stilts. Desks take off on legs resurrected from the metaphorically dead, but dukes fall off stilts, metaphorically hurled into the all-too-real abyss of annihilation and oblivion. But if the Years defeat us, there always remain the Days: Proust would have agreed with Larkin that "days are where we live."[38] He is, above all, the novelist of days, of their variable textures and rhythms (the narrative of *La Prisonnière* is structured as a sequence of "days"). The "days are not all equal," the narrator tells us, going on to compare them to automobiles with different "speeds": "There are arduous, mountainous, uncomfortable days that one spends an infinite time climbing, and downward-sloping days that one can descend at full tilt singing" (*S*, 394). The French term here for day is *jour*, but there is also the *journée*. Just as the hour is not just an hour, so the *journée* is not only a measurable unit of time but a quality of experience; the novel starts its life as recollected *journées de lecture* (reading even better than singing).[39] And there are the *journées* that are not just "like" an automobile but that are passed "en automobile."[40]

Best of all are the recollected summer days of Combray, recalled to memory ("born again") by the "chamber music" of the houseflies, which, by "containing a little of their essence," directly "guarantees their return, their presence, actual, ambient, immediate, accessible" (*S*, 85). These are the special days in Proust, the ghost-days that "return" as so many "revenants" to become once again fully embodied resurrections. But there are also the winter days, for instance, the day when on the Champs-Elysées

[38] Philip Larkin, "Days," in *Collected Poems* (London: Marvell Press, 2003), 98.

[39] The word "journée" acquired a new meaning in the early days of the French Revolution, which then settled into its historiography as the "day" that is special by being charged with the momentous historical meanings invested in revolutionary action. The paradigm case was, of course, July 14, 1789. This was to become the Day as synecdoche for History as such, a new end-time or Judgment Day ushering in the reign of universal justice. In Proust the term "journée" is less abstractly eschatological, but is rather something personally lived, attended to for what it humbly is rather than for what it loftily represents, although in the living of them there are the occasional eruptions of thrilling end-time annunciations. The revolutionary *journée* and the Proustian *journée* give us the two antiphonal structures of modern secular time.

[40] *Contre Sainte-Beuve*, ed. Clarac and Sandre, 63–69.

the narrator encounters the peculiar Madame Blatin, who sits in the same place every day and reads *Les débats*; for the narrator she is "a lady of a certain age who came in all weathers, always decked out in the same clothing, magnificent and dark" (401). Sometime later, he learns from his mother that Madame Blatin is the widow of a bailiff, allegedly on the social make, wanting to "get to know" all and sundry ("she always had to cultivate a new acquaintance. She's horrible, vulgar, and a trouble-maker into the bargain," 417). Maybe, but Madame Blatin is also interesting. Resembling Legrandin in her social aspirations, she also talks like him: "This snow—you'll laugh at me—reminds me of ermine!" This is not far from the narrator's "the snow of the moonlight" (*SG*, 369) or even the moonlike milky whiteness of Madame Verdurin's temples ("her temples, like two beautiful burning spheres, pain-filled and milky white, in which Harmony rolls undyingly around"). If this isn't self-parody, I don't know what is.[41] Perhaps Madame Blatin—one of the strangest of his minor characters, strange because there is no obvious reason for her being in the novel at all—finds her purpose here. For no sooner does she compare the snow-covered carpet of the park to ermine (the narrator is with her in referring to "the mantle of snow" that covers the balcony at home and to the "snowy lawn" on the Champs-Elysées that the sun converts into "the metallic worn surface of an old brocade," 402), than, in addition to surmising that her interlocutors will laugh at her simile ("you'll laugh at me"), she starts to laugh at it herself ("And the old lady began to laugh," 402). First Madame Verdurin, then Oriane, then Albertine, now Madame Blatin—tropes no laughing matter?

[41] In conversation with Albertine the narrator has a line on "literary" moonlight in conversation: "I repeated lines of poetry to her, or prose phrases, about the moonlight, showing how, having once been silvery, it had become blue for Chateaubriand and the Victor Hugo of 'Eviradnus' and 'Theresa's Party,' before becoming metallic yellow again for Baudelaire and Leconte de Lisle" (*P*, 378). An arbitrary business, poetic color-investments, Proust seems to be saying.

CHAPTER SEVEN

Bodies and Ghosts

WHEN PROUST OUTLINED TO Anna de Noailles an ideal of style that would approximate a uniform, malleable substance, a *fondu*, such as the artist's impasto or the baker's dough, might he also have been imagining a relation of style to matter that was a relation of language to body or a version of the word made flesh? The latter notion Proust himself gestured at in the letter to Daudet in which he spoke of his literary ambitions on the "eucharistic" analogy of the "miracle of transubstantiation." I have already referred several times to this remarkable aspiration, and the moment has now come for a fuller reckoning with it. But might there not have also been another influence here, deriving from his passion for *The Arabian Nights*? There is no evidence of any direct acquaintance on Proust's part with Arabic script, but, if only secondhand in the context of his occasional musings on different writing systems, he may have come into contact with the altogether less theological and more materialist idea of the letters of Arabic calligraphy as based on the forms of the human body. There is also the narrator's attraction (understandably emphasized in the context of Albertine's maddening evasions) to words and phrases that would be like spontaneous bodily reactions (such as the blush), the so-called indexical sign or the sign that cannot lie: "I relied on words only when I could read them like the rush of blood to a person's face" (*P*, 77).

Yet, if the body is the ground of an "incarnationalist" dream of expression, on the subject of the body itself Proust's views are largely disheartening, as in the following observation—at once post-Cartesian and proto-Beckettian—from the closing pages of *Le Temps retrouvé*:

> I really had to start from the fact that I had a body . . . having a body is in itself the greatest threat to the mind . . . The body encloses the mind in a fortress; before long the mind is besieged on all sides, and in the end the mind has to give itself up. (345)

This definitive statement may bring welcome relief to intellectual digestive systems suffering from an overdose of contemporary body-talk (the supply seems to be inexhaustible and the addiction very strong), but it also suggests that the Proustian body may turn out to be something of a dead end, at least relative to Proust's restlessly curious interest in the vicissitudes of the mental life. Brunet's *Vocabulaire de Proust* gives an impressively long entry for the word "corps," but Brunet himself glosses his entry with the comment that Proust rarely describes the body other than negatively.[1] Although this is not quite right, it captures an important truth. In *Proust et le monde sensible* Jean-Pierre Richard posits "three great Proustian axes of the lived: body, place and time."[2] Yet, in relation to the first of these, whatever it is that we carry away from the cornucopia of Proust's sensory world, it is unlikely to include vividly coherent images of the human body. There is, of course, the intricate registration of bodily life, but a trawl through Richard's inventory of the sensorial universe of the novel instructively yields few accounts of individual bodies. This is in part an effect of the cut-up technique for which Richard is justly famous, disassembling motifs from their local contexts and redistributing them across the grid of large thematic configurations. But it also connects with something intrinsic to Proust's own text, where typically the body appears less as an individuated object than as a depersonalized space across which physical experience flows and disperses in a manner cognate with the psychological dispersal of the unified Self into a multiplicity of selves.

A simple test works well here: try to visualize bodies in *À la recherche*, and what typically comes into focus is either nothing at all or bits and pieces, corporeal fragments. But when we ask the question, "What do Proust's characters look like?" (in the sense of that question that demands the conversion of fragments into wholes), the text does not supply us with the kind of answers so readily forthcoming in, say, the novels of Balzac and Dickens.[3] The one exception to this inbuilt resistance to coherent visualization is the spectacle of the aging body, the body marked by time, decrepitude, and mortality, the *corps* on its way to becoming a corpse. Our physical sense of Charlus, for example, is never more acute than when we are presented with the signs of his bodily decline. This sort of precise notation becomes a veritable carnival of sadistically gleeful description in the Guermantes *matinée* of *Le Temps retrouvé*, with its procession of bodies altered and disfigured by the ravages of time (what, in connection with d'Argencourt, the narrator calls "the transformations of the human body," 923). This produces for the narrator a parody of a recognition scene, but in which the initial misidentification of which bodies go with which identities in no way obscures the precision of bodily notation itself.

---

[1] Étienne Brunet, *Le vocabulaire de Proust* (Geneva: Slatkine-Champion, 1983), 1:151.

[2] Richard, *Proust et le monde sensible*, 171.

[3] The best study of Proust's disruptive relation to the convention of the "legible" body in the nineteenth-century novel is Liza Gabaston's *Le Langage du corps dans "À la recherche du temps perdu"* (Paris: Champion, 2011).

These, however, are last appearances, terminal states both biologically and narratively. Consider what happens with first appearances. In Balzac first descriptions are strategic: modeled analogically as "portraiture" and functioning semiotically as pointers to some larger pattern or theme, initial images of the body are fully legible tokens in a controlled economy of signs and meanings. By contrast, take one of the first appearances of Odette in "Un amour de Swann."

> as for her body, which was admirably formed, it was difficult to discern its continuity . . . because its blouse, jutting out as though over an imaginary paunch and ending abruptly in a point, below which the balloon of the double skirts swelled out, made a woman look as though she were composed of different parts poorly fitted inside one another, because the flounces, the flutes, the vest followed so independently, according to the whimsy of their design or the consistency of their material, the line that led to the knots, the puffs of lace, the perpendicular fringes of jet, or that directed them along the corset, but were in no way attached to the living person, who, depending on whether the architecture of these frills and furbelows approached too closely or moved too far away from her own, was either encased or lost in them. (200–201)[4]

However we engage with this passage, it is scarcely one we can hold in what is called the mind's eye. What starts as an account of Odette's body ends with the body "encased" and "lost," beneath not only the structures of her clothes but also the overlays of syntax and trope. Whatever the moribund expression "admirably formed" might mean in relation to the "living person," the text willfully obstructs passage to any secure visual hold on that relation. Where in Balzac and Dickens elaboration of this sort produces an effect of hypervisuality, in Proust vision is decisively blocked, and perhaps nowhere more so than in representations of the organ of vision. Proust returns obsessively to the eyes of his characters, but, whatever it is we as readers might do with these instruments of seeing, we ourselves do not, and cannot, see them. Proust's manic habit of metaphorical extension means that the descriptive notations are often drowned in a figurative flux. Here, for example, are Legrandin's eyes: "I saw a little brown notch appear in the centre of each of our friend's blue eyes as if they had been stabbed by invisible pin-points, while the rest of the pupil reacted by secreting the floods of azure." However it is that these jovially rhetoricized eyes, stabbed by pinpoints and secreting azure overflow, look at us, it is not clear that we can, so to speak, look at them in any normal sense of imaginary seeing. We do not see eyes here; we read

---

[4] See Richard, *Proust et le monde sensible*, 199–201. Odette's appearance is later recalled as making "her look like a creature of separate parts unlinked by any individuality" (*JF*, 194).

tropes.[5] And then consider the eyes of Albertine, as a first stop on a tour around the most elaborately yet elusively staged body in the whole of the *Recherche*:

> the eyes, like two polished oval plaques still trapped in their surrounding ore, had become more lucent than metal while remaining harder than light; they shone, among the blind matter overhanging them, like the mauve silk wings of a butterfly in a case.

The eyes belong in a description of a body that ranges freely over legs, hands, face, and, above all, hair, whose curls also acquire figurative wings with which to take flight into an extraordinary constellation of images, where what curls ordinarily and recognizably look like is left far behind:

> the hair, black and curly, showing different patterns of locks as she turned towards me to ask what she should play next, now a splendid wing, pointed at its tip and broad at its base, black, feathery and triangular, now a mass of three-dimensional curls like a mountain range, powerful and varied, full of ridges, watersheds, precipices, whipped up into a richness and multiplicity that seemed to exceed the normal variety of nature, as if a sculptor were accumulating difficulties so as to show off the suppleness, the dash, the freedom and lifelikeness of his execution, brought out more strongly, by covering and breaking it in places, the lively curve and, as it were, the rotation of the smooth, pink face, which had the shiny yet matt quality of painted wood. (*P*, 354)

Apart from the sheer pleasure of sensuous play with language in the way the sculptor can play with clay, there is a reason for this complicated game of displacement and dispersal. For the most part we encounter the human body in the *Recherche* less as something objectively described than as something subjectively fantasized, imagined, seen, or "read" through the prism of desire (or its lack). It is in relation to the high drama of imagining desire that the one solidly descriptive emphasis of the text (on the fragility of the human body) finds much of its point. Images of bodily decrepitude are the text's ironic rejoinder to this fantasizing activity, a reality check on our desiring compulsions. There is thus a primary opposition: between the body desired (the imago-body) and the body revealed (frail, infirm, wasted, grotesque). In itself the opposition is banal, a variation on Proust's way with the theme of *vanitas vanitatum*. The plot thickens considerably, however, when we consider the extent to which the first term of this opposition, the body desired, turns on the paradox

---

[5] David Ellison makes the interesting argument that faces in Proust are not described in accordance with mimetic codes of "recognition" but rather as "autonomous" aesthetic objects in their own right. *The Reading of Proust* (Baltimore: Johns Hopkins University Press, 1984), 16.

of being nowhere more absent than when present or more distant than when close. This is the paradox crucially enacted in the narrator's tortured relationship with Albertine.

The body of Albertine is the object of an intermittent yet developing exploration of this paradox and its implications, from *Sodome et Gomorrhe* through to *La Fugitive*. At various junctures the narrator stares at Albertine's body in the determined but vain attempt to match the corporeal and the essential (an essence of Albertine or more generally an essence of "girlness"). The more he looks, the less he finds, repeatedly encountering in the "notebook"—that is, Albertine—a series of blank pages,[6] a fundamental illegibility around and on which the imagination spins with increasingly frantic desperation:

> What a deceitful sense sight is! A human body, even when loved, as was that of Albertine, seems from a few metres, a few centimetres away, distant from us. And the soul that belongs to it likewise. Except that, should something come violently to alter the position of that soul in relation to us, to show us that it loves other human beings and not ourselves, then, by the beating of our dislocated hearts, we feel that the darling creature was not a few feet away, but inside us. Inside us, in more or less superficial regions. (*SG*, 519)

The perverse logic of this relation to the body is twofold. First, there is the experience of distance-in-proximity (the closer the body in physical space the further away in psychological space). Second, there is the process whereby distance is overcome, in the triangular format of Proustian desire within which our knowledge (or suspicion) of the desired one's desire for another (here Mlle de Vinteuil) instantly abolishes distance in the mode of a painful introjection; the body of the other comes close, is experienced as moving "inside us," only, however, to wreak emotional havoc. There are but two remedies for this invasive laceration. One is the emetic slowly administered by time and the process of forgetting, whereby the invader is eventually expelled; but that is not effective until late into *La Fugitive*. The other is to put a stop to the interpretive frenzy, to cease trying to "read" the fluid and treacherous signs imprinted in the notebook, by the reduction of the unmanageable living person to a controllable thing of "dumb nature." This is the operation performed by the narrator over the *sleeping* body.

There are several such scenes in the novel, the longest the wonderful four-page dawdle in *La Prisonnière* over Albertine as captive sleeping beauty.

---

[6] "I longed, not to tear off her dress and see her body, but to see through her body to the whole note-book of her memories and plans for further ardent lovers' meetings" (*P*, 82). For the issues surrounding the attempt to "read" Albertine's body, see Gabaston, *Le Langage du corps*, 200–205.

She had drawn back into herself all the parts of her that were normally on the outside, she had taken refuge, enclosed and summed up in her body. Watching her, holding her in my hands, I felt that I possessed her completely, in a way I never did when she was awake. Her life was subject to me, was breathing out its light breath in my direction.

Possession, however, comes at a price—in the passivity of sleep, Albertine is dispossessed of her complex and difficult humanity: "By closing her eyes, by losing consciousness, Albertine had put off, one by one, the various marks of humanity which had so disappointed me in her." The next step is toward outright reification, in a first moment as organic plant-life ("in her sleep she had turned into a plant . . . she was animated only by the unconscious life of plants"), and in the next as inorganic, inanimate matter ("no longer just a plant" but "a whole landscape . . . one of those inanimate creatures we call the beauties of nature"), the final stage of which is her fantasmatic subjugation as "dumb nature" (59–62).

This last reduction has a sexual aspect. The narrator gazes at the sleeping body of Albertine as at a "thing" tamed and owned, but, along with looking, he also touches, with sexual intent.[7] He lies down beside her and brings himself to climax, in a sexual consummation that is indistinguishable from a self-pleasuring: "as my own pleasure reached completion, I could kiss her without breaking into her sleep. It seemed to me at those moments that I had possessed her more completely, like an unconscious and unresisting part of dumb nature" (62). In general, there is not much touching in À la recherche, and when there is it is often of the furtive kind, as bodily statements of the vices that otherwise dare not speak their name (the wandering hands in search of erotic adventure in the blackout of the wartime Metro, or Charlus "slipping his arm into mine" as he and the narrator walk down the boulevard). To be sure, touch will have its ecstatically revelatory moment in Le Temps retrouvé, when after taking petits fours and orangeade in the Guermantes waiting room, the narrator brings to his lips the starched napkin that will instantly transport him (in the sense of both movement and bliss) back to the hotel dining room of Balbec. Yet, of the five dimensions of the human sensorium, representation of the tactile in the Recherche is pitifully thin relative to the abundance of the others. While, analytically speaking, word counts don't necessarily count, it is a statistical-lexical fact of the novel that (according

---

[7]Anna-Magdalena Elsner has also noted the paucity of moments of touching in the Recherche, while dwelling on the hand-touching fantasy the narrator weaves around Albertine ("the fortuitous thrill of touching her hands") that informs the game-playing with the young band of girls on the picnic outing in À l'ombre des jeuenes filles en fleurs (JF, 495–96). Mourning and Creativity in "À la recherche du temps perdu" (PhD dissertation, University of Cambridge, 2011).

to Brunet's concordance) the term "tactile" itself appears but twice.[8] The first belongs in the description of Chopin's musical phrase mentioned in chapter 2; the other, and far richer, occurs in *À l'ombre des jeunes filles en fleurs* as the narrator's curious and wandering eye sweeps desirously across the band of young girls, and Albertine in particular, in what, even by Proust's prodigal standards, is a riot of imagined sensations:

> when our eye ventures in the direction of a young girl, it is as though it acts on behalf of all our other senses: they seek out her various properties, the smell of her, the feel of her, the taste of her, which they enjoy without the collaboration of the hands or the lips; and because of desire's artful abilities in transposition, and its excellent spirit of synthesis, these senses can draw from the colour of cheeks or breast the sensations of touching, of savouring, of forbidden contact. (470)[9]

There can be few passages in the novel to rival the synesthetic delirium of this one, its wild swirl of commingled primitive sensation. On the other hand, the fantasy of touching (along with smelling and tasting) is entirely generated from and governed by the more distanced relation of seeing; it is an effect of what in the same passage is called the "greedy eyes" of Desire.[10] The latter's transpositional and synthesizing powers are accorded the grade of "excellent," as if the desiring eye were a kind of artist, a worthy companion perhaps to Théophile Gautier's art of transposition. Yet this is tactility at one remove, mediated by vision, the will to

---

[8] Forms of the verb *toucher* are manifold but also include the two figurative meanings of "move" and "concern."

[9] Since no translation can do proper justice to it, we must here quote from the original: "c'est comme déleguée des autres sens qu'elle [la perception visuelle] se dirige vers les jeunes filles; ils vont chercher l'une derrière l'autre les diverses qualités odorantes, tactiles, savoureuses, qu'ils goûtent ainsi même sans le secours des mains et des lèvres; et, capables, grâce aux arts de transposition, au génie de synthèse où excelle le désir, de restituer, sous la couleur des joues ou de la poitrine, l'attouchement, la dégustation, les contacts interdits" (*ARTP*, 2:246–47).

[10] Derrida comments at length on a tradition that runs from Plato to Bergson, in which vision is subjugated to touch (or "contact"), in *On Touching—Jean-Luc Nancy* (Stanford, Calif.: Stanford University Press, 2005). The tradition is both extended and modified by Deleuze and Guattari as "the becoming-haptical of the optical." *A Thousand Plateaux* (Stanford, Calif.: Stanford University Press, 2003), 123. Deleuze and Guattari themselves write: "'Haptic' is a better word than 'tactile' since it does not establish an opposition between two sense organs, but rather invites the assumption that the eye itself may fulfil this non-optical function" (ibid., 492). In Proust, however, it seems to be the other way around—touch subjugated to the distancing control of vision, the indirect touching of the voyeur with all its removal of the subject from the messy complexities of physical contact. As Benjamin writes, "Proust's pointing finger is unequalled. But there is another gesture in amicable togetherness, in conversation: physical contact. To no one is this gesture more alien than to Proust. He cannot touch his reader either; he could not do so for anything in the world." "The Image of Proust," in *Illuminations*, ed. Arendt, 207.

touch as obscurely wound into a kind of voyeurism.[11] In the relationship with Albertine, the preferred occasion of actual touching is while she is asleep, as a quasi-dead or ghostly form. In the episode where he rubs himself against her sleeping body to the point of orgasm, touch belongs in onanistic fantasy rather than in a mutual exchange; the spasm of orgasmic pleasure is also a spasm of evacuation in another sense, the emetic expulsion of the other even as the other's body is instrumentally used on or with which to "play" (in a later instance of Albertine asleep, he touches her as if playing a musical instrument: "I could put my hand in hers, touch her shoulders and her cheek . . . Only her breathing was affected by my touching as if she had been an instrument I was playing," *P*, 100). Breath and touch, the auditory and the tactile, join in the production of yet another synesthetic image mutating into an aesthetic one, the body (of the other) an object of "play" in both the sexual and the musical senses. It is an image at once sensorially rich, but also humanly poor, intimacy framed and contained by another set of oppositions or distinctions: the sleeping and the awake, the vulnerable and the powerful.

While the narrator's relations with Albertine in *La Prisonnière* are clearly sexual, the text is coy as to their exact nature, and it has been maintained that he never has "full" sexual relations; he does not "enter" her (physically), in contrast to her moving "inside" him (psychically) in a manner that will shatter him. The quasi-masturbatory scene may then be as "intimate" as it gets between the narrator and Albertine. Narrative and psychological guessing-games are not, however, my purpose here, which is rather to consider, if but briefly, a potential link to another, more visceral brand of skepticism, widespread in the early modern period and later theorized by Freud. This was a form of skeptical thought and feeling combining the somatic and the solipsistic, in which the negation of the reality of others rests on a phantasm of ingestion and expulsion, a bodily experience of "taking in" the other only to expel or "vomit" it out as unwanted, alien substance; a skepticism of the gut or the entrails.[12] I have already mentioned the felt need "to vomit" stemming from the nar-

---

[11] The closest Proust's text gets to it being the other way around, to the genuinely haptic understood as vision converted to touch, is the mad fantasia around Albertine's breasts quoted in the opening chapter.

[12] See David Hillman, *Shakespeare's Entrails: Belief, Scepticism and the Interior of the Body* (London: Palgrave, 2006). Jean-Luc Nancy links the experience of expulsion to the Christian topoi of the Last Supper, the Eucharist, and the Resurrected Body: "There is no getting away from it, one is caught up in a vast waste of images stretching from a Christ who daydreams over his unleavened bread to a Christ who extirpates from himself a throbbing Sacred Heart . . . all the ways of thinking about the body proper . . . end up with nothing but the expulsion of what one wished for." *Corpus* (New York: Fordham University Press, 2008), 9. We might relate this to the scene of the agonized dawn at the end of *Sodome et Gomorrhe*, the flaming, "bloody" spectacle of the sudden eruption of the sun; the narrator compares this to the laying of a "golden egg," but it could easily also be read as an extirpated heart.

rator's overexcitement by the name "Venice" and the nausea that can be a reaction to a surfeit of "sweetness."[13] The rhythm of intake and ejection (as of an unwanted food) also figures in the passage affirming the "unreality of others" and the emptiness of our social relations: "the sign of the unreality of others is surely shown clearly enough . . . for instance in the case of social pleasures, which at best result in discomfort caused by the ingestion of awful food" (*T*, 183).[14]

But it is primarily in connection with the sweetness of the "sweetcheat" Albertine (as Scott Moncrieff represented her in his translation of *La Fugitive* or *Albertine disparue*) that this rhythm is most fully instantiated. In the passage that speaks so deliriously of wanting to touch her, Albertine is also represented as a sweet, honeyed substance (*mielleuse*), and the "eye"/I that converts her into an object for the other senses includes the move from the tactile to the gustatory (*dégustation*). On the face of it, the implied thought of savoring, licking, and swallowing Albertine is the opposite of the "darling creature" imagined as moving threateningly "inside" the narrator's psyche and its eventual ejection by means of the work of forgetting. Yet the synesthetic bonding of taste and touch to the distant but controlling point of view of the eye opens a perspective in which both taste and touch converge on the kind of reserved, self-protecting physical contact exemplified by the narrator's "playing" with Albertine's passively sleeping body. One might furthermore hazard the suggestion that, in this context, the synesthetic experience, so primordial in Proust, is also a form of vicariousness (touching and tasting via seeing are substitutes for the real thing). It is not a plunging of self into the sensory motility of bodily life but a way of having some dimensions of that life at a remove, a place in which the self remains "intact" (the word deriving from Latin "intactus," meaning both "untouched" and "uninjured").[15]

---

[13] See chapter 4.

[14] In the commentary on Ruskin, Proust associates the "refusal of food" as a "modification of the state of mind, as for instance in asceticism" (*On Reading Ruskin*, 87–88).

[15] Also pertinent here is the relation of touch and aesthetic response, what one "feels" in the tactile sense, in the hands and between the fingers. This was to be a major theme in the late nineteenth-century cult of *japonisme*, in particular the collectors' craze for Japanese netsuke described by Edmund de Waal in his memoir of Charles Ephrussi. On the one hand, unencumbered by the specialized erudition and connoisseurship that were the badge of distinction and the measure of "value" in respect of the ownership of Western art, the lovingly held small object promised an innocence of artistic sensations (an art to which we "could come as innocently as we could," in the words of the American painter John La Farge in 1884). On the other hand, the collecting frenzy was quickly assimilated to the canons of connoisseurship as a new sign of refinement. Edmond de Goncourt, adept at positioning himself ahead of the pack as arbiter of taste in the matter of Japanese art, wrote that "[t]he man who handles an object with indifferent fingers, with *clumsy* fingers, with fingers that do not envelop lovingly, is a man who is not passionate about art" (emphasis in original). Both sources (La Farge and Goncourt) are quoted by Edmund de Waal (*The Hare with Amber Eyes*, 50), who captures very well the ambiguity of "having it in your hands," the sense of

There is an interesting line of inquiry here, especially for those tempted by the view of Proust as himself tempted by the solipsist stance. It is not, however, to be mine (I have already given some reasons for maintaining that the solipsist variety of skepticism makes no useful sense of Proust). There is, however, another, more resonant example of the relation between touch and doubt: the biblical story of Thomas the Apostle. There is nothing comparably explicit in Proust to parallel Joyce's use of the source—along with the other Thomas (Aquinas)—for the exploration of the theme of doubt;[16] the only mention of the apostle is Elstir's, while talking of the sculptural motif on the facade of the Balbec church that depicts the Virgin Mary handing Thomas her girdle as "the proof of her resurrection" (*JF*, 420). Nevertheless, there is something of the noli me tangere imperative in Proust's "message" of redemption through art.[17] The example of Thomas is notoriously ambiguous; on the one hand, in Christian orthodoxy he is a shining example of doubt superseded by faith; on the other hand, his insistence on "verification" is an awkward challenge to the demands of faith. There is, perhaps, a parable here that we can carry over to Proust. An act of faith is required of both Proust and his readers to accept that his version of the Book can bring us within sight of the resurrection and redemption of time-bound experience, that it can restore to us what we have lost, or indeed never had. The belief can, however, be sustained only by not getting too close, not poking and prying, not wanting to "touch" to check if it is for real. But that is to ask a lot, too much for Thomas and his ilk; "miracles" require "proof," but it is the nature of miracles that you cannot prove them. Thomas's skepticism has nothing to do with solipsism. It is the skepticism of the critical

---

owning as well as touching, in the historical context of the vast trading network that linked Tokyo to Paris (buying cheap in Tokyo and selling dear in Paris), a saga of greed and cupidity on a grand scale. Goncourt was also notoriously a specialist in the collection of erotica and pornographic memorabilia, where it is the relation of looking—the voyeur before the vitrine in the more private rooms of the commercial art dealer—that is paramount. Where commodity fetishism and pornography meet, there is nearly always beneath the surface of "interested" looking a streak of pure bestiality. Proust understood these connections well, as did Henry James. The opening pages of *The Beast in the Jungle*, for example, take us to a large country house in which the various guests are ambling through the many rooms adorned with "the fine things, intrinsic features, pictures, heirlooms, treasures of all the arts that made the place almost famous." The strolling viewers are represented as persons to be observed, singly or in couples, "bending towards objects in out-of-the-way corners with their hands on their knees and their heads nodding quite as with the emphasis of an excited sense of smell." The "sense of smell" is developed on the next page as "the movements of a dog sniffing a cupboard" (*Henry James: Complete Stories, 1898–1910* [New York: Library of America, 1996], 496–97). Food is tamer than sex, of course, and perhaps James added "cupboard" to soften the more startling image of looking as sniffing the erogenous zones.

[16] See Jean-Michel Rabaté, *Joyce upon the Void: The Genesis of Doubt* (Basingstoke: Palgrave, Macmillan, 1991).

[17] I am greatly indebted to Dominique Jullien on this point.

rationalist.[18] It would therefore be consistent with the case I have been making throughout this book (that Proust himself is fully aware that the demand of "faith"—in the work of art—is open to critical questioning) to see him, in one of his many modes of thinking, as a doubting Thomas in relation to his own enterprise. It is also relevant to this analogy that in the tradition of commentary Thomas is sometimes represented as looking at the body of the resurrected Christ as if confronted by a "ghost."[19]

II

Albertine is the novel's outstanding instance of what Deleuze says of Proustian love in general: "the reasons for loving never inhere in the person loved but refer to ghosts."[20] In À l'ombre des jeunes filles en fleurs she is "not quite the mere phantom that a passerby becomes, whom we have barely glimpsed, of whom we know nothing and who may haunt our life thereafter" (451), but she will come to haunt him like no other. In Sodome et Gomorrhe it is the relationship with Albertine that brings him to reflect that "my fate was to pursue only phantoms, beings whose reality lay in large part in my imagination" (407), while the memory of her in La Fugitive becomes the realization "that my vast, protracted love for her was as it were the ghost of the feelings I had felt for her" (497). Swann naturally precedes him and is indeed cited for his tastes in the sphere of the feminine-spectral (JF, 101). However, the category of spectrality in the Recherche has a much wider remit than the will-o'-the-wisps of the besotted. Most of the ghostly apparitions are figures of speech built from impressionistic perceptions of light: the "fantasms" produced by the play of moonlight in the letters of Mme de Sévigné, which so delight the narrator and which he compares to the art of Elstir (JF, 232–33);[21] material forms "looking like pallid evening ghosts of themselves" in the fading light of the Balbec dusk (JF, 394); the "phantom of brightness" cast by the morning sun on the trees in the Bois de Boulogne (S, 426); the Duchesse de Guermantes in her box at the opera as "the spectre of an ideal figure projected against the darkness" (CG, 39). It is also in the

---

[18] Although John's gospel makes no mention of Thomas actually touching the body of Christ, the possibility of doing so is conceived as an empirical test of truth.

[19] Some of the ancient texts have Jesus saying to the apostle: "Take hold, handle me, and see that I am not a bodiless demon."

[20] Deleuze, Proust and Signs, 30. Rabaté posits Albertine as the ghost that is never laid to rest that survives and haunts as a trace (of writing) beyond the processes of forgetting and the experience of indifference. La Pénultième est morte: Spectographies de la modernité (Paris: Champ Vallon, 1993), 20.

[21] On the "spectral" effects of paintings and their "ekphrastic" descriptions in Proust, see Thomas Baldwin, The Picture as Spectre in Diderot, Proust and Deleuze (Oxford: Legenda, 2011).

dark (of the railway station at night) that Brichot semihallucinates M. de Cambremer and company emerging onto the platform as ghosts from the Norman past (*SG*, 501). Scared witless at the prospect of encountering a vengeful Charlus, Morel appears as "the shade of Morel . . . an apparition of Morel, a spectral Morel" (*SG*, 473). And there are those who are figuratively spectralized as an effect of end-times: the desolate hotel manager at the end of the Balbec season who "called to mind the ghost of a king haunting the ruins of what was once his palace" (*JF*, 527); the "doleful, elongated features" of Legrandin at the spectral procession par excellence, the *bal des têtes*, resemble "those of Egyptian gods. Gods? Ghosts would be more appropriate" (*T*, 244), as indeed the term proves to be for the former Boulangist minister who crosses the room "looking as if he were imprisoned in the myriad ties of the past, like a little ghost led about by an invisible hand" (256). And although the analogy is not explicitly used, the narrator himself, returning to Paris after an indeterminate number of years in a sanatorium, reappears like a specter observing a party of specters.

While metaphorical ghosts abound, there are, of course, no "real" ghosts in *À la recherche*, and the only character who appears to (half-) believe in them is the "superstitious" Françoise.[22] After Albertine has left (an outcome greatly relished by Françoise), the narrator feverishly imagines a return every time the lift in the apartment building stops at his floor, but pauses in the midst of high anguish to point a mocking finger: "she has come home, Françoise will come to say, more in fear than in anger, for she is even more superstitious than she is vindictive, and would

---

[22] For the historical and anthropological context of nineteenth-century folk beliefs, see Thomas Kselman, *Death and Afterlife in France* (Princeton: Princeton University Press, 1993), 58–64. In intellectual culture, there was the growing interest in spiritism and psychical research in France and England (what in 1882 the *Saturday Review* called the fashion for "spookical research"). Cited in Shane McCorristine, *Spectres of the Self: Thinking about Ghosts and Ghost-Seeing in England, 1750–1920* (Cambridge: Cambridge University Press, 2010, 145). Bergson, for one, took spiritism seriously (in his presidential address to the English Society for Psychical Research "he defended the immortality of the soul on the basis of apparitions of the dead" [Kselman, *Death and Afterlife in France*, 143]). Schopenhauer's essay on ghost-seeing was highly influential; it argued that ghost-seeing was a form of memory ("retrospective second sight"), particularly active in connection with the recently dead. He also posited a connection between ghost-seeing and the "waking dream": "His theory [was] that the ghost-seer is a person who is dreaming while awake" (*Spectres of the Self*, 74–76). There is a line of connection here to Proust, *The Arabian Nights*, and the theme of the *rêve éveillé*. There is also that "astral body," the doorknob of the magic lantern scene in which Golo appears as a supernatural being (*S*, 13–14), which has some sort of echo in contemporary Theosophy, where "astral" meant "made of starlight" and was "used to designate that aspect of a human being which is called up after death in séances, as well as that which leaves the body during sleep and goes time traveling in the fourth dimension." Leonard, "Proust and Ruskin 2000," in *Proust in Perspective*, ed. Mortimer and Kolb, 220.

be less afraid of the living woman than of a woman she might perhaps believe to be a ghost" (*F*, 487). The mockery ill becomes him, however, since this is precisely what, in another register, Albertine will prove to be for the narrator himself. The French term here translated as "ghost" is "revenant." It is one term in the array deployed by Proust for ghostlike manifestations: "ombre" (shade), "fantôme," "apparition," "spectre." But the most important is the least translatable, the *revenant*, the ghost as the one-who-comes-back.

Françoise's peasant beliefs are also on display in connection with that other *revenant*, the ghost of the dead grandmother, although it is more the reaction of the narrator's mother that tells us what the Proustian phantom looks like: "while we were watching over her dead body, Françoise, who half-believed in ghosts and was terrified by the least sound, had said 'I think that's her' . . . But it was not fear, rather an infinite sweetness that these words aroused in my mother, who would have longed for the dead to return and to have her mother with her sometimes still," and who herself comes to resemble in her son's eyes "a supernatural apparition . . . her eyes seemingly gazing after a being who had flown off" (*CG*, 341–42). She will return—to the narrator—in the emotionally climactic episode of the *intermittences du coeur* ("the anachronism which so often prevents the calendar of facts from coinciding with that of our feelings," *SG*, 158). It is part of the meaning and the effect of that return that the narrator is wholly unprepared for it. The narrative, however, does a lot of preparatory work, starting with a spectral manifestation delivered via a piece of modern technology (literally the ghost in the machine), the disembodied voice ("the ghostly image . . . evoked by her voice") of the grandmother on the telephone to the narrator in Doncières: "but all that I had beside me was her voice, a ghost as bodiless as the one that would perhaps come back and visit me when my grandmother was dead" (*JF*, 132, 137).[23] "Would" means, and becomes, "will." In *Sodome et Gomorrhe*, as the narrator ("suffering from an attack of cardiac fatigue") bends down to remove his boots, she returns "as a convulsion of my entire being" that is a compound of grief, love, and guilt, and that bears the dreadful knowledge that "on meeting her again . . . I had lost her forever" (*SG*, 158–60).

[23] When the narrator first registers that his grandmother is sick and dying, he sees her as if in a photograph. The association of ghosts and photography became commonplace and included the notion that the ghost was a "photograph" in the spirit world of the once living person (as, for example, in Newton Crosland's "Spiritual-photographic theory"). In *Quand j'étais photographe*, Nadar referred to Balzac's reflections on the daguerrotype as offering a "théorie des spectres," while later in the nineteenth century there was Strindberg and his "celestographs" (the photograph plate exposed to the firmament without lens or camera and allegedly capturing "souls" without lens or camera). See Jérôme Prieur, *Proust fantôme* (Paris: Gallimard, 2006), 93–94.

The ghost, of course, resides solely within ("the dead exist only in us," 162), and the "resurrection" is as much of him as of her ("the self that I had suddenly re-become," 161). Lost selves and dead ancestors are the related inner phantoms awaiting the call to return (the call that may, however, never come): "Once we pass a certain age, the soul of the child we used to be and the souls of the dead from whom we spring come and scatter over us handfuls of their riches and their misfortunes, asking to bear a part in the new feelings we are experiencing" (P, 68). The ghosts gather where involuntary memories are deposited, in the body and bodily memory. The body recalling "faithful guardians of a past my mind ought never to have forgotten" (S, 10), but whose forgetting is the very condition of their ghostly being, is where the novel begins, with memories stored in the "limbs" of the sleeping narrator (the theme "returns," in connection with Albertine, at the end of the novel, as "an involuntary memory of limbs," T, 5). Limbs that do their work of recollection as if isolated from the rest of the body to which they belong are what we might call "ghostly parts," the fragmentary sites of the scattered, random, but powerful sensations that support the "edifice of memory" (S, 49).[24] On the one hand, they reveal what, again in respect of remembering Albertine, is termed "the body's terrible ability to keep records" (F, 392), sending forth the bad ghosts, the ones that haunt in the sense of coming back as torment. On the other hand, there are also the benign ghosts, "phantoms of a past dear to me," the ones that come, unbidden to be sure, but as joyful apparitions bearing the treasures locked away in the bodily memory bank.[25]

The bank, however, also requires an external key (an Open Sesame) with which to unlock the deposit-box. In "Combray" Proust invokes the Celtic belief in metempsychosis whereby the "the souls of those we have lost are held captive" unless and until we happen to "come into possession of the object that is their prison. . . . Then they quiver, they call out to us, and as soon as we have recognized them, the spell is broken. Delivered by us, they have overcome death and they return to live with us" (47). How much more Proust might have admired the corresponding Hindu belief in the transmigration of souls, which has it that residues of

[24] Heller-Roazen uses the expression in connection with studies of the condition of delusional limblessness in late nineteenth-century neurology and psychiatry (*The Inner Touch*, 270). One of the key research scientists in the field was Jules Cotard, best known for his account of the so-called Walking Corpse delusion. Adrien Proust was acquainted with Cotard and his work, and it is not at all unlikely that the syndrome was a topic of conversation in the Proust household (there are those who maintain that Cotard is one of the sources for Cottard). The experience of the body as dismembered and ghostly was an extreme form of how "thinking about ghosts came to express the spectralisation of the self in the modern world" (McCorristine, *Spectres of the Self*, 218). It is a striking fact of the narrator's bodily existence in the novel that, while powerfully endowed with sheer sentience, we have no sense of what any of the body parts look like.

[25] *Against Sainte-Beuve*, ed. Sturrock, 6.

past lives and selves are to be found in bodily memory, above all in the sense of smell.[26] Although he may have come across aspects of it in his reading of Schopenhauer, Proust refers to Hindu doctrine but once, and in a very different connection (the attachment to a rigid "caste" system in Swann's social world; no transmigration possible there). Nevertheless, it is on the very same page where the narrator speaks of Celtic beliefs that he links resurrection of past selves to the power of the olfactory (along with the gustatory) as the primary building blocks of recollection: "But, when nothing subsists of an old past, after the death of people, after the destruction of things, alone, frailer but more enduring, more immaterial, more persistent, more faithful, smell and taste still remain for a long time, like souls, remembering, waiting, hoping, on the ruin of all the rest, bearing without giving way, on their almost impalpable droplet, the immense edifice of memory" (49–50).

One example given of the Celtic belief in the incarcerating and embodying object is "the tree" ("when we happen to pass close to the tree"), and is a foretaste of the trees at Hudimesnil:

> I saw them as ghosts from my past, beloved companions from childhood, sometime friends reminding me of shared moments. Like risen shades, they seemed to be asking me to take them with me, to bring them back to the realm of the living. (*JF*, 298)[27]

On this occasion the call is not heeded, and the phantoms slip out of reach as the narrator's carriage turns a corner in the road. One reason the call goes unanswered is because he is not yet in a position to grasp the error in confusing inner and outer. There are hints, even as he refers to Celtic belief and readies for the narration of the madeleine: "[t]he past is hidden . . . in some material object (in the sensation that this material object would give us)." In the parenthesis there is already a displacement across the bridge of sensation, from material object to mental state, which is repeated in the struggle to locate the "meaning" of the madeleine and the cup of tea: "it is clear that the truth I am seeking is not in the drink, but in me" (*S*, 48). These are the first indications of a progressive shift of emphasis away from the embodied toward the disembodied and

---

[26]The anthropologist, Wendy Doniger, summarizes it thus: "all of us are subject to what the Hindus call *vasanas*, 'perfumes,' scents that cling to our transmigrating souls, even in new bodies." "Where a Kiss Is Still a Kiss: Memories of the Mind and the Body in Ancient India and Hollywood," *Kenyon Review* 19, 1 (1997): 119.

[27]Proust writes of the past as ghostly in the concluding paragraph of the preface to the translation of *Sesame and Lilies*. With the two columns of Saint Mark's, we encounter "the past familiarly risen in the midst of the present, with that rather unreal complexion which a kind of illusion makes us see a few steps ahead, and which are actually situated back many centuries; appealing in its whole aspect a little too positively to the mind, overexciting it a little, as should not be surprising on the part of a ghost from a buried past." *On Reading Ruskin*, 129.

a relinquishing of "a fetishistic attachment to the old things which our belief once animated, as if it were in them and not in us that the divine resided" (428). The lesson will gather pace throughout the novel, reaching its conclusion in *Le Temps retrouvé*: "I had realized that it is only coarse and inaccurate perception which places everything in the object, when everything is in the mind" (221). It is the lesson above all confirmed in the Guermantes library, where the productions of involuntary memory are distilled into something "freed of whatever was imperfect in the external perception, pure and disembodied" (177).

The error of believing that one can close the gap between matter and spirit by "possessing a thing materially" (*CG*, 350) takes us back to Albertine's body and to another set of terms: symbol and allegory. The latter is often associated with the image of the spectral (Coleridge termed allegory a "phantom proxy"[28]), while the former is associated with embodied presence rather than proxy representation. Both terms are used to describe the narrator's relation to Albertine's body. The condition of "captivity" in which the narrator seeks to keep Albertine expresses, among other things, a drive to material incarnation, the attempt to hold and contemplate a putative essence of Albertine in a "material symbol of my possession of her" (*P*, 158). This, we have seen, is the drive ceaselessly frustrated by the experience of Albertine as "enigma," the resistance of the body and the person to capture by interpretation, one further term for which is "allegory": "I looked at that entrancing body, at those pink features of Albertine's, raising the enigma of their intentions in front of me . . . It was a whole state of being, a whole future existence, which had assumed in front of me the fateful, allegorical form of a girl" (*SG*, 415). In its mute refusal of embodied meaning, Albertine's body occupies the open form of the allegorical as the form of questions asked and answers withheld, the very figure of allegorisis as endless reading for hidden meanings beneath a literal surface (her skin and "pink features"): "So I stood there, still in the overcoat in which I had returned from the Verdurins, looking at that twisted body, that allegorical figure of what? Of my death? Of my love?" (*P*, 334).

III

What then hangs by this way of representing the body, and what, from a literary point of view, does it mean to be a ghost in *À la recherche*? Viewed in a larger historical perspective, Proust on bodies and ghosts

---

[28] Samuel Taylor Coleridge, appendix to *The Statesman's Manual*, in *Collected Works*, ed. Kathleen Coburn (Princeton: Princeton University Press, 1972), 6:30.

involves his complex relation to an ideal of "embodiment" inherited from nineteenth-century aesthetics.[29] A shorthand illustration of the relation is provided by the contrasting examples of two of the novel's artists: on the one hand, the capacity of Vinteuil's music to summon "disembodied spirits" as if "called up by a medium and interrogated about the secrets of death," spirits that, like the shades of the underworld visited by Odysseus (and evoked by Proust), come from a "lost homeland" with which Vinteuil's music remains "unconsciously in tune" (*P*, 235–36); on the other hand, La Berma's vocal and gestural delivery of lines from Racine as a special kind of "transparent" or nonopaque embodiment—the stylized bodily art of the actress as the "embodiment of an idea represented by a line of poetry (an embodiment that unlike human bodies does not stand in the way of the soul like an opaque obstacle that prevents us from seeing it, but is there like a purified, vitalized garment in which the soul is diffused and can be discovered)" (*CG*, 46).

If we run these contrasting conceptions—the conjuring up of the disembodied specter and the bodying forth of the soul—through the formal categories of romantic literary thought, we are brought back to the distinctions between symbol, sign, and allegory. All three terms appear regularly in the *Recherche*, though for the most part in a free-wheeling, ad hoc manner, such that it would be foolish to read a rigorously coherent, theoretical design into their usage. Many have tried,[30] the starting point normally Proust's reflections on Ruskin, in particular, the reference to allegory as "allegory of reading" (in one of the notes to the translation of *Sesame and Lilies*) to designate an open-ended process whereby a text or oeuvre is not to be grasped in terms of a preconceived schema but as a collection or montage of fragments whose unity becomes clear—to both its writer and its reader—only retrospectively; this is the pattern that, in connection with Ruskin's works, Proust describes as "the secret outlines," which, once glimpsed, retrospectively give a kind of order to the whole.[31]

---

[29] "Proust's aesthetic theory belongs to the nineteenth century." Compagnon, *Proust Between Two Centuries*, 8.

[30] The most carefully argued account is David Ellison's *The Reading of Proust*, 96–104.

[31] Proust, *On Reading Ruskin*, 144–45. As a model for Proust's own working method, Compagnon links what Proust claims to have detected in Ruskin to the remarks in *La Prisonnière* on the open and incomplete compositional processes of Wagner, Balzac, and Hugo, where unity becomes visible in retrospect, *après-coup*. Compagnon's theoretical inspiration is Benjamin's distinction between allegory (as montage, construction working from fragments) and symbol (as imposed organic form), related in turn to Benjamin's arresting reference to Proust's text as woven from the "Penelope work of recollection" (*Proust Between Two Centuries*, 226–27). Luc Fraisse has analyzed how the Kolb edition of the correspondence discloses "a work written in all directions and left open-ended, without an author's guide to its use," allowing us to see the loose patchwork compositional method in action. "Philip Kolb Behind the Scenes," in *Proust in Perspective*, ed. Mortimer and Kolb, 27.

But if modern critical theory, especially from the stable of deconstruction, has got to work on this deep in the trenches, it is not clear how much assistance Proust's text lends the enterprise in any explicitly formulated sense.

Proust often uses the words "sign," "symbol," and "allegory" as if they were more or less synonymous, or alternatively to express a range of different meanings, but in relation to which the terms themselves are not assigned stable values.[32] For instance, in the sequence that has attracted the most comment in this connection—the comparison of the Combray kitchen-maid and Giotto's frescoes—the word "symbol" recurs throughout until finally yielding to one use of the adjective "allegorical" without, however, any implication of an intended change of meaning; the terms are clearly synonymous.[33] Moreover, in addition to lexical blur, there is also conceptual unsteadiness. At one moment, the stress is on the chasm between representation and *representamen* (there is nothing charitable in the expression of the figure who stands for Charity, nor anything envious in the figure of Envy), which thus seems to call for the work of interpretation normally associated with the allegorical. On the other hand, the narrator tells us that he later comes to understand that "the special beauty of these frescoes was due to the large place the symbol occupied in them and the fact that it was represented, not as a symbol, since the thought symbolized was not expressed, but as real, as actually experienced" (*S*, 83–84).[34] In short, we are dealing here with two paradigms of "embodiment," variously seen as either disjunctively related to its more abstract meaning, or as a fully concrete, immediately present instantiation of what it signifies (a "symbol" that is "not a symbol").

There is a compacted potpourri of terms and concepts here, and Proust does not seem to have seen decompacting them with a view to fine analyt-

---

[32] Uncertainty and instability of meaning are also indicated by Proust's quoting of Ruskin on the sculpture of Christ as "no more than a symbol of the Heavenly Presence and not an idol, in our sense of the word—only a letter, or sign of the Living Spirit" (*On Reading Ruskin*, 22). "Symbol" here is synonymous with "letter or sign," although in another idiom it would be "allegory" (with "idol" the partner of "symbol").

[33] Paul de Man's analysis of this sequence (six dense pages) simply inverts the lexical pattern of the original: in de Man's commentary, the term "allegory" is used repeatedly and the term "symbol" just once (in quotation of Proust's text). This is either willful manipulation of the text in the service of an agenda or a tacit acknowledgment that the two terms are in effect interchangeable (but the whole of de Man's work contests that). On other hand, de Man is right to read Proust inside out, so to speak, in the sense that it is clear from many contexts that Proust himself uses "symbol" in ways that would normally be represented as "allegory." Gabaston interestingly relates the Giotto/Charity sequence to the account of La Berma's art of the theatrical gesture in terms of an aesthetic of embodiment (*Le Langage du corps*, 293–96).

[34] In the later return to the frescoes of Giotto's images of Christ and the Virgin Mary in the side-trip to Padua during the stay in Venice, the angels in flight are painted as real flying beings, like birds, as distinct from the angels of later Renaissance art where wings are purely "emblematic" (*F*, 612–13).

ical distinctions as one of his literary priorities. Nevertheless, in however jumbled a form, they can be tracked back to the distinction in romantic literary thought between allegory as a conventional or arbitrary sign and symbol as an embodying instance of what it symbolizes, presented to us rather than represented for us. One wonders, for example, if in his introduction as a student to Schelling's thought, Proust came across the definition that echoes his own striking formulation (a "symbol" that is "represented not as a symbol . . . but as real"): "An image is symbolic whose object does not merely signify the idea but is that idea *itself*"; symbols "do not signify, they *are* the thing itself."[35] Even closer is Goethe's famous definition: "It is the thing itself, without being the thing, and yet the thing . . . How far behind allegory remains, in contrast" (behind or in the shadows as specter to substance, Coleridge's "phantom proxy").[36] For the romantics, the exemplary case of the "living" symbol was to be found in the art of ancient Greece, an art of embodiment realized above all in representations of the body in Greek sculpture. The magisterial statement of this view was Hegel's historico-theoretical treatise on aesthetics (although the Hegelian story is terminologically complicated by the fact that, in his historical argument, Hegel reserved the word "symbolic" for so-called primitive, i.e., Egyptian art). Let us not, however, flail around in the quagmire of the *Aesthetic Lectures*. Hegel and Proust are not, after all, natural bedfellows (the one mention in *À la recherche* is Saint-Loup discussing the war as conforming to the laws enunciated by "old Hegel," *T*, 60).[37] If I mention Hegel here, it is because of a particular spin put on

[35] Cited in Todorov, *Theories of the Symbol*, 203; emphasis in original.

[36] Ibid., 209. Goethe again: "There is a great difference according to whether the poet is seeking access to the general through the particular or sees the general in the particular. From the first of these approaches, allegory is born; in this the particular has value solely as an example of the general. The second example is nevertheless properly the nature of poetry: it states a particular without thinking on the basis of the general and indicating it. But the reader who grasps this particular receives the general at the same time, without realizing it, or realizing it only later" (ibid., 204). Proust may well have acquired some knowledge of these sources in following Gabriel Séailles's course on aesthetics at the Sorbonne in 1894–95. In the article "Against Obscurity," published in 1898, Proust ran the standard distinction between "living symbols" and "lifeless allegories." *Against Sainte-Beuve*, ed. Sturrock, 139.

[37] Derrida, on the other hand, alleged a kinship, associating what he identifies as the teleological form of *À la recherche* with the dynamic of Hegel's *Phenomenology of Mind*: "The implication of the end in the beginning, the strange relationships between the subject who writes the book and the subject of this book, between the consciousness of the narrator and that of the hero—all this recalls the style of becoming and the dialectic of the 'we,' in *The Phenomenology of the Mind*." Derrida, *Writing and Difference* (London: Routledge and Kegan Paul, 2001), 25. By any reasonable measure, this is an odd alignment. If there is such a thing as a "Derridean" reading of Proust (certainly in terms of the preoccupations of this chapter), it would be more along the lines of the distinction in *Spectres of Marx* between ontology and "hauntology," and the role of that distinction in a determined resistance to a metaphysics of embodiment or material incarnation (on a spectrum from the semiotic to the political).

his interpretation of ancient art by one of his most distinguished commentators. Erich Heller claimed that Hegel's account of Greek sculpture recalls the doctrine of the Incarnation and the Eucharist, that it is indeed "the aesthetic version of the dogma of the Incarnation."[38] This is not unlike something Proust said of Ruskin: that "his devotion to Christian art never made him contemptuous of paganism," noting Ruskin's view of "the persistence of the Hellenic ideal in the works of the Middle Ages" (he quotes Ruskin's remark about the mosaics of Saint Mark's baptistery to the effect that while "not earlier than the thirteenth century . . . yet they are still Greek in all the modes of thought, and forms of tradition").[39]

This is quite a ragbag of sources and references—Schelling, Goethe, Hegel, and Ruskin; symbol and allegory; specters and bodies; Greek art and Christian doctrine—with Proust's own varied relation to them far from such as to permit any straightforward claims of "influence." Yet the formula Heller uses in connection with Hegel and the thought of his age—"the aesthetic version of the dogma of the Incarnation"—is one that comes very close to a whole way of seeing the aims of À la recherche, as a literary project best understood in terms of an interpretive model based on the beliefs, rituals, and metaphors surrounding the miracle of transubstantiation, the sacramental Host, and the Word made flesh.[40] Yet on the face of it, it is not at all clear exactly how the "Eucharistic" analogy—for that is what it is, certainly not "doctrine"—can help us in determining the kind of work À la recherche is or aspires to be. It is even less clear when used to support the claim that Proust's "world is not made of signs . . . still less of signifiers and signifieds."[41] However powerful the fantasy of embodied meaning that, along with very many others, Proust entertained, it is hard to see what else his fictional "world" is made of, or indeed, as many Christian thinkers have maintained, what else the

---

[38] "It was not in vain that we called Hegel the theologian of the Greek religiousness of his time. For his definition of Classical art is the aesthetic version of the dogma of the Incarnation . . . the vision, in short, of the Spirit's having entered, in that unique Greek moment of history, the body of the human world, providing it with the lustre of its presence, has been rendered by Hegel in the idiom of his aesthetic theology." Erich Heller, *The Artist's Journey into the Interior* (London: Secker & Warburg, 1966), 111–12.

[39] Proust, *On Reading Ruskin*, 39 and 81–82.

[40] The prime spokesperson for this view is, of course, Julia Kristeva. Here, from *Time and Sense*, are some examples (there are many more) to illustrate the insistence with which the view in question is stated and repeated: "Christian art . . . never ceased to be the model of his aesthetic all the way through to the last lines of *Le Temps retrouvé*" (129); Ruskin mattered to Proust for an experience of art as "real presence" and "transubstantiation" (132); Proust's own ideal is that of "the Word made flesh" (252) and "writing as transubstantiation" (307). Her view of Proust is moreover close to Heller's view of Hegel's aesthetics as a marriage of the Christian and the ancient Greek: "The writer [Proust] adds a Christlike ambition to the sensualism of the Greeks" (195).

[41] Ibid., 307.

Eucharist itself is made of. Doctrinally the latter has, of course, long been an object of intense theological dispute and often violent sectarian scission. In one school of thought (Tertullian and Cyprian, for example), the material Host *is* the body of Christ, a "real presence," a "symbol," in the sense of "represented as not a symbol" but as living, embodied manifestation. In the reforming school of thought (Wycliffe and the Lollards, for example), it is not a manifestation or instance of the body of Christ but a "sign" or metaphor of it (for those inwardly prepared to receive grace), and thus—in the terms of romantic aesthetics—partakes of the sphere of allegory.[42]

There can be no doubt that Proust was drawn to the analogical possibilities of the Eucharist for his own literary purposes.[43] There are many allusions to the ritual of the Host in *À la recherche*, *Contre Sainte-Beuve*, and the correspondence. In the most telling of these (the letter to Daudet), Proust appears to have conceived of a way of writing that would accomplish "the transubstantiation of the irrational qualities of matter and life into human words." This does indeed speak to an ideal of the word made flesh, a type of literary "Cratylism" decked out in the sacramental language of Eucharistic transfiguration. Perhaps this was Proust's solemn imagining of how the threads of the original tripartite scheme envisaged for the novel around roughly the same time—the Age of Names, the Age of Words, and the Age of Things[44]—might be bound together, as the attempted blending of transcendental spirit and the flesh of the world. The narrative is, of course, about the insurmountable separation of these three spheres or levels. Art cannot repair that rupture, nor can it take the place of the Eucharist other than as idolatry. That Proust understood this is clear from the extent to which the religious terms used with such high seriousness in the letter to Daudet are elsewhere more often than not rewritten as ("transubstantiated" into) a comedy of loss, perversion, and desecration. The more casual sources include the tongue-in-cheek compliment bestowed on Robert de Montesquiou (reading his latest poems is like taking Holy Communion) and, in the same year (1907), the flirtatiously playful letters to Anna de Noailles (if insufficiently virginal to be a new Virgin Mary, she is nevertheless so beautiful as to form the "object of a new religion based on the miracle of the incarnation").[45] This already skirts obscene profanation, as does the curious talk in *Carnet 3*

---

[42] See Miri Rubin, *Corpus Christi: The Eucharist in Late Medieval Culture* (Cambridge: Cambridge University Press, 1991).

[43] See Richard Kearney, *Anatheism: Returning to God after God* (New York: Columbia University Press, 2011), 110–18.

[44] *Corr.*, 12:232.

[45] Cited in Barbara Bucknall, *The Religion of Art in Proust* (Urbana: University of Illinois Press, 1969), 148.

of "transubstantiation" in the context of the themes of transvestism and inversion.[46] The *Recherche* itself will begin by adding the themes of incest and sadism to this perverse litany in two of the foundational scenes of the novel: the bedtime kiss and the family lunch. The first gathers into the space of a single sentence no less than three of the key terms identified with the Eucharist (host, communion, and real presence) around the ritual "moment . . . when she had bent her loving face down over my bed and held it out to me like a host for a communion of peace from which my lips would draw her real presence" (S, 17). The entire novel, however, is based on the consequences of the moment wrecked and the "presence" refused. The narrator will carry the sobbing this produces within him to the end; it is, along with the tinkling of the garden bell that announces Swann's arrival in "Combray," the permanent fixture of his inner life.

Sent to bed without the comforting kiss, the young hero is obliged "to leave without my viaticum" (31). The viaticum is the Eucharist given to the dying or those at risk of death, but it also has (or had) the more prosaic, idiomatic meaning of "travel money," a derivation from the religious idea of the crossing from this world to the other. Superimposing these two meanings already gives a hint of the incongruously humorous, and will be further developed with the trauma of the sacrament withheld acted out as a comedy of neurosis (like the "crucifixion" of the waiting room in the Gare Saint-Lazare). The staging includes the farcically theatrical maneuvers adopted to get back what has been refused (lying in wait for his mother by the moonlit window, throwing himself at her feet, all fear and trembling), along with the self-consciously enunciated double bind that undermines the cherished moment at both ends, before and after: before as a preference for delayed over actual gratification ("so brief and furtive," 30); after as the knowledge that the kiss given is but an entry into the antechamber of waiting for the next one, the infernal scene of desire and deferral whereby "real presence" is but the mask of eternal absence (the moment of the kiss "announced the moment that would follow it, in which she had left me, in which she had gone back down," 17). The impossible paradoxes of wanting, waiting, having, and wanting again constitute the point at which the human passions—whether of childhood or adulthood—invade and desecrate the realm of the sacred, as a mix of resentment, guilt, and revenge that finally spills over into a drama of blaspheming profanation: "with an impious and secret hand, I

[46]The draft mentions a certain "Maria" (a forerunner of Albertine), who, in a perspective that deliberately crosses the male/female divide, is placed alongside Racine (and we know to what provocative cross-gender uses Racine will be put in *Sodome et Gomorrhe*); if the term "transubstantiation" here "inevitably evokes the sacrament of the Eucharist," it does so in the spirit of a willful desecration. Compagnon, *Proust Between Two Centuries*, 70.

had just traced in her soul a first wrinkle and caused a first white hair to appear" (41).

For Proust, this was explosive material, however much he managed a certain comic distancing of it through the emotional antics of his hero-narrator. In 1908, when these childhood experiences were much on his mind, he wrote to François Vicomte de Paris that, whatever the complicated games he might play with sacrilege and defilement, his mother was the one person who would remain unsullied by any of it ("never . . . would I profane the memory of what I have most loved on this earth").[47] Proust's sincerity here is beyond reproach, but it is precisely *because* she is the most loved that Maman has to be the main object of defilement. Protecting her from this mess of the mind would have been tantamount to subverting the great literary project on which he was now about to embark: no anguish, no comedy, no guilt, no vengefulness around the disastrous scene of the good-night kiss meant no novel. As so often in Proust, the solution to the contradiction, the conflict between taboo and transgression, lay in indirection and delay. The real mother is replaced by the fictional adoptive mother in *François le Champi*, read to the narrator by the real mother with naturally all the passages that hint at the incestuous skipped or edited. Alternatively, the scene of sacrilege is held in reserve for elsewhere and someone else's parent, a father rather than a mother, when at Montjouvain the narrator witnesses—his first experience as sexual voyeur—Mlle de Vinteuil's lesbian partner suggesting that their mutual pleasure might be enhanced by spitting on the photograph of Mlle de Vinteuil's father.[48] And then, after a delay of several volumes, in another narrative world altogether (the beginning of *La Prisonnière*), there is the bedtime tongue-kiss proffered by Albertine (whose friendship with Mlle de Vinteuil has been the appalled discovery toward the end of the previous volume): "before leaving me to sleep, she would slip her tongue into my mouth like my daily bread, like a nourishing food having the almost sacred character of all flesh on which suffering . . . has conferred a kind of spiritual sweetness, then the analogy which springs to my mind . . . is that other night when my father sent Mama to sleep in the little bed next to mine" (4).

Albertine's tongue in the narrator's mouth is, of course, a profaning echo, at a great temporal distance, of the mother's chaste kiss on the young boy's cheek. It is also represented as a gift of "food," the nighttime offering designed to calm the tormented lover obsessed by thoughts of the depraved lasciviousness of the beloved, and compared to the "daily bread" that possesses something of the "sacred character" and "spiritual

---

[47] *Corr.*, 8:136.

[48] Proust notoriously showed photographs of his parents in one of the male brothels he frequented.

sweetness" (that word "douceur" again) of the Eucharistic Host. The "analogy" that "springs to mind" is no mere chance association; it is a deliberate violation of the self-denying ordinance affirmed in the letter to François Vicomte de Paris. The references to food and bread might also be said to prompt the recollection of a connected Combray ritual. As the church bells ring at midday, the narrator's family sits down to "our table close to the consecrated bread which had also come in, familiarly, after church" (S, 73). These contiguous places and practices—church and home, Sunday communion and Sunday lunch, hyphenated by the *boulangerie* and the freshly baked loaf—constitute a nexus for a set of ideas and associations that together go back to the earlier writings on Ruskin and look forward to the revelations of *Le Temps retrouvé*. They recall the Sundays evoked in the preface to the translation of *Sesame and Lilies*, the village church as "magic abode of . . . the blessed bread" (109), the "sacred grain" mentioned in the notes as one of the meanings of "Sesame," as well as the reflections in the notes to the translation of *The Bible of Amiens* on the "sacred character of *food* in its most general and material sense . . . the constant sustenance that food gives to thought and life."[49] The last are reflections developed in connection with Ruskin's own on the flesh and blood of Christ as sacramental motif in medieval cathedral architecture. Within the novel's own "architecture" (famously, if provisionally, conceived by Proust on the model of the "cathedral"), the remarks about Ruskin anticipate the quasi-Eucharistic "heavenly food" that in *Le Temps retrouvé* involuntary memory becomes in awakening the dead and summoning the ghosts of selves past (that "true self, which may sometimes have seemed to be long dead, . . . is re-awoken and re-animated when it receives the heavenly food that is brought to it," 181).

If this is Proust starting to sound priestly, he is distinctly less so when speaking of the provision of "nourishing food" in the sacrilegious terms of the oral-erotic, or, to return once more to the Combray family meal, when he links its preparation to the shockingly jubilant display of murderous sadism in Françoise's kitchen. The elated abandon with which Françoise slaughters the dinner chicken "put the saintly gentleness and unction of our servant a little less in evidence than it would, at dinner the next day, by its skin embroidered with gold like a chasuble and its precious juice drained from a ciborium" (123). The ciborium is the receptacle in which the Host is kept and the chasuble the garment worn by the celebrant at Communion Mass.[50] The tongue-in-cheek use of the terms here places them with the semihumorous use of the term "viaticum" for the good-night kiss. The vessel also has a more direct analogical and con-

[49] Proust, *On Reading Ruskin*, 109, 144, 87.
[50] I am grateful to Murray and Ciceil Gross for drawing my attention to these details.

textual neighbor in the cup from which the famous herb tea is drunk, as a sort of Christian chalice (as well as a Japanese porcelain bowl) that holds the miraculous liquid that is tasted with the hostlike madeleine, a whole world springing "from my cup of tea" (50). The humble pastry is, of course, the most ambivalent object in the entire novel, piously revered and yet charged with undercurrents of desecrating perversion (an ambivalence reflected in the strange lexical mix with which its shape is described as "so fatly sensual within its severe and pious pleating," 49). But the endlessly cited pastry should not be allowed to obscure its accompanying *tasse de thé* and the equally strange and comic scenes to which the theme of "tea" will also migrate. Jarrod Hayes, for one, certainly doesn't, reminding us that *tasse* is slang for a public urinal and *théière* the term for a public urinal frequented by homosexuals, while *prendre le thé* denotes a gay sexual encounter. It is to Jupien's establishment that Charlus and Morel daily repair "to take tea," though there is no way of deciding whether the meaning is demotically figurative or routinely literal (*P*, 36). *Tasse de thé* is also used in connection with the erotic practices of drinking urine and of dipping bread in urine, thus opening onto the dizzying constellation: madeleine and tea, milk and breast, penis and urine, urine and tea, bread in urine, bread and wine, the Eucharist and the Combray church, Mary Magdalene and Mother Mary.[51]

A vocabulary normally reserved for a "sacred use," whether religious or artistic, is seen to cross over into forms of obscene demotic, bearing within it all manner of feelings and attitudes. Some come from the darker side of the Proustian psychic landscape. Since these are dangerous, however (especially where they implicate the mother), there is wariness at excessive self-exposure (no doubt as much to self as to readers) and a corresponding adoption of masks and displacements. The commoner mode is the safer one of comic travesty. If, for example, Françoise's wanton savagery shocks the young hero, the episode is narrated in such a way that the reader is more likely to laugh than to shudder. The same holds for the further adventures of tea, as it travels to the worldly stage of the Guermantes receptions. The narrator's initiation into the mysteries of the Faubourg Saint-Germain is "hampered by certain difficulties, and the presence of the body of Jesus Christ in the sacrament seemed to me no more obscure a mystery than this leading salon of the Faubourg Saint-Germain being situated on the right bank and the fact that, every morning, from my bedroom, I could hear its carpets being beaten" (*CG*, 28). On the same page the twelve guests at the Guermantes dinner party are "like the golden statues of the apostles in the Sainte-Chapelle, symbolic and sanctifying pillars

[51] Jarrod Hayes, "Proust in the Tearoom," *PMLA* 110, 5 (1995): 992–1105. Kristeva traces out the full associative web that converges on desecration of the Eucharist (*Time and Sense*, 20).

before the Lord's Table." The comic analogy is moreover not allowed to rest at the threshold of baffled entry into this occult social universe. Several hundred pages later, when the narrator is himself among the guests, it is explicitly recalled as "the dinners and luncheons whose guests I had at one time imagined to resemble the Apostles in the Sainte-Chapelle. And in fact they did assemble there like the early Christians, not to partake of merely material nourishment, which was in fact exquisite, but in a sort of social Eucharist." On this second occasion, however, we are also given an indication of the "merely material," a list of some of the exquisite servings: the notorious ortolans ("prepared in accordance with recipes tastefully devised and modified by the Duc himself"); the wine (naturally Yquem) "from the recesses of the Guermantes cellar"; and additional beverages that include orangeade in summer and, in winter, *tilleul*, no less, the lime blossom tea of Combray taking another bow, this time on the menus of aristocratic Paris (512–13).

There is one further worldly displacement of the Eucharist into comedy, of which special note should be taken since it lights on the area that for Proust is "sacredness" itself, the scene of reading and writing portrayed in *La Fugitive* as the production and consumption of the "miraculous loaf." Reading as "nourishment" or "Open Sesame" was one of the themes of the preface to the translation of *Sesame and Lilies*. Responding to an inquiry by Maurice Montabre, a journalist on the staff of *L'Intransigeant*, as to what line of work he might have undertaken had he not been a writer, Proust remarked (tongue-in-cheek) that in a world without paper and in which therefore he could not be a writer, he would be a baker.[52] But since he did not inhabit a paperless world, in the meantime he would continue with a literary endeavor devoted to making an equivalent of Racine's "bread of the angels" (probably a reference to the bread that nourishes in the desert of *Athalie*).[53] And if it was not to be anything quite so opaquely celestial (and remember that "angels" and "heaven" are to turn up as metaphors for lesbian ecstasy in *La Fugitive*),[54] there was always that other image of Proust the baker in the idea of a literary style molded like dough, to which he alluded in correspondence with Anna de Noailles.[55] The very first instance of the narrator writing is not, in fact, the "prose poem" on the steeples of Mar-

[52] When Pissarro founded the Association of Artists that was to form the core of the first impressionist exhibition in 1874, he based it on the rule book of the bakers' union in Pontoise. Originating in a charter granted by Louis VII in 1162, in the nineteenth century it became a byword for militancy, especially during Commune. Philip Nord, *Impressionists and Politics: Art and Democracy in the Nineteenth Century* (London: Routledge, 2000), 52.

[53] *Corr.*, 19:290.

[54] "She had in fact indulged to the point of swooning, to the extent of biting the young laundry-maid whom she met at sunrise on the banks of the Loire and to whom she declared 'I'm in heaven'" (*F*, 491).

[55] See chapter 4.

tinville but the begging "letter" he sends via Françoise to Maman in the belief that it has the power to bring back the hostlike kiss that has been denied him. The deeply affecting meditation on the lost world of childhood, which both follows the prose poem and concludes the "Combray" section of the first volume, is the later-life recall of an irrecoverable world notably marked by the desire once more to "find among the wheatfields a church, like Saint-André-des-Champs, monumental, rustic and golden as a haystack." It is also the desire for a world in which "the mother who came to say good night to me . . . so that I could go to sleep happy, with that untroubled peace which no mistress has been able to give me since that time . . . should be her" (S, 185).

Here then is yet another web, a set of cherished terms clustered around the theme of the sacramental: mother, kiss, church, field, haystack, wheat, grain, bread. In this concluding moment, however, there is no mention of the begging letter; it is the flaw in the web, what inscribes the remembered world as already lost from the beginning, long before it becomes the "blessed bread" of memory and the "heavenly food" of art. If the letter is the first moment of writing as such, the first piece to see its way into print (in La Fugitive) is the "article" published in Le Figaro. We are not told what the article is about (Proust published several in Le Figaro, though the newspaper turned down extracts from Contre Sainte-Beuve),[56] but we know how the narrator reacts to its publication, its proliferation through mass circulation of a daily newspaper compared to Christ's miracle of the five loaves:

> Then I considered the spiritual bread that a newspaper constitutes, still warm and moist as it emerges from the press and the morning mist in which it has been delivered at crack of dawn to the households who take it to their masters with a bowl of milk, this miraculous loaf, multiplied ten-thousand-fold and yet unique, which stays unchanged for everyone while proliferating across every threshold . . . I must read this article not as an author but as one of the other readers of the newspaper; what I was holding in my hand was not just what I had written, it was the symbol of its incarnation in so many minds. (532–33)

The image of Proust as devotee of esoteric high modernism, aloof from the world of modern commercial publishing, is profoundly misleading.

---

[56] In the early drafts, the narrator mentions an article published in Le Figaro, which, by a process of "mysterious multiplication," distributes his thoughts to thousands of readers; the article is represented as a "literary page" and may well be an allusion to the Martinville prose poem (ARTP, 4:673). It is also noteworthy that Proust "originally thought of linking the crucial bedtime scene to the newspaper episode." Sara Danius, "The Mobilizaion of the Eye: Proust, Ruskin and Machines of Vision," in Proust in Perspective, ed. Mortimer and Kolb, 239.

He at first thought of publication in installments (*en feuilleton*), was insistent in wanting his novel to appear in cheap editions, and especially keen on being sold in railway stations (just like the famous nineteenth-century "yellowbacks"). Proust was, in short, fully attuned to what Françoise Leriche calls the "'democratic' logic" of the modern public sphere, with, moreover, a "heightened sense of advertising in all its forms."[57] His later exploitation by the admen from Milan to Madison Avenue should therefore neither surprise nor shock, even if much of it ("Chocolate Chip Cookies Madeleine"; "Les Rouges de Swann") trades crudely in something vaguely known and sold as "Proust."[58] On the other hand, to represent the dissemination of a newspaper article as the miracle of feeding the multitude with "spiritual bread," further backed by the loaded terms "symbol" and "incarnation," is to merge idioms and contexts either as a deliberate blaspheming or as a comic joke at the expense of his own more rarefied artistic pretensions (as well as those of his cult-admirers). The latter interpretation would be consistent with that other instance of Proust at once popularized and parodied through a mass circulation medium, the cartoon, in which a hospitalized Marcel is offered commonplace Danish pastry in lieu of sacralized madeleines.[59] "What's the difference?" is the implied question of the cartoon(ist). Both products are earthbound, sweet-tasting substances; neither is the food of the gods or the bread of the angels.

[57] Leriche, "Proust, an 'Art Nouveau' Writer?," 203.
[58] Gray, *Postmodern Proust*, 156–59.
[59] See chapter 1.

CHAPTER EIGHT

The Citizen of the Unknown Homeland

CHILDHOOD BEDROOM, family dining room, baker's shop, aristocratic salon, Jupien's "establishment," newspaper office—these are the diverse locations to which, as travesty both playful and demonic, Proust transplants the Eucharistic ritual in the course of the novel. We are nevertheless also taken back periodically to its original religious home, by, for example, the views of Charlus in pious mood on the subject of the Christian Church and the sacrament of the Word made flesh:

> the Baron was not simply a Christian, as we know, but pious in the fashion of the Middle Ages. For him, as for the sculptors of the thirteenth century, the Christian Church was, in the living sense of the word, peopled by a crowd of beings he believed to be perfectly real: prophets, apostle, angels, sacred personages of every sort, surrounding the Word made flesh, his mother and her espoused, the Eternal Father, all the martyrs and doctors, the race of whom in high relief crowd the porch or fill the nave of the cathedrals. (*SG*, 433–34)

In this account of Charlus's "medieval" piety, there is a curiously placed echo of Ruskin and Proust on Ruskin, and in particular the description of the western porch of Amiens cathedral as the "Bible in stone" (Proust's words) and the oak of the wooden stalls as containing "the sap of the living tree overflowing the passage of time," with their carvings "like living branches . . . fuller of story than any book" (Ruskin's words quoted by Proust).[1] Artistically crafted stone and wood constitute a sort of living picture-language, understood and valued not for one-to-one pictogrammatic relations of sign and meaning, but as a system of echoes, parallels, and analogies bodied forth for those who "sense" the living word through the senses, seeing, touching, smelling, and hearing it as distinct from receiving it as the dead letter of abstract doctrine.[2] As the expression of "all that can be gathered together on earth of the True and the Divine,"[3] the cathedral and its decorations were the embodied text of Scripture, permitting the type of medieval "figural" reading, a modern version of which Proust thought he had found in Ruskin.

---

[1] Proust, *On Reading Ruskin*, 18–19.

[2] As Macksey notes, the auditory aspect of the description is based partly on a mistake: Proust translates Ruskin's "sound," meaning "robust," as *qui résonne* ("which resounds"). Proust, *On Reading Ruskin*, 18n.

[3] Ibid., 14.

Charlus's view of the church as "living stone" and figuration of the
Word made flesh is, however, far more than an article of religious belief or
a statement of aesthetic credo; it is also inseparable from his anti-Semitic
ravings. We first encounter the latter in *Le Côté de Guermantes* in connection with the Dreyfus affair, the "dreadful, almost deranged remarks"
with which Charlus explains why he must "protest against the charge
of treason levelled against Dreyfus" and assert that the alleged crime "is
non-existent": "This compatriot of your friend [i.e., Bloch] would have
committed a crime against his country if he had betrayed Judaea, but
what has that got to do with France?" (284). By the same token, Dreyfus
cannot be guilty given that, as a Jew, by definition, he is not French. This
is but a foretaste of the eruption that takes place much later in *Sodome et
Gomorrhe* on learning that Bloch lives in the rue des Blancs-Manteaux,
close to the rue des Rosiers (heart of the Jewish quarter in the Marais).
Its grandiloquent insanity calls for quotation in extenso, as the longest
anti-Semitic tirade of the whole book:

> "Oh, the very height of perversity," exclaimed M de Charlus, seeming to de-
> rive a profound satisfaction from his own cry of ironic indignation. "Rue
> des Blancs-Manteaux," he repeated, laying weight on each syllable and
> laughing. "What sacrilege! To think that these Blancs-Manteaux polluted by
> M. Bloch were once those of the mendicant friars, known as serfs of the Holy
> Virgin, that Saint Louis established there. And the street has always belonged
> to the religious orders. The profanation is all the more diabolical in that,
> no distance from the rue des Blancs-Manteaux, there's a street whose name
> escapes me but which is entirely given over to the Jews; there are Hebrew
> characters on the shops, factories making unleavened bread, Jewish butchers,
> it's quite simply the *Judengasse* of Paris. M de Rochegude calls that street the
> Paris ghetto. That's where M Bloch should have been living. Of course," he
> went on, in a somewhat emphatic, lordly tone . . . "I concern myself with all
> that only from the point of view of art. Politics are not my thing and I can't
> condemn en bloc, even if Blochs there are, a nation that numbers Spinoza
> amongst its illustrious sons. And I admire Rembrandt too much not to know
> what beauty may be had from the frequentation of the synagogue. But then
> a ghetto is all the better the more homogeneous and the more complete it is.
> You may be sure, in any case, so closely bound up are the practical instinct
> and cupidity with sadism among that race, that the proximity of the Hebraic
> street I am speaking of, and the convenience of having Israelite butchers close
> to hand, led your friend to choose the rue des Blancs-Manteaux. How curious
> it is! It was there, as it happens, that there lived a strange Jew who boiled
> the Host, after which I believe they boiled him, which is stranger still since it
> seems to signify that the body of a Jew can be of equal value to the Body of
> God." (498–99)

In his own demented way, Charlus spews out a set of stock themes from the history of anti-Semitism in Christian Europe; contamination ("pollution") by contiguity and cohabitation (the ghetto—the rue des Rosiers—next door to the "Christian" street, the rue des Blancs-Manteaux); the usurpation and appropriation of what rightfully belongs to the national-religious order (the Jew—Bloch—*in* the Christian street); the threat to the integrity of a culture by the incorporation of alien signs (the "Hebrew characters on the shops"); the marking of foreignness by the use of the foreign place-name (*Judengasse*); the repeated, semivisceral preoccupation with kosher meat; profanation and desecration of the Host, as the contemptuous reference to Jewish "unleavened bread" (overlooking the fact that it was also widely used in administering the Christian sacrament) turns into the old tale of the Jew who boils the Host (a tale much in circulation during Charlus's [and Ruskin's] beloved thirteenth century, age of the great cathedrals of France). Even the "lordly" exemption of the great philosopher (Spinoza) and the great painter (Rembrandt) is consistent with the relevant social forms and contexts of "educated" anti-Semitism.

The narrator does not react to Charlus's outpouring. Reckless though the assertion might seem, Charlus is not necessarily a genuine anti-Semite (in the racial sense). His verbal behavior is more a libidinally driven "acting out," Charlus slumming it on the wild side where gutter abuse is never far from sexual instinct (he wants Bloch), in some respects (but only some) like the verbal beating he delivers to the narrator at the very moment he manifestly but unavowably desires him.[4] But if the narrator does not immediately react, perhaps it is in part from the memory of this terrible moment that, during the final exchange between Charlus and the narrator in *Le Temps retrouvé* on the subject of the stones as ruins (the wartime destruction of both the Combray church and Reims cathedral), the narrator issues his sternest warning against the fetishism of idolatry and the culture of the "symbol" as the site of a fusion between the material and the spiritual ("the whole of that mixture of living history and art that was France," according to Charlus): "I adore certain symbols no less than you do. But it would be absurd to sacrifice to the symbol the reality that it symbolizes . . . Do not sacrifice men for the sake of stones, the beauty of which derives precisely from their having for a moment embodied human truths" (104). If "symbol" is to be understood as "embodiment," the relation between symbolizing and symbolized is purely temporal and transitory ("for a moment"), inscribed in the secular

---

[4] In connection with Charlus, Eddie Hughes has perceptively commented on the "striking convergence of anti-semitic and sexual energies." *Writing Marginality in Modern French Literature: From Loti to Genet* (Cambridge: Cambridge University Press, 2001), 59.

perishability of all things, even when built to last in order to reflect a faith held to reflect eternal verities.[5]

In his remarks on the sculpture of Christ at the center of the west porch of Amiens cathedral, Ruskin spoke of the disjunction of temporal and eternal, essence and material envelope in terms of the imperative necessity of distinguishing between letter and spirit. These remarks are quoted approvingly by Proust in his preface to La Bible d'Amiens: "Of the statue of Christ itself, I will not speak here at any length, as no sculpture would satisfy, or ought to satisfy, the hope of any loving soul that has learnt to trust Him; but at the same time it was beyond what till then had been reached in sculptured tenderness; and was known far and near as the 'Beau Dieu d'Amiens.' Yet understood, observe, just as clearly to be no more than a symbol of the Heavenly Presence and not an idol, in our sense of the word—only a letter, or sign of the Living Spirit."[6]

"In our sense of the word," one among so many others, as illustrated by the sliding meanings of the term "symbol" that we encountered in chapter 7. But the general line of both Ruskin's and Proust's thinking seems to be that the symbol is problematic when it becomes symbol-worship or what Proust, summarizing Ruskin, calls "a certain fetishism in the worship of the symbols themselves."[7] Ruskin has another way of putting the same idea in what he says about the artistic desire for "perfection," the perfect—fully realized, embodied—fit of matter and spirit. True "blasphemy," Ruskin suggested, lay less in mockery than in imitation, in the belief that artistic creation can rival the creation of God the Father. One of the reasons Gothic meant so much to him was because its implicit acknowledgment of imperfection, its soaring spires a statement of longing, reach for what its makers knew could never be reached by human hand: "the demand for perfection is always a sign of misunderstanding of the ends of art . . . imperfection is in some sort essential to all that we know of life . . . Nothing that lives is, or can be, rigidly perfect; part of it is decaying, part nascent."[8] We can reasonably assume that, as, like his author, a reader and translator of Ruskin, the narrator has some of these Ruskinian ideas in mind when taking Charlus to task. Unpredictable

---

[5] Proust concludes his commentary on the springlike atmosphere of the Vierge Dorée sculpture in the porch of the Amiens cathedral as follows: "But this medieval springtime, prolonged for so long, will not be eternal, and the wind of the centuries has already stripped from the front of the church, as on the solemn day of a Corpus Christi without fragrance, some of its stone roses." On Reading Ruskin, 15–16.

[6] Proust, On Reading Ruskin, 22.

[7] Ibid., 39.

[8] Ruskin, "The Nature of Gothic," in The Stones of Venice, 11:202–3 (emphasis in original). Reynaldo Hahn wrote to an acquaintance in 1913 to say of the publication of Du côté de chez Swann: "Proust's book is not a masterpiece if one calls masterpiece a thing that is perfect and with a flawless structure." Corr., 12:333; emphasis in original.

as ever, Charlus in fact responds amicably to the rebuke ("I understand
what you mean"), and in order to signal his agreement refers to an essay
by Maurice Barrès on the bombarding of Reims cathedral by German
artillery: "M. Barrès . . . was moving and generous when he wrote that
Rheims cathedral itself was less dear to us than the lives of our infantry-
men" (104). The allusion to Barrès, however, makes of Charlus's acqui-
escence to the narrator's strictures something of a poisoned gift. The text
in question is almost certainly "Le coeur des femmes de France," from
Barrès's *Chronique de la grande guerre*:

> Perhaps one believes it is lost, the genius of men who in the Middle Ages
> sculpted the Virgins of compassion, in memory of the sufferings of the mother
> of God at the foot of the Cross. But take this letter found in the compartment
> of a train carrying wounded soldiers. Take it, read it, and you will know that
> even if the barbarian invader destroys the masterpieces of Rheims and our
> country churches, what will inspire them has not been exhausted. Beneath the
> breast of the women of France a treasure of piety exists, and that same soul
> that our ancestors had summoned and set in the stone of cathedrals. We had
> become blind, but the oldest French beauty soars up from the shadows and
> appears to us, and the great hours of battle, tocsin bells, victory bells, have
> revived us, have brought us back to living nature, to the truth of the depths of
> our race . . . I have just seen in the shadows the source from which the genius
> of our race has flowed for centuries.[9]

This rhetorically hectic confection is, as Jacques Rancière notes, both a
hairbreadth and yet a vast distance from what Proust might have written.[10]
It is at once close and far because of the complicated relation of Proust
the wartime patriot to the heavily contaminated notion of "Frenchness"
and especially what Barrès and others on the nationalist right, from the
time of the Dreyfus affair through to the First World War, had begun to
call "the good Frenchman."[11] Proust often spoke warmly of Barrès, who
in turn, writing from Vézelay, congratulated Proust for his article on the
separation of church and state, "La Mort des cathédrales," in which he
remarked that an end to the celebration of Christ's sacrifice of flesh and
blood in the churches and cathedrals would be a cultural catastrophe for

[9]Maurice Barrès, "Le coeur des femmes de France," first published in *L'Echo de Paris*,
November 19, 1914, and subsequently in *Chronique de la grande guerre* (Paris: Librairie
Plon, 1928), 151.

[10]Jacques Rancière, *The Flesh of Words: The Politics of Writing* (Stanford, Calif.: Stanford University Press, 2004), 122. Rancière does not, however, note Charlus's allusion to
Barrès's essay.

[11]The bad sort were defenders of Dreyfus, such as Zola, in fact not really French at all:
"this man is not French." Barrès, *Scènes et doctrines du nationalisme* (Paris: Plon-Nourrit,
1925), 1:43, 1:72.

France.[12] In the preface to the translation of *The Bible of Amiens* Proust explicitly stressed the relation between a cathedral and its local setting, at once historical and geographical, saying of Ruskin's own account that "he did not separate the beauty of the cathedrals from the charm of the regions from which they sprang."[13] "Charm," as we have seen on numerous occasions, is no weak compliment in Proust, but when it came to a link between the attractions of the local and the notions of Frenchness in circulation from the time of the Dreyfus affair onward, there was the risk of it getting caught up, however unintentionally, in xenophobic manipulations of the myth of *la France profonde*.

With the exception of Saint Mark's, the churches and cathedrals in the *Recherche* are all French. The cathedrals of Amiens, Reims, and Rouen are not just the "Bible in stone," declarations of religious faith, but also an expression of nation and ancestry (what Barrès, in a far more loaded phrase, terms the "genius of a race"); as national patrimony they belong to another kind of communal body, prime parts of what in the wartime sequence of *Le Temps retrouvé*, the narrator calls "the body-France,"[14] a focus for that other form of "miracle" described as "the miracle of patriotism" wherein the People, mobilized for the defense of the fatherland, "form one flesh" (82–83). The "death" of the cathedral when threatened with desertion by a more secular "lay" France is one thing, lamentable but a matter internal to the "family." Its physical destruction by the external enemy, however, is the body-France mutilated, the visible scarring of the public face of the national community. This seems to have been one of the thoughts Charlus takes from Barrès and which the narrator criticizes as a form of idolatrous symbol-worship. But Charlus's lament is also for the Combray church as much as it is for Reims cathedral;[15] it is one example of Barrès's reference to "our country churches," rooted in the *terroir* of the great Guermantes family, its stones and stained-glass windows integral to the younger narrator's romance with the nobiliary and warrior history of medieval France. For Barrès the humble country church mattered even more than the national monument. The latter embodied a memory of worldly monarchical power (Reims cathedral was where the coronation of the kings and queens of France took place), but it was in the village church that the true soul of France was found, the

---

[12] *Contre Sainte-Beuve*, ed. Clarac and Sandre, 144.

[13] Proust, *On Reading Ruskin*, 42.

[14] Proust first writes "corps France," adding the hyphen ("corps-France") when the expression is repeated some pages later. Was the addition a sign of Proust wanting to stress the idea of an "incorporating," collective entity?

[15] In fact, according to Charlus, it was destroyed by French and English forces as a consequence of having been used as an observation post by the invading Germans (*T*, 104).

buried dead in the cemetery a literal token of the roots of Frenchness in blood and soil.

In the *Recherche*, the country church on which this cultural history most insistently converges is Saint-André-des-Champs (the derivation of the name from the surrounding "fields" already signifying a relation of church to soil, wheat crop, bread, and body). There are three moments in the novel when the Frenchness of the church is brought strongly into focus. In "Combray," entranced by the perceived symbiosis of sculpted stone and everyday country life, the narrator exclaims "how French that church was!" Through the mason's work, a continuity is created between the living and the dead; the faces on the porch resemble those of Françoise, Théodore (the delivery boy at the grocery store), and "some girl from the fields" (151–52).[16] In the second moment (*Le Côté de Guermantes*), the "girl" association will reappear, though complicated by the presence of Albertine in the frame ("one of the incarnations of the charming little French country-girl typified in stone in Saint-André-des-Champs," 365). But it is also here, in the stones of Saint-André, that the fusion of Christian body and body-France is explicitly stated: Saint-André-des-Champs is "the true opus francigenum . . . the secret of which . . . is to be found . . . in those young Frenchmen, nobles, bourgeois or peasants, whose faces are sculpted with the same delicacy and boldness as those on the famous porch, traditional and still alive" (407). The living tradition embodied by Saint-André-des-Champs is moreover not just French but "something *exclusively* French" (407, emphasis added). There is a bond of church and "race," its most striking exemplum the person and the body of Robert de Saint-Loup, the "pure-blooded Frenchman." Saint-Loup is distinguished by his "unconscious grace," the endowment of "something he had inherited by birth and upbringing, his race." He is held to "embody an inner perfection in substance and shape," like one of Hegel's Greeks transplanted to the "fields around Combray" (407–13).[17] Talk of the

---

[16] Saint-André is also reminiscent of what Proust claimed to have experienced via Ruskin, a grasp of the living faith embodied by the stones of Amiens and Saint Mark's. The "notions" motivating the masons of Saint-André "were derived not from books, but from a tradition that was once very old and very direct, uninterrupted, oral, deformed, hardly recognizable and alive" (*S*, 152).

[17] In its preoccupation with social pedigree, *Le Côté de Guermantes* is the volume with the highest concentration of references to and comparisons with Greek sculpture. Of the Duc de Guermantes, for example, the narrator first observes that "he was still a very handsome man, with a profile that retained the purity, the firmness of outline of a Greek god" (221), and later that: "I seemed to be looking at the statue of Olympian Zeus which Phidias is said to have cast in solid gold" (281). In *Le Temps retrouvé*, however, the analogy is associated with idolatry: "I felt something close to idolatry for the future Gilbertes, the future Duchesses de Guermantes, the future Albertines whom I might meet and who, it seemed to me, might inspire me, as if I were a sculptor walking among fine classical marbles" (297).

"pure-blooded Frenchman" in the early twentieth century was, however, uncomfortably close to what the ideologues of nationalism meant by "the good Frenchman," and doubly disturbing to encounter in the volume (*Le Côté de Guermantes*) that has the Dreyfus affair as one of its central preoccupations. But even more charged is the third moment, the war sequence in *Le Temps retrouvé*, where the encomium linking Saint-André-des-Champs and Saint-Loup as the incarnation of a "pure" Frenchness is further developed in terms of the ideals of heroism in the name of which Saint-Loup will go to his death on the battlefield as "profoundly a Frenchman of Saint-André-des-Champs" and "in conformity with all that at this moment was best in the Frenchmen of Saint-André-des-Champs" (46).

Proust wrote to Lucien Daudet of his conception of the *Recherche* as an artistic form of "transubstantiation" in the year before the outbreak of the First World War (November 1913). Lucien's brother, Léon (also a good friend of Proust's), was, with Maurras, a cofounder and then editor of the periodical *Action française*, the principal source of the blood-and-soil narratives of nation and ethnicity in which notions of "transubstantiation" and "patrie" melded in the ideological construct of the Union sacrée (of which Daudet, Maurras, and Barrès were ardent supporters).[18] This was a territory with borders both defined and defended in the conditions of war (Alsace-Lorraine, home to Joan of Arc, the heroine of the far right, geographically and politically the most contested border zone).[19] But it was also physical earth as well as geographical territory, home to the chthonic being of the nation and the site of mystical communion with the buried ancestor; it was where the blood of the nation and the blood of the Eucharistic ceremony were as one.[20] It is doubtful that Proust had anything even remotely like this in mind when he wrote to Daudet of "transubstantiation." It is customary, and correct, to distinguish between Proust the honorable Dreyfusard patriot and Barrès, the brilliant but dishonorable nationalist (who argued infamously that to protect the nation and its sacred institution, the army, Dreyfus should be found guilty even if innocent).[21] Proust's allegiances to France stem from the sense of belonging to a territory, a history, and a language, which is indistin-

---

[18] Proust wrote an embarrassing article in praise of Léon's "boundless genius" and in the private correspondence confessed to the (disappointed) prospect of being published in *Action française* as that which "on account of your brother and Maurras, would flatter me the most." *Corr.*, 12:260.

[19] Barrès's proposal to establish a national day of remembrance of Joan of Arc was adopted by the National Assembly in June 1920.

[20] Michael Sutton, *Nationalism, Positivism and Catholicism: The Politics of Charles Maurras and French Catholics, 1890–1914* (Cambridge: Cambridge University Press, 1983).

[21] In 1906 Proust wrote to Anna de Noailles: "Barrès was very courageous and noble the other day in the Chamber," but then added, "I shan't write to him because I would immediately have to add that Dreyfus is innocent just the same." *Corr.*, 6:155.

guishable from the sentiments of the narrator-patriot who, at a time of crisis, writes of "feeling myself to be one of the cells of the body-France." At its most moving—and exactly the point where the barrier separating narrator and author simply collapses—it is the sentiment that brings him to speak with heartfelt admiration for the wartime selflessness of the Larivière family (the "real-life" relatives of Françoise, representatives of a France "redeemed by the countless masses of the Frenchmen of Saint-André-des-Champs," 154).[22]

There is nothing here that even distantly resembles Barrès's effusions (basically war propaganda masquerading as "literary" writing). Nevertheless, it is on more than just one fulsome occasion that we hear talk of blood-purity in À la recherche, and occasionally it can be heard to echo disturbingly from character to narrator. The Duc de Guermantes, not famously of enlightened or progressive views, says of the Comtesse d'Argencourt that hers is "the purest, the oldest blood in the whole of France" (CG, 445). However, the countess has a rival, sponsored by the narrator himself: the body of Madame de Marsantes is home to "the purity of blood which for several generations had flowed only with what was greatest in the history of France" (248). Atavistic bloodline can also manifest itself in distinctly "non-French" ways. Nissan Bernard, we are told, "had the atavistic love of an oriental for harems" (245). Gilberte's alleged "meanness" over money prompts the question (possibly in the form of unattributed, free, indirect speech, but it doesn't look that way): "[W]hat Jewish ancestry had thus informed Gilberte?" (F, 648). We are, moreover, often invited to "read" the transmission of heredity on bodily surfaces, as the legible signs of blood, race, and caste. There are two exceptions to the tendency of the Proustian body to obstruct or obscure legibility. One, we have seen, is the aging body. The other—and in some contexts unnervingly related—is racial body "type." The body—the face especially—exhibits atavistically generated indicators of origin and identity, "rooted" in a biological "nature predating the individual himself" (JF, 469) and manifesting "a sort of magnetism which brings together, and keeps together, certain features of physiognomy and mentality" (263).

There is a surprisingly large place granted in Proust's novel to the pseudoscience of physiognomics, which was inherited from the late eighteenth century and which was to play such a large part in the nineteenth-century novel in the presentation of "character."[23] Its uses for the purpose

[22] "Whatever the limits of Proust's own politics, the Recherche is under no illusions about the difference between patriotism and chauvinism." Michael Sprinker, History and Ideology in Proust: "À la recherche du temps perdu" and the Third French Republic (Cambridge: Cambridge University Press, 1994), 166.

[23] For an account of Proust's relation to that tradition, see Gabaston, Le Langage du corps, 86–90.

of racial stereotyping began early in the nineteenth century but were expanded greatly with subsequent developments in the biological sciences.[24] There are many traces of this in *À la recherche*, but the most flagrant concern "the Jewish nose." When, after a long gap, we reencounter Bloch in *Le Temps retrouvé*, his burning arriviste ambition to make it into the salon world has at last been satisfied, but at the cost of some masking of inheritance. In addition to having "permanently adopted his pseudonym of Jacques du Rozier," he has adjusted his look (a new hairstyle, the sporting of a monocle) such that "his Jewish nose had disappeared"; though "still large and red," it "now seemed swollen by a sort of permanent cold, which also explained the nasal drawl in which he produced his languid sentences" (261). This is a satirical comment, on Bloch's manipulation of identity, appearances, and voice to make a socially awkward feature "disappear." However, the description of the pertinent feature—"his Jewish nose"—is not Bloch's but the narrator's, with scarcely a hint of implied quotation marks; "Jewish nose" is not the hands-off citing of a racial-physiognomic discourse that is not the narrator's own. And if there is felt to be room for doubt, all equivocation vanishes with the dying Charles Swann. As the body succumbs to disease, it also reverts to origin and type: "Swann's Punchinello nose, for so long reabsorbed into a pleasing face, now seemed enormous, tumid, crimson, more that of an old Hebrew than an inquisitive Valois" (*SG*, 94).

Some have interpreted these atrociously embarrassing remarks more as an instance of Proust letting the anarchic id out to play—enjoying a sort of disreputable Punch and Judy knockabout or Ubu-style riot—than as the words of an anti-Semitic caricaturist. But then, what to do when, instead of entering the playground with daredevil bravura, Proust chooses rather to hide behind mother's skirts, with his feeble response to the arrogant swagger of Robert de Montesquiou's anti-Semitism (doubtless the model for Charlus's tirade)? On account of his Jewish mother, Proust grovelingly explains, he was "not free to have the ideas I might otherwise

---

[24]One of the more interesting aspects of the revival of physiognomics in right-wing thought of the early decades of the twentieth century, especially in Germany (in the work of Spengler, Kassner, and Klages, for example) was a renewed focus on Goethe, and in particular the respects in which Goethe's interest in physiognomics was closely related to his thinking about the nature of the symbol; the symbolic and the physiognomic (which included unguarded expressive moments such as the blush) share the property of immediacy and make possible a direct, immediate apprehension of the meanings they directly embody (Lichtenberg found this laughable, insisting that physiognomics was a semiotics that could be "read" only by virtue of an interpretive code interposed between the particular [the facial feature] and the general [the moral characteristics of the person]). See Richard T. Gray, *About Face: German Physiognomic Thought from Lavater to Auschwitz* (Detroit: Wayne State University Press, 2004).

have on the subject."[25] There is a let-out clause of sorts in the conditional "might have," although the letter, even if intended solely to gratify the flattery-addicted ego of his friend, is by any measure an egregious capitulation. Yet, the hedging, however distasteful its occasion, tells us something important: interpreting Proust in terms of "positions," whether for or against, is a category-mistake; to go looking for them, especially with a view to identifying Proust's "politics," is a waste of time.[26] Although he was not without convictions, for-or-against is not how Proust basically thought; nor is this how the world of *À la recherche* is constructed. He writes as the sworn enemy of all forms of "identity politics." If he draws in worrying ways on the language of physiognomics, he is also probably the only writer to have ever compared the human face to a "theogony," precisely in order to stress that the face is not monolithically readable but many-sided and ever-changing: "The human face is truly like that of a god in some Oriental theogony, a whole cluster of faces side by side, but on different planes and never all visible at once" (*JF*, 493).[27] That could stand as a general description of Proust's novel. It does not take "positions" anywhere, while those of his characters are themselves subject to the logic of metamorphosis (such that, for example, committed anti-Dreyfusards can become loyal Dreyfusards). As a body politic, the body-France is unstable and mutable, not a communal-corporate entity expressing a fixed essence of Frenchness.

[25] *Corr.*, 2:66. The ambivalences and evasions of the letter to Montesquiou have been discussed in detail by Jonathan Freedman in "Coming Out of the Jewish Closet with Marcel Proust," in *Queer Theory and Jewish Culture*, ed. Daniel Boyarin (New York: Columbia University Press, 2004), 343–44.

[26] Marion Schmid has, however, rightly emphasized the elements of opportunism in some of Proust's communications: "Given the highly politicized and ideologically charged milieux he frequented (amongst his friends were some of the leading ideologists and polemicists of his time: Léon Daudet, Maurice Barrès, and Charles Maurras), Proust managed surprisingly well to keep out of political debates. He cunningly manoeuvred between different political camps and happily used political personae to obtain him social honours, but was highly sensitive to rumours of his political protection . . . In a letter to Jacques Boulenger of approximately the same time, concerning an article he had undertaken to thank Léon Daudet for his support in the Goncourt jury, Proust categorically denied any personal political involvement: 'I have nothing to do with politics and never have'" (*Corr.*, 20:530). "Ideology and Discourse in Proust: The Making of 'M. de Charlus pendant la guerre,'" *Modern Language Review* 94, 4 (1999): 961. Samuel Beckett stated that Proust's work is without moral positions, but then made an exception—in exceptionally unflattering terms—for the wartime episode: "Proust is completely detached from all moral considerations. There is no right and wrong in Proust nor in his world. (Except possibly in those passages dealing with the war, when for a space he ceases to be an artist and raises his voice with the plebs, mob, rabble, canaille)." *Proust*, 49. For further details of Proust's complicated relation to Barrès and the idea of a "patriotic" literarature, see *ARTP*, 4:1263–64.

[27] Malcolm Bowie came up with the interesting formulation of "dynamic physiognomy" for Proust's descriptions of the human face in *Proust Among the Stars*, 180.

This is above all true in respect to the linchpin equation of right-wing ideology from the Dreyfus affair up to the First World War and beyond: Army and Nation (more precisely the "Army-Nation" as identical with the body-France, "the perfect emanation of the Fatherland," as General Weygand later put it).[28] The war sequence of *Le Temps retrouvé* is where the patriotic body-France represented by its military corps mutates provocatively into the transgressive sexual body, as both officers and soldiers on leave gather in the male brothel run by Jupien (it is perhaps also a delayed ironic comment on the trumped-up charge of espionage and treason on which the trial of Dreyfus was based that, on entering the brothel, the narrator is convinced that he has wandered into a gathering of spies). It is here that, unseen and aghast, the narrator witnesses the sadomasochistic orgy staged for Charlus's benefit, the baron's chained and beaten body a perversion in the sense of offering a perverted image of the martyred body of the Nation, while on the floor below soldiers chat, smoke, and play cards as they wait their turn as either customer or prostitute.[29] Jupien's brothel is also where the narrator espies a military cross lying on the floor, forgotten, debased, and without a bearer, the inverse of the publicly revered signs of the Unknown Soldier, the sacrificial victim to the holy cause of defending the fatherland.[30] It is in fact Saint-Loup's Croix de guerre (the most prestigious of all the medals conferred in acknowledgment of military valor),[31] property of the war hero who repairs to the brothel when back from the front and then forgets it, left behind as the debris of a homosexual transaction, so much anonymous lost property, unattached to a person or a name. Nor does Proust let us forget that Saint-Loup's virile-heroic ethic, though genuinely selfless at the conscious level, is unconsciously motivated by homosexual desire (as reflecting "an ideal of masculinity found in homosexuals like Saint-Loup . . . for Saint-Loup was rather the very ideal he imagined himself pursuing in his much more concrete desires," *T*, 53).

The inclusion of the war, compositionally a late decision, has proved a source of puzzlement to some (its most interesting expression is found in Rancière's commentary).[32] A tardy embrace of the aims of the historical novel, reflecting the wish to chronicle a cataclysmic moment in the his-

---

[28] See Philip C. F. Bankwitz, "Maxime Weygand and the Army-Nation Concept in the Modern French Army," *French Historical Studies* 2, 2 (1961): 158.

[29] Rancière terms it "the profaning of national heroism," in *The Flesh of Words*, 124.

[30] The monument to the Unknown Soldier was instituted in 1920.

[31] The Croix de guerre was invented in 1915.

[32] Conversely, Marion Schmid's detailed account of the genesis and successive reworkings of the episode is deployed to sustain the view of it as integral to the whole design of the novel ("Ideology and Discourse in Proust," 965). See also Colin Nettelbeck, "History, Art and Madame Verdurin's Croissants: The War Episode in *Le Temps retrouvé*," *Australian Journal of French Studies* 1, 9 (1982): 288–94.

tory of the Third Republic?[33] But the narrative approach to war is quite unlike that of *War and Peace*, *La Chartreuse de Parme*, *All Quiet on the Western Front*, *Voyage au bout de la nuit*, or *A Farewell to Arms*. We are provided with a report of Saint-Loup's death on the battlefield, but the battlefield itself we never see;[34] the air war over Paris is presented through the eyes of the narrator as visual spectacle, concerned more with the beauties of aviation than with the terror of war machines; the streets of the capital throng with exotic and enticing collections of young soldiers, occasions of possible pickups.[35] Rancière makes the brilliantly paradoxical point that the war was included to illustrate what was to be excluded, a certain conception of literature deemed to be radically alien to his own, namely, the epic as the embodying form (the "transubstantiation") of the national-ethnic community,[36] a form that in modern conditions could be reinvented only as a fraudulence. Before himself dying on the battlefield, Charles Péguy had an honorable, if unsuccessful, shot at the reinvention of the epic register. Barrès's hymn to the mother-republic at war, however, was mere feverishly eloquent noise, with its high-octane evocation of an inexhaustibly fertile body replenishing the "race" in the face of the industrial-scale waste of the trenches, a horror he chose elsewhere to exalt in a manner that earned him the infamous soubriquet of the "nightingale of bloodshed" (*rossignol des carnages*). Proust's novel goes nowhere near the trenches, and, had it done so, the trenches would more likely have resembled the brief vignette of groping hands in the Metro during a blackout. Instead of soldiers at the front, we have the scenes in Jupien's brothel. Even if this is not what Proust expressly had in mind, the latter effectively stand as a spoiling rejoinder to Barrès's text on mothers and motherland, while if one wanted a contemporaneously demystifying commentary on another Barrès text, his eulogy on the heroic meanings of

---

[33] For Sprinker the literary rationale of the war is broadly that of the classical historical novel. Its key moment is the (reported) death of Saint-Loup, which, along with the decline of Charlus, "symbolize the demise of the French aristocracy as a whole." *History and Ideology in Proust*, 160.

[34] In her letter to the narrator, Gilberte provides a brief report of the battle of Méséglise, a fictional version of the battle of Verdun.

[35] A fragment in the *Cahiers* (*ARTP*, 4:790) speaks of the "terrible beauty" of the German occupation of parts of northern France and reproaches his compatriots for, as Schmid puts it, "their aesthetic indifference to such a rare event." "Ideology and Discourse in Proust," 966.

[36] Rancière defines "the national epic" as "the book of living truth that the maternal earth carries, now turned into the spirit of the communal poem." As Rancière himself notes, this is broadly consistent with Hegel's account of the epic as the narrative poem of a collectivity and the novel as the modern farewell to the epic or the "anti-epic," disseminating the "knowledge that the word is not made flesh." Proust's farewell is brutal: "Truth made flesh in soldiers' bodies in the national epic then becomes a scenario of pure violence in a sadomasochistic system." *The Flesh of Words*, 122–23.

the Croix de guerre, one could scarcely do better than the story of Saint-Loup's lost cross.[37]

II

The body-France is part compound noun and part proper name. The question "what's in a name?" or more exactly in the "body" of the name, what does its material form "embody," runs through the whole novel and is directly bound to the attractions of magical thinking, what Proust calls "the magic world of names" (*CG*, 542).[38] We have seen how the spell is undone, as its imaginary content is emptied out when measured against the reality of what it names. The process implicates both personal names and place-names. They are always descriptive mishits, nominal versions of the "optical illusion." Place-names, however, are also a structural device as well as a thematic motif.[39] Two whole sections of the *Recherche* are themselves named by the term "place-name" itself: "Nom de pays: le nom" and "Nom de pays: le pays."[40] Initially an object of poetic reverie on the part of the narrator and of amateur etymology in the researches of the local curé, the space given over to reflection on the place-name will expand and evolve into the torrent of erudition later displayed by Brichot as scholarly expert in the subspecies of onomastics called toponymy.

Brichot brings the scientific rigor of the new positivist philology to the explanation of the origins of certain place-names (principally in Normandy), with, in part, the aim of exposing the well-meant but intellectually naive endeavors of the Combray curé (who publishes a "little book" on the subject). In this respect, Brichot is assigned the part of the demystifier, the erudite skeptic who briskly dispatches the narrator's dalliance with a pseudo-Cratylist toponomy.[41] The execution of that role does

---

[37]Barrès, *L'Âme française et la Guerre*, vol. 3, *Croix de guerre* (Paris: Émile-Paul Frères, 1916). Saint-Loup himself invokes and struggles with the idea of the war as epic poem. On the one hand, the "heroism" of the common people justifies the use of the term "epic"; on the other hand, the manufactured patriotism of politicians and press brings him to deplore the term as an abuse of language: "it is tedious to be making an epic out of terms that are worse than faults of grammar or failures of taste" (*T*, 60–61).

[38]By this Proust means something in the "body" of the name, in its syllables (for example, the "magic syllables" of the name Agrigente). *CG*, 431.

[39]Genette maintains that, in the general thematics of the Name, special values attach to place-names. *Mimologiques: Voyage en Cratylie* (Paris: Editions du Seuil, 1976), 316.

[40]In one of his letters to Lucien Daudet (August 1913), he refers to the two sections as not a "digression" (*Corr.*, 12:259). From Proust that is saying something.

[41]As Genette points out, the narrator's fantasias (especially the riff on Normandy place-names in "Nom de pays: le nom"), which variously exploit the phonic, graphic, and morphological properties of the name, are not, strictly speaking, a mimesis after the manner of Plato's *Cratylus* at all, but products of inventive poetic play (*Mimologique*, 318–20).

not, however, exactly require the manic display of Sorbonne pedantry to which Brichot treats us in *Sodome et Gomorrhe*. From a strictly "functional" point of view, the burgeoning excess of erudition is an anomaly, an extraneous textual growth that develops into a kind of monstrous carbuncle (Compagnon is even more vivid, calling it "a kind of tumour inside the novel").[42] Like the war sequence, it is another late addition, grafted onto the text but without any obvious rationale. Its apparent pointlessness has been seen as itself the point, an unusually perverse demonstration of Proust's "patchwork" compositional method and the related resistance of his aesthetic to the idea of the "organic, coherent, autonomous work."[43] But if Brichot's learned disquisitions are a sort of "foreign" body imported into the fabric of the text, there remains the exquisite irony of the importing agent himself being an anti-Dreyfusard nationalist hostile to all things foreign. Brichot may deploy the resources of modern historical scholarship to discredit the view that the meaning of a Name is embodied in and by its roots, but this does not inhibit him from openly declaring his dislike of the new German-inspired philology, not on academic grounds but for reasons of patriotism.[44]

For there was also a politics of etymology and toponomy. As a source for Brichot's discourse, Proust drew extensively on the researches into the history of place-names of the philologist and medievalist Auguste Longnon (specifically his *Origines et formation de la nationalité française*, first published in 1912).[45] Maurras wrote the preface to a posthumous edition and saluted him in *La Démocratie religieuse*.[46] For further information Proust also contacted Louis Dimier, the art historian who was also an active member of Action française (he was elected general secretary of the Institut d'Action française, the organization's think tank).[47] In these contexts, "roots" were understood and valued in more

---

[42] Compagnon, *Proust Between Two Centuries*, 227.

[43] Ibid., 226.

[44] We are told that one of Brichot's "masters," as well as a colleague in the Académie, is Renan, the most influential disseminator of comparative philology in nineteenth-century France. His treatise on the "Semitic" languages (published in 1855) reprised the distinction that went back to Friedrich Schlegel between an inferior because "agglutinative" Semitic language family ("mechanical" and "inorganic") with the "inflectional" Indo-European family, which derived its superior creative possibilities from the "germinal" power of the "root." In his incarnation as journalist during the war, Brichot also denounces German militarism in the name of "peace," not because he is a pacificist but because he is an anti-German patriot (*T*, 86).

[45] Longnon's *Lieux de France* was published in 1920.

[46] Maurras complimented Longnon's *Unité française*, noting that it was first published in *Action française*, *La Démocratie religieuse* (Paris: Nouvelle Librarie Nationale, 1921), 111. See *Nationhood and Nationalism in France: From Boulangism to the Great War, 1889–1914*, ed. Robert Tombs (London: HarperCollins Academic, 1991).

[47] Compagnon lists Proust's sources in *Proust: Between Two Centuries*, 220–21.

than just the philological sense; they were also the mark of the autochthonous "purity" of the origins of tribe, race, and people, inseparable from celebration of the rooted life of community and antagonism to its opposite, the category of the rootless, the deracinated that figures in the title of Barrès's most widely read novel, *Les Déracinés*.[48]

When, in the letter to Louis de Robert, Proust conceived the tripartite scheme—the Age of Names, the Age of Words, and the Age of Things—he did not spell out what these titles signified (the idea was floated in a tacked-on and tentative postscript), but it seems minimally clear that he understood the first as what comes first in more than the chronological sense; the age of names is the age of childhood illusion, but also the paradisiac moment of innocence in the Garden of Eden with Adam the primordial name-giver. Exiting the age of names was also to forsake the age of innocence. This was a process that involved not just the disillusion that attends the entire adventure of the Name in Proust, whether of persons or places, but also and very specifically implicated romances of a time-honored France, the door to which is unlocked by the enunciation of the place-name, as if it were a variant of the Open Sesame mantra. In this connection let us try another speculative exercise: since we are told inside the fiction that Renan is Brichot's "master" and colleague in the Académie française, let us imagine another blurring of the line separating fiction and reality, where we find Brichot chatting with Barrès in the Académie on the subject of the nineteenth-century writer retrieved from near-oblivion and identified by the nationalist right with the myth of an innocently paradisiac *France profonde*—not George Sand (too "socialist," supporter of the 1848 insurrections), but the "charming" Gérard de Nerval, author of—for those willing to blind themselves to everything in Nerval that disturbs—the sweetly nostalgic *Sylvie*, with its roll call of Valois place-names and its evocation of a lost pastoral world.

Proust was not among those willing to blind themselves, and his magnificent essay on Nerval shows us how and why. He cites and counters Jules Lemaître's view (Lemaître was a leading member of the Ligue de la Patrie française) of *Sylvie* as taking us to "the heart of France" with a question followed by a categorical answer: "Traditional, very French? I do not find it so at all."[49] On the contrary, the whole point of Nerval's story is that it takes us psychically to a foreign country, enchanted no doubt but the place of "an enchantment full of disquiet."[50] Putting Lemaî-

---

[48] See Martin Thom, *Republics, Nations and Tribes* (London: Verso, 1995). Charlus speaks of "deracinated art, as M. Barrès would call it" (*T*, 103).

[49] "Gérard de Nerval," in *Against Sainte-Beuve*, ed. Sturrock, 26. The piece that was eventually published in *Contre Sainte-Beuve* is a composite of two texts from *Cahiers* 5 and 6.

[50] Ibid., 31.

tre in his place, however, is but a warm-up for taking aim at another target, Barrès's maiden speech on his election to the Académie française in 1907 (he succeeded that other nationalist reactionary, Hérédia, who had spent his later childhood in Nerval country). Barrès went all the way with the requisite idées reçues—the church bells ringing dreamily through the autumnal mists that envelop the cantons of Chantilly, Compiègne, and Ermenonville, the traditions of local festival, the "pure" French of the songs and ballads, the memories of chivalric manners, and so on. But his main purpose was to situate Nerval in the ideological nexus where land, war, religion, chivalry, and stoutly patriotic yeomen (*terriens*) were knit together in a generalized image of uncorrupted "purity."[51]

Proust, as always, is courteous; he quotes but a handful of fragments from Barrès's text and leaves the references to war, church, countrymen, and "purity" entirely to one side. But he is immovably firm with what he calls "the charming bad taste" of Barrès, which effectively neutralizes everything that in Nerval was alien to nationalist soil nostalgia, and precisely what Proust valued in the writer whose work continually explores strange places, of both the world and the mind (his interest in the culturally esoteric, his oriental journeys, and above all his madness): "One day in Gérard there will be madness . . . it is a mistake to cite him as a model of unrestrained grace. He is a model of unhealthy obsession."[52] "Health" was one of the watchwords of Action française, which promoted the ideal of the healthy body and exploited the fear of invaders (germs as well as Germans, infecting Jews and other foreign "elements"). Thus, while there is not one word here on the politics of other-rejecting nationalism, it is everywhere its subtext. Nerval the standard-bearer of a bucolic and ancestral France, the bard who, as the church bells of Ermenonville chime through the mists, sings in "French so pure" of the old Valois times and acts as troubadour to those lovely French country maids of such "pure" stock, the future mothers of France? Proust's answer to this sentimental concoction is crisp: "there is . . . nothing very French about him," and, in insisting that there was, Barrès's great mistake (the form of his "charming bad taste") was "to recall all that was inoffensive, untroubled, almost ancient and traditional in his madness by calling him a 'delightful madman' [*fol délicieux*]."[53] I have said that it is pointless to go looking for a Proustian "politics," but, if there is one, it is perhaps here in this short piece on Nerval, modest in tone but resolute in its identification and rejection of the appropriations attempted by Barrès, Lemaître, and others.

[51] Barrès, *Discours de réception de M. Barrès: Séance de l'Académie française du 17 janvier 1907* (Paris: Juven, 1907).
[52] Ibid., 31–32.
[53] Ibid.

Another counter to the patriotic trance induced by the church bells of Ermenonville is in the *Recherche* itself, the example of another church and another place-name: the Persian or oriental church at Balbec. When, after much preemptive daydreaming, the narrator rushes off at sunrise on the day of his arrival to see the church, he finds it and its environs to be disappointingly ugly and banal. The disappointment is represented as a fall from the uplifting regime of the general and the universal ("the eternal significance of the sculptures" and their "universal value") into the banal regime of the Particular ("the tyranny of the Particular"), a fall exacerbated by metonymic contiguity—the church next door to the "local branch of the savings Bank" and "assailed . . . by the smells from the pastrycook kitchens" (the antithesis of the Combray baker's shop)—and literal contagion (the facade "stained with the same soot as the neighbouring homes"). Looking at the church, the narrator experiences another sudden collapse of expectation in the face of dead matter, a further instance of the living "symbol" disappearing into the disenchantment of the allegorical (sculpture "reduced to nothing but its own shape in stone"). The moral is to leave the Name in the sphere of the imagination: "I had broken open a name which should have been kept hermetically sealed" (*JF*, 237–39). This is the familiar pattern (we have already seen it at work in connection with the name and the stones of Venice). On the other hand, it is, as Ellison rightly maintains, also a "simplification" of Proust to see the Name solely as a stage for "the movement of disillusionment from dream to reality." If the physical reality of the place disappoints, the syllables of the name "Balbec" keep the mind focused on the notion of a "strange split city"; just as the church has something oriental and Persian, so we hear (or read) "Baalbek" (also Heliopolis, city of the sun and the sun god, Baal) in "Balbec." One of Legrandin's more extravagant flights of fancy posits Balbec as the westernmost point of Europe: "You can still feel there beneath your feet . . . the true end of the land of France, of Europe, of the Ancient World. And it's the last encampment of fishermen, precisely like all the fishermen who have ever lived since the beginning of the world, facing the eternal realm of the mists of the sea and shadows of the night" (*S*, 388). With the echo of "Baalbek," Proust turns back from the Western horizon of the setting sun to the rising sun in the East to import foreignness into the domesticated by "denaturalizing" the place-name (just as metaphor brings strangeness to the common noun). Proust indeed cracks the hermetic seal of the Name, but, if broken using the "Persian" look of the church as a tool, what, genielike, emerges is an exciting hybrid as well as a mere banality.[54]

---

[54]"Balbec/Baalbek is West *and* East, Normandy *and* the Orient." Ellison also points out that there is also a link to Venice, as "a *point de rencontre* of East and West, Roman Christianity and Byzantium," a web of associations that Ellison finally routes via Freud as

III

"Each great artist," observes the narrator, "seems to be the citizen of an unknown homeland which even he has forgotten" (*P*, 235). This may be the "lost homeland" evoked by Vinteuil's septet (236), but if it is both lost and unknown, in what sense can it be a "home" to which the wandering spirit returns or might return as to the embrace of the known? How, for Proust the artist, could it be, given what he also once claimed (in *Contre Sainte-Beuve*), that the writer inhabits his native tongue as if it too were a foreign country? Since there is an important paradox in Proust making this claim about the mother tongue in the mother tongue, the remark needs to be quoted in the original French: "Les beaux livres sont écrits dans une sorte de langue étrangère" (Beautiful books are written in a kind of foreign language).[55] Something similar can be said of the life sacrificed for France, the patriot's version of the beautiful death. Before he returns to the front where he will meet his death, Saint-Loup is overheard by the narrator singing quietly to himself. What he sings is a Schumann piece, a lied, and it is expressly noted by the narrator that he sings it in the original German (now the enemy language of the hated "Boche"): "No more German on our lips," thundered Joseph Péladan in *Le Figaro* after the outbreak of war.[56] The war-fevered embargo was soon extended to German music, and above all to Wagner, in a campaign spearheaded by Saint-Saëns and Frédéric Masson; "anti-Wagner" became a patriotic slogan. Proust protested lightly in the novel (Saint-Loup's jocular yet pointed remark to the narrator that it will take a German invasion to be able to hear Wagner once more in Paris, *T*, 66) and more vigorously in his correspondence.[57]

But if Wagner was the cause célèbre in the war against *Kultur*, as well as against Germany, Proust chose to make his point principally through the example of Schumann, selected not just because of the language of

---

a blending of the *Heimlich* and the *Unheimlich*. Ellison, *Ethics and Aesthetics in European Modernist Literature: From the Sublime to the Uncanny* (Cambridge: Cambridge University Press, 2001), 143. The echo of "Baal" as sun god also points to Sodom and Gomorrah. Proust linked his reflections on Sodom to some remarks about Zionism in terms of a rejection of "separatist" conceptions of "homeland" (*SG*, 35), while on the other hand exposing what Benjamin (in a letter to Adorno about Proust and the Dreyfus affair) referred to as Proust's grasp of "the precarious structure of assimilation." *The Complete Correspondence of Theodor W. Adorno and Walter Benjamin*, ed. Henri Lonitz (Oxford: Cambridge Polity Press, 1999), 330.

[55] *Against Sainte-Beuve*, ed. Sturrock, 93 (*Contre Sainte-Beuve*, ed. Clarac and Sandre, 305).

[56] September 1914, cited in Schmid, "Ideology and Discourse," 968.

[57] See, in particular, the letters in 1914 to Lucien Daudet and Paul Souday (critic for the newspaper *Le Temps*), in *Corr.*, 13:333 and 14:99.

the song but also because of the form of the musical genre to which the piece belongs, in particular its use of the conventions of the "ritornello," departing and returning only to depart again. The ritornello is especially associated with the imitation of birdsong in baroque music (perhaps the best known example is Vivaldi's "Primavera" in *The Four Seasons*), but is also a feature of nineteenth-century music. Saint-Loup refers to the birdsong of Wagner's *Siegfried* while also alluding to a Schumann lied ("he would only give its title in German"), both connected in his own mind with hearing "the twitterings of the dawn chorus at the edge of the forest" (*T*, 62). There may also be an association with mating rituals, the dance of flight, return and escape (we recall that in the seduction scene witnessed by the narrator in "Combray," Mlle Vinteuil and her friend are like two cooing and squawking lovebirds). More formally, the rhythms of the lied are cousin to both the sinuous divagations of the Chopin phrase (analogy for Proust's syntax) and the polymorphous energies of the Vinteuil septet.[58] Proust appears indeed to have confused Chopin and Schumann when in *La Fugitive* he compares the "delays, interruptions and hesitations" of the love affair with Albertine to the peripeteia of Balzac's stories and Schumann's "ballads" (466–67).[59] The comparison with the septet in *La Prisonnière* is even more telling. On the one hand, there is the "mystic cock-crow" of morning (229), and then the later moment of sleep and implied silence: "the phrase that had been inspired by Vinteuil's daughter's sleep . . . calmed me by its soft background of silence which underlies certain rêveries of Schumann" (232), the "silences" very probably an allusion to the "silent" melodic third line, which Schumann wrote into some of his piano pieces.

With its wanderings, its silences, and its virtualities, the musical form of the Schumann lied provides, in a very special set of circumstances (the nation at war), another model for Proust's book as a whole, reasonably seen as nothing but ritornello, repetition, digression, return, and new departure, the rhythm of "life, blissful perpetual motion" (*P*, 233).[60] The comings and goings of the ritornello structure are moreover reflected not just in the travels of theme or "motif" but also in the synesthetic texture of sound (the stimulus to the ear displaced to the eye, as musical notes evoke corresponding color values).[61] The same holds for passages in the

---

[58]See chapter 3.

[59]This at least is what the editors of the second Pléiade maintain (*ARTP*, 4:1070).

[60]For an extended account of the significance of Schumann for Proust, and especially the scene with Saint-Loup in *Le Temps retrouvé*, see Jérôme Cornette, "'Un lied de Schumann': The Politics and Aesthetics of Singing," in *Proust in Perspective*, ed. Mortimer and Kolb, 254–68. Cornette's principal theoretical source is the remarks on the *ritornello* in Deleuze and Guattari, *A Thousand Plateaux*, as a musical demonstration of the "deterritorialized."

[61]Cornette, "'Un lied de Schumann,'" 259. On synesthesia and Schumann, see Beate Julia Perrey, *Schumann's Dichterliebe and Early Romantic Poets: Fragmentation of Desire* (Cambridge: Cambridge University Press, 2002), 133.

Vinteuil septet that produce "a spell of burning sunshine" from the "repetitive clanging of unleashed bells (like those which poured their burning heat down on the church square in Combray and which Vinteuil, who
must often have heard them, had perhaps found at that moment in his
memory, like a colour ready to hand upon a palette)" (230). While also a
source of error,[62] the auditory thus comes to rank with the olfactory and
the gustatory in Proust's conception of a body without internal borders,
in which experience moves across a corporeal territory too fluid to serve
as the basis for any identity-freezing ideology of embodiment. It is one
with the very foundation of the Proustian aesthetic, the memory of sensations that belong to two moments and two places and hence to neither, in
what the narrator calls "that bundle of sensations" that is "the material
body" (*JF*, 245), a topology that no toponymy can name or classify.[63] It
most certainly has nothing in common with what Barrès tried to do with
the bells of Ermenonville in Nerval's *Sylvie*.

The bells of the septet will ring other bells elsewhere in Proust's text,
and outside the finely worked forms of music, in sounds from everyday life. They may remind us not only of the church bells of Combray,
but also—even though their sound is far from "clanging"—of the tinkling bells of the Combray garden gate and house that frame the novel
at its beginning and ending. Combray, the *fons et origo*, is the fatherland
in miniature, invaded by the Boche, the church bells silenced. Yet even
here—an occasion for patriotic lamentation or flag-waving if ever there
were one—there is at the very beginning another *dépaysement*, so delicate one might scarcely notice it, but which is on a par with the more
obviously evoked "Baalbek" in Balbec. If one is tempted by a contrast
between Balbec as the "bad" church, ugly and disappointing, too oriental, and the good Christian churches of Combray and Saint-André-des-
Champs, then what of Proust's hybridizing way with the sacred site of
origin and remembrance in *À la recherche*? For there is also "within the
name of Combray, a very different city" to which, strangely yet touch-
ingly, we are led through the early summer buttercup fields, which "perhaps had come from Asia many centuries ago, but were now naturalized
for good in the village . . . but still retaining . . . a poetic lustre of the orient" (*S*, 168–69).[64] However debilitating the contact of name with reality,
here is a form of imaginative border-crossing from which Proust's art

---

[62] Examples we have already seen include: mishearing (the sounds of a lorry confused
with humans quarreling), mistranslation (Proust taking Ruskin to hear wood "resonating"
by virtue of misunderstanding Ruskin's use of the word "sound"). To which we may also
want to add a possible misremembering (Claudia Brodsky questions whether the sound of
the bell announcing Swann's arrival in "Combray," allegedly recalled at the end, is in fact
the same bell. "Remembering Swann," 302).

[63] Deleuze, *Proust and Signs*, 166.

[64] Later described as a "flowery Delos" (*S* ,184).

never resiles, a recapturing of a distant and unfamiliar origin that once again is like the recovered figure of speech before it is "naturalized" by common usage. Proust thus opens Frenchness to welcome Eastern and Asiatic "invasions," situating them in no less than the "naturalized" buttercup fields of Combray.[65] Adjacent in Proust's text to the wheat fields of Saint-André (its soil a source of life-giving bread) and not that far from the battlefields of the Somme (soaked with the blood of those fallen in defense of the homeland), these are juxtapositions and mixtures discomfiting to nationalist "purity"-mongers and greatly complicate what, for Proust, homeland and fatherland meant.

Questions about bodies and origins, homelands and fatherlands can become readily attached to questions about fathers. In the "incarnationalist" reading of *À la recherche*, the important parental body is the maternal body (at once sacred and profane, place of both sanctuary and exile). The narrator's father is a relatively insignificant figure, his role in the novel largely restricted to that of the paterfamilias as the whimsical tyrant who prohibits the bedtime kiss but who then unexpectedly and arbitrarily relaxes the prohibition; narratively, he is not around for long.[66] There are, however, also the two artist-mentors, Elstir and Bergotte, both of whom, where the aesthetic education of the narrator is concerned, function as substitute fathers (they are for the narrator what Ruskin was for Proust).[67] Elstir opens the eyes of the young narrator to the forms of modern painting and the ways of seeing they express, but he is also the father-educator from whom the narrator must learn to take his leave. In *À l'ombre des jeunes filles en fleurs*, Elstir didactically admonishes the narrator on the need to avoid the traps of idolatry. Yet elsewhere in this episode we catch a glimpse of another Elstir, apparently caught up in the very error against which he preaches. Elstir speaks of the Balbec church in a manner reminiscent of Charlus's rhapsody on the Combray church, describing it as a "huge theological and symbolic poem," one index of which is its representation of the "nakedness" of Christ "from whose pierced side the Church gathers His blood, the liquor of the Eucharist" (420). The narrator is, of course, all wide-eyed attention. There is further-

---

[65] "The Orient of *La Recherche* owes little to Orientalism: rather, it shows a desire to disorient Frenchness, to take its origins elsewhere." André Benhaïm, "From Baalbek to Baghdad and Beyond: Marcel Proust's Foreign Memories of France," *Journal of European Studies* 35, 1 (2005): 88.

[66] For another view of the importance of the narrator's father, see Edward Bizub, "La surprise du père," in *Marcel Proust: Surprises de la Recherche*, ed. Coudert and Perrier, 45–56. Particular note is taken of Adrien Proust's medical research and Marcel Proust's interest in multiple selves and the life of the unconscious.

[67] The other artist-father, Vinteuil, is defiled by his daughter and her lesbian friend but finds an ardent disciple in the latter, who after his death edits the score of the septet and other pieces (*P*, 240).

more a correlative of this embodying view of the splendors of religious art, in an aspect of Elstir's career as a painter with which the narrator becomes acquainted only "at a later stage," but which is recalled by the narrator in the same sequence of *À l'ombre des jeunes filles en fleurs*. It concerns the moment of Elstir's "mythological" nudes, around which is elaborated "a certain model of beauty" in which Elstir "had once seen something almost divine," an "ideal [that] had become a form of worship," and that he believes he discovers for the first time "externally manifested, in the body of a woman who later became Mme Elstir," a corporeal manifestation, "which now in a mysterious incarnation offered itself for a sequence of efficacious sacraments" (429).

It is but one moment of the Elstirian career, but it is one that with time and "mental fatigue" comes to predominate ("he was reaching the age at which one looks to the body and its fulfillments to stimulate the energy of the mind, when we are inclined by its weariness to materialism . . . when we begin to accept that there may be certain bodies . . . which achieve our ideal very naturally," 430). The moral of the tale is drawn, again with the benefit of hindsight understanding, through a comparison with Swann: "So it was that, even for Elstir, a day would eventually come when he regressed to the attitude to beauty (which I had seen in Swann and beyond which he had never gone) . . . a day when his creative genius would begin to dissipate, gradually giving way to idolatry, mere worship of the forms which had once nourished it" (431). It is the more dispiriting lesson Elstir imparts to his protégé; the narrator does not forget it and makes sure we do not forget it, when in *Le Temps retrouvé*, he describes "sacramental" Elstir as "inclining increasingly to the materialist belief that a substantial part of beauty resides in objects themselves, as at the outset he had adored in Mme Elstir the type of rather heavy beauty he had pursued and caressed in his paintings and tapestries" (78). This is precisely the belief that the narrator has to learn to renounce; in this respect, Elstir, otherwise the exemplary artist-father, proves to be the failed father.

In the case of Bergotte, the identification of artist with paternity is more explicit: the narrator imagines the writer, or more precisely his books ("his pages"), as the site of a paternal homecoming: "I had wept over the writer's pages as though the arms of a father I had found again" (*S*, 98). Bergotte the artist seems to offer the narrator an equivalent of Hegel's fantasia in which Greek art as embodiment and presence is linked to the dream of a homecoming, the "spirit" finding its way back from wandering and exile to its natural habitus (or *bei sich*), albeit that in the *Aesthetic Lectures* the medium of the final reconciliation of spirit and world will be philosophy rather than art. But if we fast-forward to the time of Bergotte's end in *La Prisonnière*, what we find is the dispatch of that fantasy in the spectacle of what is left after the dispatch of bodily remains to the grave:

They buried him, but all the night before his funeral, in the lighted bookshop windows, his books, set out in threes, kept watch like angels with outspread wings and seemed, for him who was no more, the symbol of his resurrection. (*P*, 170)

The irony is in the effect of the zeugma, the incongruous yoking of terms from religion ("angel," "resurrection"), art ("symbol"), and commerce ("shop windows").[68] This is the printed page as object of consumer display and the symbol as commodity (precisely the form defined by Walter Benjamin, echoing Marx, as "spectral," a magic lantern show of pure illusion). First, there was the idea of writing as an equivalent of the "bread of the angels," then as the "spiritual loaf" provided by the mass circulation newspaper, and now books like angels with outspread wings. The lighted shop windows in which Bergotte's books are exhibited cast a searching light over the whole drama of symbol, body, and incorporation in *À la recherche*, and are the sign of its distance from traffic in ontologizing conceptions of literature and related origin myths of paternity and *patrie*. Bergotte's last days—the days not where we live but where we prepare to die—also furnish Proust with a miniature illustration of a more general, apocalyptic view of the End, in particular the prospect of "an end to resurrection" and the time when books will no longer be read because there will be no one left to read them: "Thus he grew colder and colder, a little planet offering a foretaste of what the last days of the big one will be, when first warmth and then life recede from the Earth. Then there will be an end to resurrection, for however far into the world of future generations the works of men may cast their light, still they will need human beings to see them" (*P*, 166).[69]

IV

In Proust the body is where we live but not where we are at home. There is a miserably constraining reason for this as well as an expansively nomadic one, and it brings us to the first of three loosely stitched codas or postscripts. The first, in *Le Côté de Guermantes*, is the superbly cadenced sentence that, in holding back its point (the syntactic equivalent of a whole narrative logic of delay), ends by delivering it with the force of a shock-effect:

[68] Bowie notes the incongruity in *Proust Among the Stars*, 69.

[69] On the other hand, obliquely self-ironizing to the last, Proust also constructs a mildly comic version of the melancholic contemplation of the end-times, in Charlus's grandiloquent (and self-satisfied) roll call of the dead: "Hannibal de Bréauté, dead! Antoine de Mouchy, dead! Charles Swann, dead! Adalbert de Montmorency, dead! Boson de Talleyrand, dead! Sosthène de Doudeauville, dead!" (*T*, 171).

It is illness that makes us recognize that we do not live in isolation but are chained to a being from a different realm, worlds apart from us, with no knowledge of us and by whom it is impossible to make ourselves understood: our body. (*CG*, 294)

Here we have another inflection of the theme of exile, in which what is radically alien, incommensurably "other" to us, is not some enemy body-nation but our own corporeal selves, the body as a foreign country we are compelled to inhabit and can never leave, but in which we can never feel at home because it is so devoted to busily and patiently preparing our extinction. This is not, of course, the only place where Proust's literary imagination resides, and, although the preoccupations of this book have been overwhelmingly focused on a view of what Proust is *not* (a "celebrant" of one kind or another), its intention has not been merely to negate. It has been rather to stay alert, with one of the most alert minds of modern literature, and to do so in a manner that has tried to remain faithful to the incomparable brightness of Proust, in every sense of that term. It includes the spirit of what I have attempted to describe as Proust's skepticism. I began that inquiry with a remark of Nietzsche's from *The Gay Science* ("I approve of any form of scepticism to which I can reply 'let's try it'", characterizing the remark and the more general attitude that underlies it as "sprightly." It is an adjective that applies to Proust's own idiom, as itself the sparkling science of what—in the best description, at once simple and deep, of *À la recherche* I have yet encountered—his novel is about: a man thinking about what it is to be alive.[70] The thinking extends to all the things—the hours, days, and years; the seasons; colors and atmospheres; the places and the people; the hopes and disappointments; the stories told and untold (what actually happens to Maman in the end?); in short, everything hauled in from the Sea of Time Lost—for which the entire vast net of *À la recherche* is required. But it crucially involves a long, cool look at the things we think we "do" with time, in the folly (that other mad belief) of viewing time as the object of a transitive verb: "waste" or "kill" or "find" or "spend" or "save" are the standard metaphors, to which we might add another less aggressively or avidly anthropocentric verb ("to run out of"). Bergotte runs out of it, struck down by cardiac arrest (possibly triggered by eating a dish of undercooked potatoes) while looking at Vermeer's little patch of yellow wall and seeing in it a prototype for what his art might have been, now too late for anything other than the bitter counterfactual of a might-have-been that can never be.

---

[70] Andrew Marr in the radio broadcast, "Start the Week," BBC, Radio 4, December 6, 2010.

At the moment of discovering his vocation as a writer, the narrator worries that he too might not have enough time for its completion. But along with the dread of having no more time, there is that other writer's fear—of a lack of paper (though, as Proust said to Maurice Montabre, were he to find himself without paper, there was the consoling alternative of becoming a baker). The second coda is prompted by the experience of a paperless world on a miniscale. It is another comment, private and nonchalantly humorous, on illness, on different kinds of ailment (the recoverable and the irrecoverable). But, in its playful way with the cliché that Time is both on your side provided you have the right kind of illness, and yet, when all is said and done, on no one's side, including that of the artist who wrote (on paper) to redeem Time, it serves as a perfect envoi. It is from Proust's "revelations on the continuation of his novel" (the reflections written on the blank pages of the copy of *Du côté de chez Swann* for his friend Mme Scheikevitch). This was Proust in 1915, engaging with a set of questions that, with the benefit of hindsight, appear somewhat premature for the writer who was to spend the remaining years right up to the end deferring the end with the manuscript addition of further "continuations." "You wanted to know, Madame, what became of Mme Swann as she aged," sets the tone. It concludes with a passage that sits with Proust's best jokes:

> among bodily ailments, we must distinguish those which act upon the body only through the agency of memory. In the case of the first, the prognosis is generally favourable. After a certain time, a patient suffering from cancer will be dead. It is very uncommon, after the same length of time, for an inconsolable widow not to have been cured. Alas, Madame, I have run out of paper just as it was about to get rather good.[71]

An alternative to the scenario of running out of paper is that of patching it up. This is the task of Françoise as seamstress, and the source of our third and final coda. I have already maintained (in chapter 2) that Proust's best joke is delivered by, or rather through, Françoise obliquely (in the way the best often are), in words uttered not in jest but as the unself-conscious declaration of a "faith" that demands little of this life, or of any life: "my time is not so precious; He who made it did not sell it to us." Françoise also has one final entrance as a corrective voice, that of the finer sort of skeptic, practical and earthbound, while remaining affectionately loyal ("Françoise sensed my happiness and respected my work"). In her very last appearance in the novel, she is imagined as a helpmeet (arguably as a replacement for Maman) "who, in the way that

---

[71] "Proust's reflections on the continuation of his novel." *Against Sainte-Beuve*, ed. Sturrock, 241–42. A version of this finds its way into *La Fugitive* (608).

all unpretentious people who live alongside us do, had an intuitive understanding of my task." Retreating from the monumentalizing idea of
the work as church or cathedral ("Think how many cathedrals have been
left unfinished!") in favor of "thinking about my book in more modest
terms," the narrator changes "the comparison by which I could best and
most materially represent the task on which I was embarking." Françoise
provides the basis for that change: "I would work next to her, and work
almost the same way as her (at least in the way she used to in the past: she
was now so old she could hardly see at all); for, pinning a supplementary
page in place here and there, I should construct my book, I don't dare say,
ambitiously, as if it were a cathedral, but simply as if it were a dress I was
making." In the closing moments of the search, the narrator abandons the
grand for the humble, stone for thread, the body-Nation for two fragile,
individual bodies, one already half-blind, the other not long out of a
sanatorium, seated together "at my big deal table," as figures in a tableau
of writing that is seen as an activity of sewing and stitching (*T*, 343).[72]

The image is moreover not merely analogy. It has a material, and thus
a mortal, dimension. Just as the body falls apart (it is at this point that
the narrator inserts his maxim to the effect that the body is the enemy
within—"having a body is in itself the greatest threat to the mind"), so
does the manuscript; Françoise has already done her best to "patch" the
narrator's earlier literary endeavors (mentioned in *La Fugitive*). There
are, however, the bits that cannot be rescued or "saved," too far gone to
lend themselves to repair, and, alas (once more), they may be the best bits,
the ones where it gets or got truly interesting: "the papers that Françoise
called my manuscribbles kept getting torn. But Françoise would always
be able to help me mend them, just as she put patches on the worn-out
parts of her dresses or, while she was waiting for the glazier, she would
stick a piece of newspaper over a broken pane in the kitchen window.
Françoise would say to me, pointing to my note-books, eaten away like
wood that insects have got into: 'It's all moth-eaten, look, that's a pity,
there's a page here that looks like lace,' and examining it closely like a
tailor: 'I don't think I can mend this, it's too far gone. It's a shame, those
might have been your best ideas' " (*T*, 344). We will never know.

---

[72] The other homely analogy is from Françoise's cooking repertoire: braised beef in aspic,
with its processes of extraction and reduction (*T*, 344).

Index